CHAPTER I

INTRODUCING THE FOUR CHIEF CHARACTERS

WE often pride ourselves on our originality but actually we are made in a certain limited number of patterns and we possess very little that we can claim to be unique. At birth we are given the plastic material which life begins to mould, namely a number of innate physical and mental qualities and capacities some of which we have inherited. We can claim, therefore, the originality of clay or of wax, but although we own the medium we must borrow its final form. This simile illustrates yet another truth. As clay or wax that is stale loses its plastic powers, so do we, as we grow old, become less and less responsive to the power that shapes us. Childhood is pliable; age is rigid. 'Give me a child up to the age of seven and I will make of him anything you like', wrote a Jesuit. It is an idle boast, for a Jesuit can only make Jesuits, but it contains an element of truth. The child is the ideal plastic medium, but the sculptor life must move quickly for with increasing age our capacity to be moulded into new forms is lost. As we have been made, so must we remain.

A dismal philosophy, this, that new thoughts, novel emotions and fresh reactions become rarer and rarer as we advance in years; dismal but true. Is not this the source of the eternal conflict between youth and age? It is not that the old refuse to understand the wild schemes of youth, it is rather that they are generally incapable of understanding them. Each generation has its characteristic responses and adjustments to life, so youth must for ever rebel and age be the protector of outmoded things.

The material is ours but we borrow the shape. We borrow when we imitate, and as the leaf insect reproduces the appearance of the leaf on which it lives, so do we imitate everything around us, taking our opinions from the press, our religion from the church, our laws from the Romans and our British code of honour from the public schools. The greatest of all borrowers is the child, who by imitating those around him, learns to think, to feel and to act. Soon he learns to read, and then he borrows wildly from a whole new world of books. I tremble to think what a debt or a grudge — I am not sure which — I owe to such writers as Henty, Manville Fenn, Gordon Stables and Fenimore Cooper. I also feel called upon to express a belated apology to the editors of *The Boy's Own Paper* and of *Chums* for having purloined from their pages so many thoughts, sentiments, aspirations and illusions. From the Bible that was treated with such reverence by my elders I took much less, and seldom what they intended I should take. I was interested in the orderly procession of the animals, big and small, all walking in pairs into the Ark, but Christ held up to me a model of behaviour that even in my most exalted moments I recognized as being beyond my powers to imitate. For the majority of characters in the Old Testament I had little liking, and Jacob, for all his godliness, was clearly mean and a cheat. Joseph left me cold and critical, and Elijah's behaviour to the jeering children was frankly outrageous. A man who was old enough to have a long white beard was surely old enough to have known better. It was surprising that the bears had obeyed him.

From what a heterogeneous and accidental mixture a child selects his own outfit for life. In my own case the actual living models around me were quiet Scottish folk, but in my innermost being I felt their limitations and their lack of colour. They were good, but like so many good people, they were wanting in interest and not very companionable. I needed something more heroic, something more in keeping with the splendid figures that had been caught between the covers of my books and which sprang to life whenever I began to turn their pages. I developed a strong partiality for Indian braves, knights on horseback, crusaders and explorers, and as they passed before my respectful eyes I filched from each of them a trifle for myself. At a tender age I became a plagiarist of the most shameless sort, a despoiler of other people's splendours.

What is the discriminating agent in the child which chooses the models for his own behaviour? This is a mystery. When David Hume set himself the task of discovering *himself* by turning his eye inward and watching the flux of thoughts which made up his being, he could find nothing of a permanent nature, nothing that he could call himself. He wrote: 'For my part, when I enter most intimately into what I call myself, I always stumble on some particular perception or other . . . I never catch myself.' So also am I now unable to discover that part of me which selected or rejected models of behaviour. All that I know is that the engine-drivers, buccaneers and pirate chiefs favoured by other boys were to my way of thinking unimpressive people, whereas my own band of stalwarts were all that the heart could desire. Between me and them there existed the closest of links, a natural affinity strengthened by a bond of blood brotherhood. With the passage of time our mutual understanding became so complete that all separateness disappeared and we were as one flesh; they lived in me and I in them. We were followers of noble causes, heroes who at times rose to the heights of being demigods.

This, it will be said by the Freudian, is the picture of an imaginative child, and it suggests that the writer of this book, the third and youngest member of his family, compensated for a feeling of inferiority by taking refuge in fantasy. This, I reply, is the history of an ordinary human being, living with the rest of humanity to a large extent in the imagination. Dreams are not dispelled by opening the eyes, and fantasy, like the heart, never stops working. Daydreams are so woven into the texture of our lives that it is difficult to unravel the real in us from the imaginary. It is possible that the property I borrowed for this masquerade of life was a little more theatrical and bizarre than that selected by the more discriminating of my fellows, so that my disguise was more apparent than was theirs, but it is by no means certain that this is the case. Anyone who examines his life as critically as I have tried to examine mine, anyone who makes the effort to look below the surface of it, will find that it contains as much of the fantastic as does the fabric I am about to display.

When I survey that medley of thoughts, emotions and imaginings which was and still is *myself* I become bewildered. How can I contrive to produce some order in all this confusion? It is as though I had made a raid on some theatrical emporium, had gathered up as much of the property as I could carry away, and had then strewn my spoils on my own private floor. There is so much disorder around me that I am at a loss to know what by rights belongs to me and what I have stolen from Clarkson's. By what means can all this gear — some of it my own property and some of it stolen — be sorted out so as to clothe the four characters which are to represent my life? It is a hard task, rendered still harder by the fact that in this dark lumber room of my being there is plenty that I have not yet discovered, let alone labelled and placed on an inventory. Yet this preliminary stocktaking and assorting of theatrical properties must be skilfully done if an ordered tale is to be told. Should however the complaint be made that my characters are oddly clothed, that my Redskin sometimes wears the mask of an Inquisitor and my Knight the collar of a Scottish divine, let it be remembered that I lay no claim to be consistent. With Walt Whitman I am able to exclaim: 'Do I contradict myself? Very well then, I contradict myself (I am large, I contain multitudes).'

The first small heap of clothes I am able to gather together on my floor is obviously the scanty wardrobe of a Redskin, straight from the pages of Manville Fenn. The clothes are few because Black Hawk's reactions, like his equipment, have been reduced to a minimum; he is remarkable for what he does *not* do rather than for what he does. By long training he has divested himself of as many of the usual human responses as possible. For example, he can squat motionless in front of a fire for hours, with his feet so close to the glowing embers that the soles become blistered. He could easily move them, but he would not deign to do so, for by practice he has acquired an aptitude for suffering. Is he not Black Hawk, the Indian brave, who has risen above the weakness of feeling pain, or, indeed, of feeling anything? What is comfort to him? What is anything to him? I have a shrewd suspicion that my parents were in part responsible for Black Hawk's contempt for the amenities of life. They lived in the Victorian age and 'comfortable' and 'wholesome' were favourite words in their vocabulary. To Black Hawk their preoccupation with such drab things as comfort and wholesomeness seemed an ignominious weakness and it was only his taciturnity which prevented him from openly express-ing his contempt when he sat with them at table and listened to their reminiscences of the various dull hotels in which they had spent bygone holidays.

A play cannot be run on a character whose qualities are mainly of a negative nature and another character, Selous, supplied the drive which Black Hawk so badly lacked. He came to me straight out of a big yellow volume in the dining-room bookcase, but whereas the authentic Selous was an explorer who confined his attention to Africa, my Selous pene-trated into every corner of the globe. 'The world is my adventure', he would cry, as he disappeared into an Amazonian swamp, to reappear later, weary but still persistent, in the uncharted wastes of Greenland. Selous was not one of those phlegmatic heroes who have insufficient wit to realize the greatness of the dangers they run. On the contrary, he was always aware of the existence of peril and when on certain occasions it was lacking, he would supply it out of the rich stores of his imagination. An adventure was always improved by the addition of just a spice of danger. Indeed without this it could scarcely be termed an adventure.

The third character in my private theatrical party is a somewhat incongruous figure whose motley appearance is due to the fact that alterations had to be made in his original make-up. At the start this third character was simply one of the paper knights pasted by my father on to the lavatory window of my home so as to confer on it the decorous opaqueness of stained glass. There were four of them, belonging to the orders of St. George, St. Andrew, St. Patrick and the Temple. Every morning I paid homage to them, studying their knightly equipment and becoming better and better acquainted with their distinguishing features. It was to the Scottish Knight of St. Andrew that I eventually made my own knightly vows, dedicating myself like him to a noble cause, and swearing never to marry. Never? Well, perhaps I would marry at the age of forty, for at forty—it was my parents' age—it would matter little what I did. At forty one was finished and when married one was equally finished. Although for a brief period (the fairy-story phase of my childhood) my errantry veered to rescuing golden-haired princesses from villainous hands, on the whole I was true to my bigger aim; at heart I remained a crusader.

It was my grandmamma who was responsible for the changes which at a later date spoilt my Knight's appearance. She was deeply religious, and therefore keenly interested in the work of carrying the light of the Gospels into the dark corners of the globe. Her own hero happened to be a certain Scottish medical missionary, named Dr. Paton, who at the end of many years of noble labour had apparently won a martyr's crown in a Marquesan cooking-pot. (Later in life I discovered that I was mistaken in this and that Dr. Paton's end was fortunately less distressing than I had deemed it to be; he died comfortably in bed.) Sitting on a footstool at the foot of my heroic old grandmamma — heroic because within a few years she had lost her husband, her sight and her money, and yet never doubted the loving wisdom of her God — I learnt so much about the reverend Dr. Paton that in the end I took him for my own. His outline and that of my Knight-Crusader gradually came together and in the course of time coalesced. This had certain disadvantages, for there were many things about the reverend gentleman that I frankly disliked. My grandmother had told me that, on the one occasion on which he had been persuaded to ride, his steed had immediately bolted with him and had all but dashed his head against the low arch of the stable door. Could a knight be a bad horseman? Obviously this was impossible and some adjustments would have to be made. My composite figure was allowed to maintain a high standard of horsemanship and for that ignominious end I substituted martyrdom in a large city square crowded with admiring onlookers. Ever afterwards during the singing of the 'Te Deum' in church, and at that precise moment at which the chant suddenly changes to a minor key and the 'noble army of martyrs' praises the Lord, my scalp would begin to tingle and the well-attended scene of my own martyrdom would rise vividly before my eyes. But even in these ecstatic moments I cherished in the recesses of my heart the secret hope that the stake would be avoided and that Knight-Paton (as I have now called my composite character) would obtain his crown without payment of the customary due.

The fourth figure in my company stood for Greatness, but from the very beginning I had difficulty in deciding in what his greatness lay. This fourth character resembled an unfinished portrait in which only the background has been painted in. Or perhaps it would be more apt to liken it to a piece of descriptive writing broken off at the end of the first paragraph: 'As he entered the crowded building, a hush fell upon the waiting multitude, and as he made his way with slow and dignified steps to the dais that had been erected at the far end of the hall, a sea of faces turned in his direction.' That was all I knew for certain, for at this point both painting and writing always stopped. Once during a sermon I thought that out of the corner of my eye I had caught the gleam of scarlet and ermine on the shoulder of my figure of greatness as he passed up the aisle, but of this I could never feel sure. What was true greatness? Thirty years elapsed before I could make any progress with my picture, and when I took up my brushes again, it was not for the purpose of painting in the figure of Greatness in the foreground, but of obliterating the whole of the background. 'Away from the marketplace and from fame taketh place all that is great', wrote Nietzsche, and by the time that I read his words I was able to appreciate their truth. The crowd and dais have therefore disappeared from the later painting and the central figure stands there solitary and unacclaimed. But the fact that my childhood portrait had no face troubled me very little for the whole world clearly recognized his worth, and that was surely enough. He was the Personage of Personages.

It is not to be supposed that these four figures of mine sprang, like Mars, fully developed and armed, from the conceiving head. They were born of a mortal and they required time, nourishment and exercise for their development; above all, exercise.

Never take the play of a child lightly for it is the most serious and the most urgent of all occupations, of greater importance even than a grown-up's affairs, since it is the father of these. I doubt whether I have ever completely forgiven my mother for her irreverent attitude to my play. Somewhere in those unlit and not very pleasant cellars of the mind, which the analysts are always seeking to enter, there lie the remnants of an old grudge against her for her lack of understanding. But then all women, to my way of thinking, were like that. To be called in from exploring the wild lands that lay between the back of the bicycle shed and the garden wall, and to be told that I must change my damp stockings in case I caught cold was nothing less than an insult. Black Hawk did not wear stockings, and were he, like me, forced to do so he would not notice that they were damp, or if he did, he would never be so feeble as to catch cold. Dry stockings and wool next the skin did not belong to my world, and I bitterly resented these interruptions. It was ignominious to be messed about by women. At such times I felt how wise I had been to make that vow of celibacy to St. Andrew.

During the earlier years of my life my environment was more suited to the needs of Selous and Black Hawk than to those of Knight-Paton and the Personage. All that the first two of these characters needed were hunting grounds and opportunities for displaying resource and imperturbability, and the uncultivated strip of our London garden between the bicycle shed and the garden wall was sufficient for these purposes. But in course of time this region became too small and, what was worse, too familiar. Selous then began to peer over the garden wall at the neighbouring domain. On the other side of the wall lay Mr. Sewell's garden with its carefully trained espaliers of apple and pear planted along the trim paths. What made the next door garden particularly perilous, and therefore a fitting place for an adventure, was the fact that Mr. Sewell's son, Frank, was always lurking in it. He was a tall unhealthy youth, white-faced, pimply, and with a weak fluffy chin. By a careful study of the gardener's habits one could generally tell when he was safely at work in the potting-shed and could therefore judge when an expedition could be launched, but Frank's movements were so erratic as to defy all prediction. Dressed in shiny black clothes, Frank would be seen moving towards the house, and, at the precise moment at which Selous had dropped down into this new world, he would stop, hesitate and then turn unexpectedly in the direction of the bottom of the garden. Frank, therefore, supplied the incalculable element that must exist in every true adventure; he was the danger hovering in the background, from which Selous derived that tingling of the nerves which he found so pleasant.

A few years later my father provided all that the great hunter could possibly need by renting a small estate in Suffolk. No father could have possibly made a better choice of a country residence. At the bottom of the new garden ran a stream, crossed by a ramshackle rustic bridge, and this bridge linked more than a garden and a meadow. It spanned a mighty chasm between two worlds, the humdrum world of lawns, visitors, flowerbeds, women and vegetables and the world of adventure and romance. Never was there a more abrupt transition between the known and the unknown, the commonplace and the exciting than that experienced in crossing this stream; once over the bridge and anything might happen.

Poor Frank was now as out-of-date as my old wooden horse (covered with real skin) that had long ago been presented to the Children's Hospital in Hackney. I had no more use for Frank now than I had for my discarded catapult, for I was the proud owner of a rook-rifle, not just an airgun, but a genuine lethal weapon firing real brass cartridges and conical bullets. By raising the highest sight and lying flat on the ground Selous could hurl a bullet across two vast meadows and, a few seconds later, hear it plop into the trunk of a big elm tree that stood at the boundary of our land. In the air of Bealings he grew lusty and skilful both in forest lore and marksmanship. Many a water-vole and moorhen fell to his gun as he walked along the banks of the stream and on one memorable day he invaded Mr. Cracknell's adjoining property and shot a partridge. The big brindled bird was squatting on the grass at the time, but then Selous was armed only with a rifle, and he could not afford to be finicky about the nicer laws of sportsmanship. How companionable was that stream, every twist and turn of which was as familiar to me as the back of my own hand. Could anything be more delicious than to lie on its banks on a hot afternoon with arms plunged deep in its brown coolness, so deep that one could feel the water thrusting round one's elbows as it pushed its way downstream. As I lay there I could see a little way off a shoal of tiny brown fish struggling to make headway against the current, a shoal which immediately broke rank and darted helter-skelter, in all directions, whenever my hands moved a little nearer to it. Everywhere there were little unnoticed living things, all going about their urgent business. With my face close to the grass I could make out ants engaged in prodigious labours, carrying burdens sometimes bigger than themselves. In that position everything was so large that grass stalks looked like trees and stones were as big as mountains. What a host of things there were in those two meadows of whose existence the dull grown-ups who lived on the other side of the bridge knew nothing.

The needs of Knight-Paton were equally well catered for at Bealings. In Mr. Kersey's yard were two horse-boxes, one for Netty, the sturdy and very reliable cob, and the other for Prince, the strawberry-roan and the not very reliable pony. Mounted on the first, Knight-Paton was able to enact the part and to display the horsemanship of a Knight, but mounted on the second, he often unwillingly enacted that of the Reverend Paton. Earlier in his life Prince had learnt the trick of throwing his rider by stopping abruptly in the middle of a gallop, and seven times in a morning poor Knight-Paton was prostrated on the heath which stretched between Bealings and Felixstowe. It was a hard school of horsemanship but in the end it yielded excellent results. Fortunately both of the mounts were at my disposal now, for my elder brother — whose lack of prowess I heartily despised — had given up riding. At teatime on a sunny Saturday afternoon Netty had taken control and, invading a neighbour's drive, had galloped full tilt across a lawn on which three ladies and the vicar were finishing an exciting croquet match. My brother had social aspirations and he never forgave Netty for this gaffe. Netty was now at my entire disposal.

My life at this period was particularly pleasant and Black Hawk, who thrived on discomfort and pain, found little sustenance in the pleasant village of Great Bealings. It was only by the exercise of considerable ingenuity that he discovered opportunities of displaying his powers. Fortunately I happened to come across an article on tattooing in a magazine, and in this subject Black Hawk immediately became interested, chiefly because tattooing entailed the infliction of pain. By means of a penknife and a nib dipped in Indian ink, he succeeded in tattooing my initials on the back of my wrist. Two subsequent events were also marked as red-letter days on his birch-bark calendar. The first was when, as a sequel to jeering at the cook through the kitchen window, I contrived to get my head painfully wedged between its iron bars, so that one of them had to be filed through in order to liberate me. The second was the day on which I discovered a strange weapon of torture in my father's study. Its manufacturers had intended it to be used for the pressing of papers, but by placing one's hand between the two iron slabs and then turning a large screw Black Hawk found that it provided a splendid means of testing his capacity to endure.

With Selous and Knight-Paton taking so much of the limelight it was inevitable that my figure of Greatness should be pushed into the background, there to remain, an aspiration, yet at the same time in some ways a present possession. Although I never formulated the idea clearly I had a feeling that deep within me lay the germ of something big, something which when the right time came would suddenly burst into splendour and astonish my relatives and their dull friends. It was a hidden possession, something which lay in a locked room that no one was allowed to enter, not even my cousin Ruth, who, now that her parents had returned to Ceylon, had come to live with us. She was a faithful companion, so far as girls went, but there were limits to the confidences I was prepared to share with her. It was impossible to share with her this secret of the seed of something big which lay quiet in the depths of my being, biding its time. The Great One, the Personage, as he is called in these pages, would reveal himself in the future, and, I hoped, in the not very distant future.

CHAPTER II

INTRODUCING THE INTRUDER

WITH so much to do, with so much that was satisfying in the well-regulated world over which Queen Victoria presided, there was little temptation to bother one's head about any spiritual world that might exist alongside of, or within, that to which I so obviously belonged. My brightly-coloured material home was so tightly packed with novelties and incidents that it provided all that anyone could need, whilst heaven was very far away and merely a subject for pious talk on Sundays. Like all other children, I plied the grown-ups with questions and to my 'Why this?' and 'Why that?' they supplied answers that were more or less satisfactory. But sometimes they would look disconcerted, and fumble in their replies, and on occasions they deliberately trailed a red herring across the path. Then I knew that I had touched on the fringe of one of those great taboos to which all grown-ups would seem to subscribe. There was, for example, a mystery about the behaviour of animals and the origin of kittens which it was wiser not to pry into. There were also a great many questions the answers to which would appear to depend on the existence of God. Things were thus because God had so willed it. From this there was no appeal and it was useless to carry the matter further, for God always had the final word. Nor was it difficult to accept the idea of an autocratic ruler over all things. There were many orders that for me were based solely on the illogical whims of my elders, so that I was not surprised to learn that in the background, or somewhere high above the sky, there lived One to whose will even they were forced to submit. I had no idea what He was like, but the grown-ups appeared to know Him so well that they could tell at once when He was angry and when He was pleased, when my conduct irritated Him and when it met with His approval. A little disconcerting was this all-seeing eye, that had time to watch a boy helping himself to jam out of the dining-room cupboard. But if God spied on me He had the decency not to interfere with me. There was no objection therefore to my taking as much jam as could be extracted without lowering too obviously its level in the pot. God would not give me away. It was possible, of course, that later I might have to pay something for my pleasure because this stern, loving God had been known to take it out of wrongdoers even when at first He had allowed them to have their own way. Witness the story of Adam and Eve in the Garden of Eden. An apple — it seemed such a little thing and yet an angel with a flaming sword had been specially summoned to drive them out of the garden for ever. But I accepted whatever was in store for me in the spirit in which my grandmother had accepted her blindness, as part of the inscrutable wisdom of the all-knowing and all-loving heavenly Father. She knew God even better than did my parents, and her acquiescence in the punishment He had seen fit to inflict upon her, although difficult to follow, must be right. In the meantime, jam was jam.

Man is a spiritual being and he cannot indefinitely silence the voice within him which asks the first of all religious questions: 'Who am I, and who is this "I" which takes stock of its existence?' Carlyle describes with characteristic vigour those vivid moments in our lives in which we face the miracle of our existence and search for some explanation of it, however tentative that explanation may be. ' ... there come seasons, meditative, sweet, yet awful hours, when in wonder and fear you ask yourself that unanswerable question: Who am I; the thing that can say "I"? The world, with its loud trafficking, retires into the distance; and, through the paper-hangings, and stone walls, and thick-plied tissues of Commerce and Polity, and all the living and lifeless teguments (of Society and a Body), wherewith your Existence sits surrounded, the sight reaches forth into the void Deep, and you are alone with the Universe, and silently commune with it, as one mysterious Presence with another.' The 'meditative, sweet, yet awful hours', described by Carlyle, come perhaps more often in childhood, before routine and custom have had time to dull that sense of wonder from which religion springs. It is the child rather than the man who is aware of mystery, and because this autobiography deals with inner responses rather than with external actions this response of the spirit to the mystery of its existence must find some place in its pages.

Western psychologists, with the notable exception of William James, have strangely neglected the study of the more spiritual sides of man's nature and have shown a greater interest in his lower and less conscious faculties. Freud has indeed gone so far as to proclaim that all spiritual manifestations, from the inborn wonder of the child to the illumination of the saint, are symptoms of what he calls the world's 'great obsessional neurosis'. It is only in the East, the birthplace of all religions, that the nature of that special faculty in man which can reach out to truths beyond the range of the intellect has been carefully studied. But neglectful though we may have been in the West of the study of our higher faculties we cannot as individuals escape from their influence on our lives. I have had to make provision therefore in this autobiography for the sporadic activity of the more spiritual part of my being and I have done so by creating yet another character, whom I have called the 'Intruder'. The name is well chosen, for on those rare occasions on which he appears his presence is so much resented by the other characters that they leave the stage. Why should the more regular actors in my cast be so disturbed by a part of me which so seldom functions? Is it because when he appears more light falls on the dark stage of my being and, thus illuminated, they are discovered to be what they are, the fantastic figures of a dream? It would seem that this is the case and that the actors within me are akin to the unsubstantial images projected on to a screen by my father's magic-lantern. They are images which can exist only in the dark. All that I know for certain is that between my band of strolling players and him whom I have called the Intruder, there lies the distance that separates two different kinds of world, the imaginary and the real.

Looking back on those rare moments at which the Intruder has appeared I find that they are so vividly impressed on my memory that I can recall, not only my thoughts and my feelings at those times, but every detail of my surroundings. They are moments also of a new understanding, when confusion begins to give place to order and when glimpses are caught of the real behind the façade of ordinary living. A brief account of an incident in my early childhood will convey what I mean better than any general description. The occasion was a visit of my family to a certain Mr. Bushby who lived at Rustington, a few miles from Littlehampton; and a comfortable and leisurely vehicle, suitably named a Victoria, with a coachman in livery, had been hired to convey my parents, my sister and myself from Littlehampton to Rustington. A visit to Mr. Bushby was always an enjoyable outing, for he lived on the outskirts of that village in a wonderful house surrounded by spacious lands. One could visit the cowsheds and watch the cows splashing streams of milk into frothing pails or wander at will in the garden and find the pond in which goldfish were fanning themselves under the shelter of overhanging rocks. One was even allowed to drop in front of their blunt noses tempting lumps of dough moulded on to bent pins and, if one was lucky, to land one of them, glittering and gasping on the lawn. Over all these possessions reigned Mr. Bushby himself, a massive and kindly old man with a face like a bird's nest, and tweed clothes that gave out a pleasant earthy smell. He was like a Father Christmas enjoying a summer holiday.

This particular visit had proved to be a specially profitable one, and seated between my parents on the return journey, my mind dwelt lovingly on all the events of the afternoon. Not only had I explored a hitherto undiscovered corner of the garden, but I had been allowed to touch the rubbery udder of a cow and, best of all, I had been lucky enough to catch three large goldfish. They were actually there beneath the seat in a funny tin with a perforated top, my own goldfish, to do with as I liked. Glimpses of trees, french windows opening on to stretches of lawn and a table loaded with tea things passed through my mind like dissolving views in my father's magic lantern. Mixed with these realities were visions of Indians, of wild animals lurking behind bushes and of a host of imaginary beings that had become so mixed up with what had actually happened that it would have been difficult, had I attempted to do so, to have separated what was real from what was the product of fancy. Then suddenly I realized that everything had changed. The stream of images had stopped abruptly, as though the light in the magic lantern had fused, or somebody had drawn back the curtain to let the daylight into the room, and there I was, a little boy sitting in a Victoria at a bend in the road, staring at the buttons on the coachman's coat in front of me — I, and all this other that was not I. How strange and how frightening it was. This sudden and stark realization of my existence. My mother was smiling and was pushing the end of my muffler under my coat, but I was alone. I was alone and I was looking at myself as though I had suddenly 'come-to'. What did it mean, this acute realization of being here, and this stark sense of isolation? In my heart I knew that I had stumbled across a question to which nobody could give me any answer. I was face to face with a great mystery and I felt mortally afraid. It was not that there was anything terrible about this clear sense of existence; it was frightening because it was so strange and new. I had a feeling as though I had suddenly awakened to find myself perched on a mountain top and I wanted to get down into the familiar valley below. My wish was soon granted. The fuse in the lantern mended itself and a stream of images and thoughts carried me back into the unthinking world to which I really belonged, the world in which I just did things without knowing I was doing them, thought things without realizing I was thinking them. The moment had passed, but like a sun that has sunk below the horizon, it left a glow in the sky behind it. There were mysteries of which grown-up people did not speak, perhaps because they were inexplicable, perhaps because they did not even know of their existence.

Life is so exciting in boyhood that there is little temptation to think for long about things that are clearly beyond the understanding, or to ask questions which are unanswerable. But from time to time these moments of wonder would return and I would stop in whatever I was doing and look with new eyes, not only at what was happening around me, but at myself and at the procession of sensations, thoughts and feelings which made up my inner world. What was this part of me that felt its existence so vividly, and what was this new state of being in which the more familiar aspects of my life seemed so much less important and less substantial than the things I saw then? I waited, but no answer came. Sometimes there was the feeling that if I could only manage to struggle a little further I would discover the explanation of the mystery of my existence, but however hard I strained the answer to it stayed just out of reach. It was there but I could not get to it. Then the surge of life would carry me onward again, and, ceasing to wonder, or even to see that there was cause for wonder, I would continue what I had been previously doing.

All philosophy and religion are born out of this sense of the mystery of our existence and in course of time these moments of clearer understanding became linked up with the idea of God. But it was not with the distant, patriarchal God of the Bible that they became connected, but with something much nearer, and yet so big and so difficult to grasp that it was impossible to put it into words. At such times I would feel the same sense of isolation, but in some vague way the tiny separate thing that was 'I' stood in relationship to a higher order of existence which permeated the whole universe. I was in the presence of something divine which lay within as well as without, and, filled with awe, I would stand quiet for a moment and would listen with bowed head, as one stands silent and reverent in a great cathedral.

I was sent to a public school and public schools do not encourage speculation on subjects outside of an already crowded syllabus. Nor would such efforts on the part of a boy to break through the outer crust of living be considered healthy. Many people look back on their schooldays with disfavour, but having an aptitude for taking on the colour of my surroundings I soon found the arrangements at the Leys School, Cambridge, to be to my liking. To be at a boarding school was in itself a kind of adventure and Black Hawk made things easy for me by showing considerable ability at 'rugger'. It was a game which involved the giving and taking of many bumps and bruises, and within a year of entering the school he gained a beautiful headdress of royal blue velvet with a silver tassel, the first school colours. The Personage also obtained for himself some recognition at Cambridge. The secretary of the Rugby Football Club and the senior prefect of a house is not necessarily a great man, but he is a person of local distinction and entitled therefore to adopt a certain swagger in walking across the 'quad'. It was pleasant to see small boys looking at one and showing gratitude for the barest nod of recognition and, smiling in anticipation of greater triumphs to come, the Personage dispensed his favours with a certain discrimination. Knight-Paton was not much in evidence, but his portrait had a place of honour in my study, for on becoming a prefect I had purchased an immense engraving of a knight in full armour setting out to conquer. Behind him lay a wood in which men of lesser calibre, dressed in silken finery, were dallying with damsels, a wood on which this dedicated knight had resolutely turned his back. How heartily I approved his choice and how much I despised the effete young men in the background.

Although excellent in every other respect, the religious sustenance provided by the Leys School was not to my liking. The school had been founded by Wesleyans and there was much in nonconformity which offended my aesthetic taste. How was it possible to worship a Divine Being, who to my mind was in some mysterious way connected with the idea of beauty, in the unsightly tabernacle of varnished pine to which we repaired on Sunday? At that time the school possessed no chapel of its own and we attended the services in the Hills Road chapel. Obviously such a place was as out of keeping with my feeling for the divine as was the lusty singing, in which we gave praise to the Spirit of Infinite Goodness and Beauty, an insult to music. The Personage was in entire agreement with this disapproval of Wesleyanism, but for a different reason. He was convinced that the great ones of the world naturally gravitated towards the more modish church and that they were rarely, if ever, to be seen in a chapel. He veered therefore violently in the direction of the High Church.

During those two years at boarding school I thought very little about those questions to which we must look to philosophy and religion for an answer, such as the question of the meaning of life. For a few weeks I attended prayer meetings held in one of the class-rooms and, on two or three occasions, I took the sacrament after the evening service, but the loud voice of the senior prefect leading us in prayer and the unctuous behaviour of the clergymen officiating at communion convinced me that I was in the wrong place and that it would be more honest to retreat again into agnosticism. All the cleverest scientists were agnostics, and as I was now studying science, it was only right and proper that I should join their company. I would no longer bother my head therefore about religion, but would confine my attention to the study of facts. Someday, perhaps, I would try to penetrate more deeply into the heart of the mystery of my existence, but in the meantime there were more important things to do. Why should I puzzle over matters which everybody else seemed to take for granted? It would be wiser and healthier to leave such things alone.

CHAPTER III

THE PLAY BEGINS

THE players in my private company have now been introduced and the play can proceed. Would that I could look back on my past and see myself as a producer, comfortably seated in the wings of the theatre, directing the actors and prompting them when they forget their parts. Unfortunately there is no such person. In this theatre, which is to represent myself, the actors appear on the boards when and how they like, and as each of them has a different idea of what constitutes a good play and none of them takes any notice of what others are doing, it is not surprising that, when examined in retrospect, the play appears to have been utterly chaotic. Nor is it strange that the scenes about to be presented have little or no connection with each other. This play is not a planned work of art, but it represents life as it is lived; it is a portrayal of what actually happened and not of what ought to have happened or of what I would have liked to have happened.

I suppose that the day on which a boy chooses his career must be considered to be one of the most important of his life and it is therefore a fitting moment at which to raise the curtain. I can recall the particular Sabbath afternoon on which my father discussed the question of my future. We had enjoyed the usual Sunday meal of roast beef and York-shire pudding, followed by apple tart and cream, and my father and I were alone. My sister had gone out to afternoon Sunday-school, my brother was away, and my mother was upstairs resting. My father and I always treated each other with mutual toleration and respect, and we were here this afternoon to discuss this important question, not as parent and child, but as two intelligent people sitting in committee. He opened the proceedings.

'What do you want to do?' he asked, putting down his pipe on the table beside him, leaning back in his chair and crossing his knees. 'There is, of course, a place for you in the family business, but perhaps you have other ideas?'

'Most certainly I have,' shouted at least a dozen voices within me. A vision of silken or bowler-hatted men, dressed in sombre clothes and climbing into the eight-thirty train from Finchley Road to Moorgate Street, passed before my eyes. Each of them carried a little bag, and from the pockets of their overcoats protruded a corner of the *Financial Times*. 'Good God, an office!' muttered Selous, 'what an awful suggestion.' For a moment there was silence, the deep silence that precedes the giving of a verdict. It was the Personage that spoke first. 'The Foreign Office.' He had seen the arrival of an ambassador, Her Majesty's Plenipotentiary hurrying up the steps of an imposing building with a great many people looking on. My father looked thoughtful and waited a minute before he replied.

'The Foreign Office needs money and influence. I'm afraid that I could give you very little help in such a career. Unless you are absolutely set on it, it would be better to choose something else.'

Again there was a silence in the room, but inside me I heard a low rumble of protests — 'anything but an office' — 'anything but the City' — 'anything but the eight-thirty in the morning to Moorgate Street' — 'anything but a top-hat and spats.'

'Then I will be a doctor,' I heard myself say, just as though some catch in me had moved and a new gramophone record had slid on to the revolving disc. It had been Selous' suggestion. He had suddenly caught sight of himself in a foreign land (doctors had no offices and could travel) astride an Arab horse, with a black bag, quite different to the kind carried by business men, tied to his saddle, galloping, galloping to save the life of the favourite wife of a sheik. Knight-Paton approved of any career that served some cause, even although the cause of succouring ailing humanity was not as thrilling a one as that which he personally would have selected. He therefore supported the suggestion made by Selous. My father was also obviously pleased with it.

'A noble profession,' he said. 'I think that you have chosen well, and I will do all in my power to help you.'

Knight-Paton repeated to himself my father's words, 'a noble profession', with evident relish, and before the eyes of Selous passed visions of the many strange lands he would be able to visit as a doctor. So I was committed to the career of healing not so much because I had a burning desire to pry into people's interiors, or felt much sympathy at that time for invalids — Black Hawk had a hearty contempt for them — but because

Selous and Knight-Paton wanted to gallop across a desert with a little black bag tied to their saddles. 'A race with death!' How thrilling it sounded. Fortunately for me their blind choice had happy results and I have never regretted this accident that made me a doctor.

The factors that determine our actions are so complex that when we assert that it was this or it was that which prompted us to behave in a certain way, we are in all probability naming only one of the many forces to which at that time we were being subjected. It is an over-simplification therefore for me to say that my decision to become a doctor was based on nothing more substantial than imagination and that I had no desire to pry into people's interiors. Early in life we display certain qualities and propensities which exert a considerable influence on our future and it is not surprising that a boy who dissected rabbits and who bleached their skulls and bones on the lawn at Bealings eventually took up medicine. However powerful the influence of Selous and Knight-Paton might have been it is doubtful whether they would have succeeded in making me into a doctor unless they had been aided by a natural bias in this direction.

To become a medical man at that time cost anything from one to three thousand pounds and my father had no intention of cutting the price. In order to discover what would be best for me he took counsel of Dr. George Ogilvie, a Scottish consultant then practising in Welbeck Street. 'Send him to Cambridge,' was the advice he received. 'They are beginning to object in London to what they call the Celtic invasion, and a degree from Cambridge will carry more weight than one from Edinburgh. Mind you, I'm not saying that the training at Cambridge is any better than in Edinburgh, but it's more canny to humour these Sassenachs.' So I took the Littlego and entered Cambridge university.

The transition from the Leys School to Gonville and Caius College was an easy one, and my new room in Trinity Street was a natural sequel to my prefect's study at the school. My dedicated knight now hung on more spacious walls and the oriental draperies I had bought at Liberty's curtained taller windows, and that was all. My new life, like my new room, was more spacious than the old one and furnished like it with many new conveniences. I would no longer be disturbed in the morning by the insistent clamour of that bell with which Harry, the school servant, awoke us from our slumbers. I could get up more or less when I liked and do whatever I felt like doing. There were lectures to be attended, but if I failed sometimes to put in an appearance nobody would make any fuss about it. Life, like music, is full of recurring themes, and at Caius much that had happened at school was repeated. Black Hawk again made things easy for me by gaining his college cap, this time a parti-coloured affair of light-blue and black. The cap gave me an immediate entry to good society, that is to say, to the society which congregated in small noisy groups in the court, and shouted to each other through its open windows. Caius boasted of two learned clubs, the 'Science and Art' and the 'Shakespearean', and the day following my election to the team I found a polite note on my table which invited me to become a member of the first of these erudite circles. I never reached the heights of the 'Shakespearean'. For that a blue, or at least a half-blue, was required, and although on three occasions I turned out against the 'varsity, I was never selected to play for it.

Those who aim at taking a First in the 'stinks' Tripos (a name derived from the smells emanating from chemical laboratories) have but little leisure. If I misused my time at Cambridge — and in retrospect I am sometimes inclined to believe that this was the case — my error lay in the direction of an over-devotion to work rather than of too much play. Science provides an arid soil for the development of some parts of the mind and I now agree with Stevenson that: 'An intelligent person looking out of his eyes and hearkening in his ears, will get more true education than may another in a life of heroic vigils.' But looking out of the eyes and hearkening in the ears is an art which the young man has not always acquired and by temperament I was more inclined to be engrossed with the affairs of science than with what Stevenson calls 'the warm and palpitating facts of life'. This does not mean that I became a college hermit poring over my books and neglectful of all else. I have memories of magnificent three-course Sunday breakfast parties continuing till long after lunch, of walks with friends to Grantchester, of expeditions up the river and of interminable discussions about the fourth dimension and the existence or not of telepathy and of ghosts. No, it was not all work at Cambridge. Nor were Knight-Paton and Selous entirely neglected. On a fine afternoon the former was sometimes to be seen on a spirited chestnut curvetting along the King's Parade in the direction of Trumping-ton, whilst a loiterer in Tree Court by night might have espied a figure climbing out of a top-floor window on to a ledge which ran round the buildings. Selous had heard of the famous Trinity College Climbing Club and it was his ambition to be the founder of a similar club at Caius. From Tree Court it was possible to reach the two older courts of the college and then to return again to the starting point by traversing the roofs of the dining-hall and the chapel. A visitor to Caius may still note that there is a ridge-tile missing from its dining-hall roof, and if he cares to climb the spire which overlooks King's Parade, and to examine the terminal of its lightning conductor, he may find a few shreds of a hand-kerchief tied to it forty years ago. I had time for diversions at Cambridge in spite of my now-to-be-regretted devotion to work.

At the end of my third year I passed out of the college gates and entered the square of St. Bartholomew's Hospital with a First Class Honours degree, a complete ignorance of the world which lay outside Cambridge, a suspicion of women, and a conviction that the male population of the world was divided into two categories, 'varsity men and non-'varsity men. It is to be regretted that the Personage had such a limited view of what is meant by a gentleman, but it must also be admitted that he was a snob. St. Bartholomew's Hospital was as different from Caius as were my new lodgings in Bloomsbury from my old quarters in Tree Court, and the change was so abrupt that I was inclined to feel aggrieved. It was obvious that the old days of elegance and freedom were over and that an earnest devotion to my profession was now being demanded of me. Nobody at St. Bartholomew's seemed to have any free time. White-coated figures were to be seen hastening across the square at all hours of the day, telephones rang, ambulances drew up at the entrance to the casualty room and students were for ever streaming in and out of the out-patient departments and the lecture halls. Almost before I had realized what had happened to me I found myself in what was apparently called the Surgery, a vast gloomy room divided into cubicles by screens, in which all the halt, the blind and the sick in London seemed to be collected. It was an utterly new world and a dirty, smelly world at that. It was also a world which had its own language, a lingua-franca of medicine made up of terms borrowed from the tongues of ancient Rome and Greece. Mistura gentianae cum rheo alkalinus, Lini-mentum Saponis, Haustus Calumbae Alkalinus — I selected one of these high-sounding medicines out of my new hospital pharmacopoeia, copied it on to a coloured prescription form and handed it to a patient, trusting that it was the right remedy for his particular disease. Fortunately most of these medicines were entirely innocuous and I had been assured that it was generally safe, when in doubt, to prescribe a mild purge or a rhubarb and gentian mixture. But one was not only a physician but also a surgeon, and it was the 'surgical case' that imposed on me the severer strain. The ulcers which these people exposed to my view could only be described as being horrible, and when one unrolled the bandage, the gauze dressing was generally stuck to them. What was one supposed to do? One could either spend hours slowly and painfully teasing off the gauze, or else one could tear it away with a single convulsive jerk. Which was the better, a protracted discomfort, or a shortlived intense pain? There were many such questions to be answered, and the house-surgeon in charge of one had far too much to do for every decision to be referred to him. It was here that Black Hawk often lent a useful hand, for having a contempt for pain, he was able to remain unruffled even in that awful surgery.

Every evening I retired gratefully to my lodgings at the corner of Guilford Street, but for the first few weeks I sometimes found it difficult to sleep. In my dreams I was back again in that surgery, flinching as I removed the dressings from some appalling sore or shutting out from my ears the screams of a child going under an anaesthetic. And there could be no doubt of the piercing quality of those screams. But when I awoke it was to find that they came from a yard just outside my bedroom window where two Bloomsbury cats were engaged in settling their marital differences. Could I continue the career which I had chosen, or would it be better to take up work of a less harrowing nature? I began to wonder whether I would be able to stand the strain of it all, but within a few weeks I had grown accustomed to the hospital surgery, and to all that I was called upon to do there.

The heart of St. Bartholomew's is the fountain in the centre of its fine square, and around this vital centre collected the dressers, the medical clerks and the house-physicians and house-surgeons awaiting the arrival of their chiefs, the members of the honorary staff. At two o'clock in the afternoon these great consultants from Harley Street would arrive in their carriages and pairs, and the Personage enjoyed witnessing this magnificent spectacle. He took a special pleasure in the smart shining broughams of Sir Lauder Brunton, Sir Dyce Duckworth and Sir Henry Butlin. How splendid were the horses of these noble knights and baronets, and how dashingly they entered the square. He noted with pleasure the cockades in the hats of the coachmen, the painted crests on the panels of the doors, and then whispered in my ear, 'There's greatness in Harley Street'. His words brought me comfort, for I had to admit that the life of a doctor was very different to that previously pictured by Selous. So far as I could see, it contained no place for a horse galloping across the desert and for romantic meetings with sheiks. But perhaps that would come.

Life in a big London hospital turned out to be less unpleasant than I had at first thought possible. The square of St. Bartholomew's, with its fountain, its shelters and its seats under the old plane trees had much in common with the cloisters of a monastery, the forum at Rome, the Platonic Academy and the village pump. It was here that we met to exchange the news of the day, to discuss clinical problems, to sharpen our wits and, on very rare occasions, to lay bare to our friends the secrets of our hearts. There were several old cronies of mine of whom, had I wanted to do so, I could have made confidants, for to the mother of all London hospitals had come many whom I had previously known at Cambridge; Podge Oulton, the burly Cambridge three-quarter, Gillies and Taylor, the rowing blues, Sammy Dickson from King's and Chandler from Jesus. There was also Patrick Brown, the famous Caius wit, who was as busy as ever with his quips and his jokes. 'Have you heard Patrick's latest?' was a well-known opening to an amusing anecdote. Patrick had long ago established a reputation as a wag in the courts of Caius, and so far he was managing to maintain it in the square at Bart's. He was our professional jester, but a jester into whose quips and jokes was beginning to creep an element of bitterness and spite. It was better to be on good terms with him, for if one was not, one was likely to become his butt.

In due course I 'went on the district'; in other words, I took up my residence in the broken-down house in Cloth Fair which was the head-quarters of those who were studying midwifery. For some reason or other, known only to nature, the ladies we attended in Clerkenwell usually required our services in the early hours of the morning. The clang of the loud-voiced night-bell would be heard just before dawn and, throwing on old clothes, the clerk on duty would hasten down to the front door to accompany some agitated husband along the deserted streets until he reached a lamplit room in which lay a woman in labour.

Why had not nature devised some better method of achieving her purposes and why was she so often in need of our help? Fortunately Podge Oulton, my usual companion in these nocturnal expeditions, seemed less puzzled by these mysterious happenings than I was, and only once did he let me down. We had retired for a breath of fresh air after a four hours' vigil culminating in a birth, whilst the patient's friend was tidying up the tousled room. In a few minutes, after having packed up our bags, we would be free to return to Cloth Fair, there to enjoy a well-earned breakfast. This work had its advantages, and there was something godlike in handing over to its parents a long-expected child. Suddenly our self-congratulatory reflections were cut short by the opening of an upper window and a piercing cry from the room that we had recently left. We looked gravely at each other and threw away our cigarettes. Something had obviously gone wrong, and two steps at a time we darted up the long and twisting staircase. 'I was only just in time,' said Oulton to me, when we talked the matter over, an hour later, on our way home. 'I had no idea that she was going to floor us with twins, had you?' I hadn't, but then, childbirth has always been to me a mystery, and I have never acquired nor ever hope to acquire that prescience of future events which every skilled accoucheur seems to possess.

The medical curriculum is a very exacting one and the picture that Charles Dickens once drew of the riotous life of the medical student is utterly out-of-date. Willingly or unwillingly, the student of medicine must devote himself to work and there is very little of interest to be recorded of those far-off student days at St. Bartholomew's. It is the dramatic incidents that arise in my memory when I look back at my life, and such subjects as the signs and symptoms of cholecystitis and the differences between lobar and bronchial pneumonia are devoid of all dramatic interest.

CHAPTER IV

SELOUS' FIRST EXPEDITION

Now although Selous and Knight-Paton had accepted the life at Bart's as a necessary interlude, they had no intention of leaving me entirely alone there. For them medicine was merely a preparation for future adventures and from time to time they would grow restless and would point out to me the advisability of leaving for a while my studies and of seeing something of the greater world which lay outside the hospital gates. A short holiday abroad would give me valuable experience and, in the end, make me into a better doctor than I would become if I remained the whole of my time in London. I had only to look at some of my fellow students to see how narrow was the outlook of a man who allowed himself to be too much the slave of his work. These and many similar arguments were used to tempt me from my studies.

In the rooms below me in Guilford Street there lived an unusual variety of the species medical student, a man who deliberately cultivated an aura of mystery and who, according to our landlady, spent most of his time studying Chinese. Wilkinson soon attracted the attention of the romantic pair within me, and sometimes of an evening I would abandon my studies and pay him a visit. What tales of adventure he could have told me had he been at liberty to do so! Without definitely stating this, he implied that he was engaged in work of the utmost secrecy and importance, and one night he displayed to me a gold watch on the back of which was engraven 'Remember Servia'. 'I was in the palace at the time', he said, 'at the very moment that King Peter and Queen Draga were being murdered. It was touch and go, but I kept my head and it was afterwards that I was presented with this watch.' Yes, but what was he doing there, in the palace? Was he in the plot to murder the King and Queen, or was he supposed to be protecting them? I was too tactful to put this question to him, but after listening to those stories which he was able to recount I discovered in them certain surprising features. There was, for example, that account he gave me of amputating a man's leg, single-handed and in the middle of a desert. 'He was bleeding like a pig, and I knew that unless I was pretty quick, he would be gone. Luckily I spied a piece of gas-piping and twisting it round his thigh to act as a tourniquet, I did the job with the simple instruments I happened to possess. He recovered.' How strange that there should be scraps of gas-piping lying about in the desert, thought Selous. 'That's not the sort of desert that I'm accustomed to travel in.' I began to wonder whether this big man Wilkinson, with his strange habits, his hints of secret missions in the Balkans and North Africa and his studied neglect of medicine — he rarely appeared at the hospital — was all that I had first thought him to be. In spite of the watch and the old Spanish coins presented to him by the Sultan of Morocco I became suspicious of him. Several years later, when I had acted on his invitation to visit him at Marraquesh and had actually landed on the coast of Morocco at Mogador, these early suspicions were fully confirmed. Wilkinson was a consummate liar. The armed escort which he had promised would be awaiting me there to conduct me to the Sultan's palace, in which he said he was living in the capacity of private medical adviser to Muley Hafid, never arrived. On inquiry of the resident British consul I learnt that there was a strange Englishman, whom the consul had once met travelling through Morocco seated on a donkey and accompanied by a similarly mounted lady, whom he introduced to everyone as 'La Princesse de Moroque'. She looked suspiciously like an ordinary Jewess. Wilkinson undoubtedly had adventures, but they were not always the adventures which he narrated.

It was not only in Guilford Street that Selous and Knight-Paton waylaid me to tempt me away from my dull work and to induce me to go out into the wide world in search of adventure. Suddenly and surreptitiously they would appear at my elbow in the library or the pathological museum. What was I studying? A map of Europe showing the famous centres of learning in the Middle Ages. How interesting; did it not show equally well how little of the world I had yet seen? What was that strange-looking island shaped like a duck on the very edge of the duck-pond of Europe? It was Iceland, a land not only of ice, igloos and reindeer-sledges, but also of polar bears and seals. They met me also in the hospital museum. What was in this specimen case in the corner? It was a great canine tooth from the jaws of a sabre-toothed tiger. Then, what on earth was I doing peering through glass at this fragment of majesty when by rights I should be stalking the tiger itself. This was not the way to spend one's life, messing about amongst a lot of dry bones and pickled specimens. Little did it matter to the heroic pair that long, long ago in the great glacial epoch, the last of the sabre-toothed tigers had lain down and died.

A revolt against hospital discipline was bound to happen sooner or later, and it did. Within a few months of the beginning of Selous' whisperings I found myself a passenger in a small Danish vessel which was ploughing its way through a broken sea in the direction of Iceland. The small company that met for meals in the saloon was an odd assortment of beings. At the last moment I had induced Archie Brandon to accompany me, and he was now sitting with me at the long table that bisected the saloon. Archie had a small allowance from his people and, because his health had not been too good, he had been forced to abandon the medical career on which he had started with me at Cambridge. He was now a gentleman at large, with no fixed occupation and with three pounds in his pocket with which to defray all future expenses in Iceland. I had guaranteed that it would not cost more, though on what grounds I would have had difficulty to say. Later in life Archie developed such a strong passion for stamp-collecting that he was in the habit of taking up his residence in that particular part of the globe that seemed best able to provide him with new specimens for his album. But at the present moment he was in ignorance of what later would prove to be an important directing force in his life, and he was coming with me to Iceland chiefly because I had pointed out that it looked funny hanging on to the edge of the map of Europe. Archie had agreed with me and had immediately felt sympathy for Iceland on the grounds that few people seemed to want to visit it. Opposite us at the table sat an elderly man with the complexion and the expression of a dried fig, and with limbs that gave at the joints whenever he moved, but otherwise remained rigid. He turned out to be Colonel Fraser of the North-West Frontier Force. Next to the Colonel sat his opposite number in the way of physical form, Van Noorden, the fat Dutch cigar merchant. Van Noorden's face was pink and white and his movements were as jointless, smooth and round as those of a jellyfish. Last of all — and how many times did we wish that he was not there — was the man from Nottingham. He was obviously an outsider, and we had as little to do with him as possible. The Personage looked on him with extreme disfavour and detested the sound of his uncultured voice. It was whispered that in addition to the passengers at the table there were two Icelandic ladies on board. As they never appeared at meals I concluded that Icelandic femininity lived under some system of 'purdah'. Later in the voyage, when our little ship struck the full force of the Arctic Ocean, unpleasant noises were to be heard coming from the direction of a cabin the door of which had remained closed since the day we had sailed from Leith. These suggested to me that the hidden ladies might not be so much in 'purdah' as in dire physical distress. This turned out to be a correct diagnosis.

We caught sight of Iceland on the evening of the third day. It appeared on the north-west horizon mixed up with the splendour of the setting sun, and the scene made such a vivid impression on me that 'sunset in the Arctic Ocean' became one of the favourite subjects of my imaginative painting when, at a later date in my life, I took up watercolours. With the unthinking courage of the beginner I attempted to portray colours which might possibly have been mimicked in some great stained-glass window, but which could never have been put down on paper. I doubt whether Turner himself could have caught the contrast between the long line of purple cliffs of Iceland and the shining splendour of its ice-capped 'jokylls' towering high above them. Romance lay not only in the distance but in the tiny ship in which I was tossing. Collected at the bow was a group of Icelanders, emigrants to America who were now returning to their country after an absence of many years. Children who had never seen the fatherland were being held up to catch their first glimpses of Iceland before its golden splendours had faded through orange, red, blue and violet into the dull indigo of night. And when the light had gone the sound of old Icelandic songs, wild and stern, like the music of all mountain races, reached us from the deck below.

We were due to drop anchor in Reykjavik Harbour early the next morning and the time had come for a decision as to what we were going to do after we had landed there. Until this moment Archie Brandon and I had given no consideration to this problem, but now it appeared that our more provident fellow passengers had long ago made their arrangements. They were all bound for the famous hot-springs and geysers which lay two days' journey from the capital. Apparently there were no roads in Iceland and the only method of travelling about the island was on ponies. As these were very small each traveller required at least three of them, one to ride, one to carry his equipment and the third to act as a spare mount. Ponies could be hired for five kronen a day, and since a guide was essential, and he also would need three mounts, Brandon and I could not get away with less than a stable of nine. The Colonel had also a great deal to say on the subject of equipment and supplies. He had brought with him the saddlebags he formerly used on the North-West Frontier, a primus stove, a serviceable tent that could be wrapped up and strapped to the saddle, a picnic basket fitted with collapsible mugs and two canvas bags filled with an assortment of tins of everything from ox-tongue to chutney.

Having gained this information Archie and I retired, rather dispirited, from the saloon to the darkness and the privacy outside. What were *we* going to do? Our joint equipment consisted of two battered bags, a camera and the remains of a tin of ginger-nuts. After reviewing this shabby collection we counted out our money on a seat lit by the light coming through the saloon window. Changed into Iceland currency this represented three hundred kronen. If we could secure berths in the next boat back — and apparently there was some doubt about this — we had to budget for at least eight days' residence in Iceland. Could we live on our limited means, let alone become the owners of a travelling circus of ponies. We soon decided that we had misstated the problem. There could be no doubt that we were going to acquire the circus and it only remained for us now to decide how we were going to live. 'Horses', announced Archie defiantly, 'are in every way superior to human beings.' Later in his life, while completing his set of Ceylon stamps, Archie became an amateur jockey in Colombo, and horses became his passion. 'I can do without food', boasted Black Hawk within me, 'and if need be, a stone will serve me quite well as a pillow.' So within a very short time we decided that we would hire ponies, and having acquired them, that we would trust to luck to find food. We pocketed our kronen and returned to the saloon. There good fortune was awaiting us.

'Hello', said the Colonel, as soon as we had joined the table, 'we're drawing up the plan of our campaign. If you boys haven't already engaged a guide, why not join our party?' We had not engaged one, and even at the cost of riding cheek by jowl with that dreadful man from

Nottingham, we thankfully fell in with the Colonel's suggestion. The initial guide difficulty had been settled and the food problem could easily wait. Elijah had not worried himself about any catering arrangements, and the ravens had supplied all his physical needs. We would follow his example.

Next day we climbed down the side of the ship into a small boat and, steering a course through a bobbing flotilla of eiderducks, we landed in Reykjavik. It was a very different place from the igloo town we had pictured. Low wooden buildings stood side by side with long sheds of galvanized iron from which emanated an overpowering odour of dried fish. Some of the houses were built of whitewashed stone, and some of tarred wood, so that the capital of Iceland, at that time, was not unlike a large fishing village in the north of Scotland. The Icelanders conformed as little with our previous picture of Icelanders as did their town. Two of them had come on board to claim the bleached and shrunken occupants of the inside cabin and from one of these, a Mr. Magnuson, I received a polite invitation to visit him in his Icelandic home. I accepted this and some hours later I found myself in a plainly furnished, but very comfortable, dwelling on the outskirts of the town. The link with my host, namely the drooping black figure that I had watched being helped down the ship's gangway, had again gone into purdah and we were alone.

'So you are surprised at us Icelanders,' said Mr. Magnuson, in excellent English, taking from a tail pocket a red bandanna handkerchief marked with a curious brown stain, and burnishing his glasses. 'You expected to find us dressed in skins, and so on? Why, Iceland had her culture and her literature in days when your countrymen were painting themselves blue. Have you never heard of the Icelandic sagas?'

Indeed I had. The Colonel had brought with him a small pocket edition of Icelandic sagas, and I had been reading them during the voyage. Three of my inner company were thrilled with them.

'When you get to Thingvellir you must make a point of visiting the island on which our heroes used to fight. You remember that Gunnlaug was in love with Helga the Fair and that during his absence at the wars she married Hrafn.'

'Such things are apt to happen,' I answered. 'He ought not to have left her.'

'But he had made a vow,' explained Mr. Magnuson. 'Let me see — how does the saga go? Ah, yes.

> "Thus runneth my vow,
> To voyage and visit
> In court and castle
> Three kings and two earls:
> Then back turn I hither,
> When he calls me to battle,
> Who giveth gold arm rings,
> The rich kings great heir."

And while he was away Helga married Hrafn.'

'So he lost her because he wanted gold arm rings. What happened next?'

'Well, when he returned and found that she had left him, he sought out Hrafn and fought with him on the island near Thingvellir.'

'And slew him?'

'No. That was later, in the final combat which took place in Norway. But the most famous of all the sagas is the Njal saga, and it is the one I like best. You haven't read it? Well, I will tell it to you.' And there in that room, after he had lit the oil-lamp and seated himself in a comfortable chair beside me, Mr. Magnuson talked of Harold the Fair and of heroes and kings, of troll-wives and gnomes, of blood feuds and mortal combats, till I seemed to be no longer living in this matter-of-fact world but in the pages of some fairy-book. Every now and then he paused, and drew from his pocket a small round metal box, the lid of which was decorated with a pattern that I had once seen carved on a stone in the island of Iona. From it he took a pinch of snuff, sniffing it up the right nostril first and then the left, with his head tilted to one side like a robin and with a smile of amusement on his face. Now I knew the explanation of the brown stains on the red handkerchief.

'It is an old custom with us,' he said, as though answering my thoughts. 'I believe it is beginning to die out in England.'

Beginning to die out! Why, this old Icelander belonged to the age of Dickens. Soon he would be inquiring of me about the mail-coach to Portsmouth and be asking what quadrilles were being danced in the fashionable world of London. But I answered only that this was true and that people now seemed to prefer cigarettes.

'A dirty habit,' he said, as he wiped away a tiny trickle of brown that was emerging from one nostril. 'With cigarette ash all over their houses I am not surprised that English women are beginning to get restive.'

Mr. Magnuson had evidently heard something about the new feminist movement and he had his own views as to the causes of British women's discontent. A few minutes later I rose, thanked my host for all the interesting stories he had told me, shook him warmly by the hand and made my departure. 'Don't forget to visit the island where our warriors fought', said Mr. Magnuson, just before he closed the front door, 'and if there is a moon, visit it by moonlight.'

On reaching the small hotel in which our modest luggage had been deposited I found that Archie had made good use of his time while I had been away. He had found a man who could let us have five ponies at the reduced price of four kronen a day each and, as we had very little luggage, one pack-pony would be enough for the two of us. The bargain was clearly an excellent one and Archie had promptly closed with it. Afterwards he had visited a strange shop at which was sold dried fish, sealskin, leather straps, fishing-tackle, aniseed and bread. Having no knowledge of the cooking of dried fish, and no use for sealskin, aniseed, straps or fishing-tackle, he had only purchased bread. There, under the chair, was our sole sustenance for the journey. I looked at the strange amorphous mass lying on the floor and was startled by its octoroon colour. It did not look appetizing but, clearly, it would travel. Archie had done wonders. Now for Thingvellir and the geysers.

We started early next morning. The cavalcade consisted of the Colonel (an obvious leader of men), Van Noorden, the man from Nottingham — how I hated his golf-trousers and his vulgar new leggings — Archie and myself. With us rode two Icelanders, one our guide and the other a personal attendant to the Dutch cigar merchant. Each of us was astride a small Iceland pony, our feet so near to the ground that from a distance we must have looked like a Bank Holiday party mounted on donkeys. Before us scampered a troop of thirteen ponies, some carrying equipment, and amongst it Archie's octoroon mass, and some enjoying a temporary freedom. Selous was reminded of days out West rounding up cattle and he sat his mount with the insolent air of his favourite character, Black Gully Dick. Archie rode like the jockey he was.

Reykjavik was left behind us and we were soon in a country of low hills covered with scrub. The Colonel, with his long thin legs trailing on each side of a diminutive pony, resembled a lead soldier that had got into another box and had been stuck by a careless child on to the wrong mount. Yet in spite of the fact that his feet barely missed the ground, he contrived to ride like a cavalryman.

'Extraordinarily like a valley in Tibet,' he remarked, pointing to a depression between the two hills towards which we were riding. The land in front of us had obviously in some past age been the site of much volcanic activity and it was as bare of vegetation as was the back of the Colonel's head. Looking at its desolation I understood why mountain races are forced, for the sheer need of living company, to people such inhospitable regions with gnomes and spirits from another world. After two hours' riding through this barren scenery we changed mounts, our liberated ponies scampering away in front of us with joyful kicks and plunges. At length the Colonel called a halt and announced that it was time for 'tiffin'. Archie and I looked at each other and without exchanging a word we retired together behind a large rock.

Our action might appear unsociable, but we had private reasons for preferring to eat alone. The man from Nottingham noted our disappearance and, being very touchy about his native town, he appeared to regard it as a direct affront on the part of two Cambridge graduates to the university that had recently been established on the banks of the River Trent. I distinctly heard the words, 'unsociable' and 'standoffish' as I turned the corner of the boulder. Archie had unstrapped the canvas bag containing our supplies and the bread now lay on the ground in front of us, looking like a first cousin of the boulders that lay strewn around. We munched for some minutes in silence and then exchanged glances. From behind the rock were coming sounds, the creak of the opening of the Colonel's picnic basket and the rasp of openers cutting into tin. The air of Iceland was invigorating and our appetites were keen, so it was only because our jaws were fatigued that we again wrapped the brown mass in its sacking and corded it on to our baggage pony. Then, lighting cigarettes, we sighed, rested our backs against the boulder and waited patiently. Twenty minutes later there were new noises on the other side of the rock. 'Now then, you boys,' shouted the Colonel, 'we've a long way to go, and we must be off.'

'All right', answered Archie, 'don't wait for us. We haven't quite finished, but we'll catch you up.'

'What do you mean?' I protested. 'Not finished!' But Archie held up a warning finger.

'They're bound to have left behind some tins, and there may be something in them,' he whispered. And he was right, for when the party had got to a safe distance we crept from our lair like two marauding Indians and pounced on the remnants of the feast.

'Thank God for litter,' said Archie, fishing two battered sardines out of a tin.

'Heaven bless Nottingham,' I answered, drinking 'absent friends' in peach juice.

'Now we must hurry,' said Archie, and having mounted our ponies we galloped after the party.

Our guide was a serious and disturbingly well educated Icelandic youth, who spent the long winter nights poring over the classics and the long days of summer earning money for his winter's studies by acting as guide. He spoke Icelandic, Danish, French and English fluently and, discovering that Archie and I had been at Cambridge, he engaged us in a conversation on the relative merits of Virgil, Cicero and Horace. I fear that he was somewhat disappointed by the vagaries of our answers, and by the rapidity with which we drew his attention to the beauties of the country through which we were passing. After five hours' riding, by which time the sun had sunk beneath the distant hills, we arrived at Thingvellir of the sagas, the meeting-place of the Thing, that most ancient of all parliaments. In the half-light of an Arctic summer night it looked the home of mystery, a place built, like the Giant's Causeway, out of basalt pillars, shaped and hammered together by volcanic force. Before me stood a solitary building, the local inn, a wooden hut with light streaming through the windows. After such a long ride it looked extremely inviting.

Having dismounted I accepted Archie's offer to look after the ponies and opened the outer door and then another to enter what I believed would prove to be the main room in the building. Heavens! where was I? Seated at a table and facing me was the most kingly person that I had ever imagined. Harold the Fair had come to life again and had taken up his residence in Thingvellir! Small wonder that it was said that the blood of the gods ran in his veins, for here was someone who seemed to me to be more than a man. Before me sat a veritable demi-god, with a fine head, clustered with flaxen curls, the chest of a warrior, eyes of piercing blue and the limbs of a Greek statue — Hector, perhaps even Hercules himself had come back to earth. He was dressed in a leather doublet, with breeches of blue-green sailcloth, and he was talking to two quite ordinary men, seated on either side of him. On his fingers flashed two enormous jewels, one an emerald and one a diamond, and from each ring there ran tiny gold chains to a bracelet round his wrist. A smile flickered in his eyes. What does one do when a demi-god smiles at one? I had no idea, so I hastily closed the door and retired in confusion.

Outside they were tying the ponies up to a line stretched between two stakes. Archie had secured our team and he was now approaching the hut with that blasted mummied meal under his arm.

'Hello,' he said, 'have you seen a ghost, or are you merely faint from hunger?'

'There's a man in there, and I can't think who he can be.'

'Nothing in that,' said Archie. 'I'll introduce you, and you can invite him to dine with us. Hello, here's the Colonel, and he'll know all about him.'

The Colonel did, and in a few soldierly words he explained that there would be just sufficient accommodation for us all if we dossed down in two rooms. Philippe, Duc d'Orleans, had unexpectedly arrived at Thingvellir only a few hours before us and with his retinue he was occupying the rest of the house. He had just returned from exploring the north coast of Greenland and his ship was now lying at anchor off Reykjavik. The Colonel had met him when he was shooting in India some years ago, and later he would take the opportunity of introducing us. It was either his father or his grandfather, he did not remember which, who had been the last king of France and had lost both his popularity and his throne by indiscreet speculating on the Bourse. He was a great traveller, the duke, and, for a Frenchman, he was a very good fellow, quite a sportsman indeed.

That evening will never be forgotten by Selous, Knight-Paton and the Personage, and when it was arranged that the duke's party and our own should combine forces on the morrow and should ride together to the geysers, they could barely restrain themselves from shouting. Never before had they been so heartily in agreement in their admiration for one person, for here in Philippe d'Orleans were united an explorer, a mighty hunter, a fighter of duels and a king. It was true that he had lost his throne, but once a king, always a king, especially when the crown jewels of France are worn on the finger. The only dark spot on that otherwise scintillating evening was the man from Nottingham. To see him smirking before the royal eyes and to listen to his dreadful accent was nothing less than torture. After he had said, 'Yes, Dook', for the third time, I left the room in dudgeon and strode away into the outer darkness.

No, it was not dark. There was a strange flickering in the sky that lit up the ground and allowed me to find my way without difficulty around the great boulders scattered over the earth as though by some petulant giant. A path led downwards towards a stream which ran between two cliffs of black rock, and when I had reached the end of this path, I sat down to think. Somewhere near me must be the island that Mr. Magnuson had urged me to see by moonlight, the island where the old heroes had fought. But what was this strange flickering that had suddenly grown stronger? And looking up again I saw that the sky was lit by lambent flames of light, the aurora borealis. Before this splendour of the heavens, dukes, heroes and demi-gods sank into the earth, the clamour within me died down and there was I, a tawdry little snob sitting on a boulder thinking my shabby little thoughts — I and all this bigness around me. It was as though I had come-to from an anaesthetic. For a moment I saw myself as I was, stripped of all the finery lent to me by my imagination, and, like a blustering beggar who has suddenly caught sight of himself in a mirror, I was ashamed. How petty were the thoughts, vanities and grievances which had been troubling me a few minutes ago and yet they had been in complete control of me. Apart from them I could not be said to have existed. Was this in truth all that I was, a sequence of reactions?

Plessner, the German physiologist, has written that man is unique in having the capacity to struggle out of the current of blind living and to look at himself a little more objectively, as he is and not as he imagines himself to be, but it is a power which he is seldom able to use. Only at rare moments does he become a startled spectator of the sequence of sensations, emotions and thoughts which make up his psychic being and then, so swiftly that he does not even register the change, he is swept along again in the swift current of unconscious living. So now did it happen to me. For a moment my eyes had been open and then they closed so that I saw myself no more.

We set off next day on the long journey to the geysers and my heart went out to the pony that carried the duke. He was an excellent horseman, a veritable centaur, but a centaur whose top half was so much bigger than his lower half that I expected at any moment to see him topple over. Fortunately our Iceland ponies' legs, like those of the Somalis I was later in life to meet, were much better than they looked, and we reached the region of the hot springs without such a mishap having occurred. During the journey Archie and I adopted the luncheon tactics of the previous day and with even greater success. The Colonel was suffering from a liver attack, possibly due to the celebrations of the night before, and his appetite was so poor that he left behind half a tin of bully beef. Our rations were also considerably improved by the addition of some excellent pickles supplied by a fashionable West End firm patronized by the duke. The ravens were feeding us and we had been right when we had elected to follow the example set by Elijah.

We had no longer need to worry about ourselves, and having been relieved on this score, our anxiety was promptly transferred to the geysers. Our guide had warned us that although the smaller of the two hot springs could be relied upon to give a good performance several times a day, the behaviour of the larger was very erratic. Sometimes it would remain sullenly underground, refusing to show itself to visitors and sometimes it would give a stupendous display. On our arrival the small one was working splendidly, but, as the guide had warned us, the great geyser, the one we had come all this way to see, was, like the Colonel, distinctly 'off colour'.

The party sat patiently round the great steaming cauldron for hours but during the whole of that time no bubble of steam broke the glassy smoothness of its surface. Clearly something must be done about it. On being approached on the subject the Icelander who kept the small inn at which visitors stayed shook his head mournfully, but he agreed to take a look at the geyser. The good repute of the neighbourhood and of his hotel was at stake, and he gazed at the water that refused to blow up with the disappointed expression of a parent whose child has the bad taste to sulk before visitors. His attitude, though sympathetic, was not helpful, so we consulted the only other local authority on geysers, a neighbouring farmer, and from him we obtained real practical assistance. To make a sick geyser work one must apparently dose it with butter. This, the farmer explained, was not blind empiricism, but therapeutics resting on a sound scientific basis. By spreading over the surface of the cauldron the melted butter would prevent the escape of gas, and when the pressure of steam had risen to the necessary height, the geyser would blow up. It was really very simple, and fortunately the farmer was able to supply us with the proper medicine. The party looked at Archie and me. The doctors must decide. Geyser ailments did not happen to be in our line, but we had sufficient medical knowledge to know that a verdict, given in no uncertain voice, was required of us. We held a brief consultation and then agreed with the farmer. We had done our part and we could now honourably retire and allow the Colonel to take charge.

'How much do you give it?'

'Twenty pounds,' replied the farmer, 'and I can let you have it by this afternoon.'

'It seems a lot,' murmured the Colonel.

Archie and I agreed with him, but we held our tongues. Half a pound of butter would never be missed by a geyser, and we knew where it was needed even more than by a pool of sulky hot water; our bread was not yet finished. But by now we should have known the Colonel better, for when the butter arrived it never left his sight.

'It is essential,' said the Colonel, as though contradicting our unvoiced thoughts, 'that everything should be done properly. First it must be sewn up in a canvas bag, and then the bag must be thrown right into the middle of the pool. I myself will be responsible for all the necessary arrangements.'

Like two cats sniffing round a parcel of kippers we watched him at work, and when he had finished the sewing we followed him down to the brink of the mighty cauldron. The Colonel swayed backwards and forwards and then suddenly threw with such gusto that butter, bag and thrower disappeared momentarily from view. As we dragged a sodden, perspiring and partially cooked Colonel from the edge of the sulky geyser's maw, we heard an angry growl. Two immense bubbles of gas had risen to the surface, and then all was peace again. We waited in vain, for the geyser, that great brute who had taken all the butter, was giving nothing in return.

'What a wicked waste,' said Archie, as we made our way back to the inn.

'What a clever farmer,' I answered.

The duke now parted company with us but before doing so he invited us to pay him a visit on board his ship when we had completed our trip and were back in Reykjavik again. We reached the capital a few days later than he, only to discover that the vessel on which Archie and I were to make our return journey to England had been delayed and that we had, somehow or other, to defray the cost of four extra days of living out of a by now exhausted capital. But again our luck was in. There were two minor casualties in our party to whom I was now acting as doctor, one being the Colonel, with a scalded foot, and the other the Dutch cigar merchant. I would take no fee from a leader who had suffered in the common cause, but I had no scruples in accepting an honorarium from a wealthy Dutchman. Evidently nature did not forsee that man would eventually take to horseback, for if she had done so she would have taken the precaution when creating him of toughening his skin where toughening is needed for comfortable riding. Thanks to her lack of foresight I earned a welcome fee by applying fomentations to the resentful integument of a man who never before had ridden a horse, let alone an Iceland pony. This materially eased our, by now, extremely difficult financial position; indeed but for this help of the Iceland ponies we could not have met our hotel bill.

On a beautiful summer morning, the day after our return to Reykjavik, five of us rowed towards the solid wooden ship in which the duke had spent the greater part of the previous winter, shrouded in mist and locked in the ice of northern Greenland. Selous ran a professional eye over the reinforced timbers as we approached the massive hull, and he noted with a thrill the spearlike object projecting from the bow, obviously a harpoon. We clambered up the steep gangway that had been let down for us and then stepped on to the deck of a ship which was literally chock-a-block with wonders; two polar bear cubs in a roomy wooden crate, a black retriever dog which had been found alone, adrift on an ice-floe, pelts from seals and walruses, a collection of arctic birds and studies made by the duke's artist of many strange creatures — what more could anybody want? Then, thrilled by all these astonishing sights, we gathered in a little group in the bow of the ship and, raising glasses as fragile as soap-bubbles, we drank our host's health in excellent champagne. The Personage noted with pride the labels on the bottles, resplendent with the royal arms of the House of Orleans. He thought how glorious it would be to make his return journey, not in that old Danish tramp, but on this ship as private (although without a diploma) physician to the duke. How glorious, yes, but in life the appropriate ending is much less likely to happen than it is in a play. Instead, Archie and I returned to Leith in an old Danish tramp, together with some two hundred Iceland ponies destined for the mines. On arriving in Scotland we discovered that owing to the delay in our sailing the excursion tickets we had taken from London to Edinburgh were now out-of-date. But in a corridor train it is possible, by the exercise of a little cleverness, to evade the collection of tickets, and when we reached London we both agreed that we had had a splendid holiday, a holiday during which we had seen an astonishing number of things and at a surprisingly small cost. This was particularly gratifying to a Scot.

CHAPTER V

THE PARTY GIVES UP MOUNTAINEERING

LIFE moves unevenly over the recording wax of the mind, at one time cutting deeply into it and at another leaving on its surface only the faintest impression. When I look back on my days as a medical student at St. Bartholomew's it is my holidays which I remember best and my work at the hospital which I have difficulty in recalling. Although by now I was enjoying this work and becoming enthusiastic about my profession, it was only during my brief holidays that I was able to indulge that innate desire in me for adventure and romance. Adventure for me was anything that was sufficiently startling and unusual to lift me for a moment out of the deep ruts of ordinary living. Romance was closely allied to it and might almost be described as adventure dressed up in foreign clothes. If one were to encounter a burglar in one's home and were to become friendly with him, it would be an adventure, but if one were to meet a bandit in a picturesque garb and were to become his guest in some Corsican cave, that would be the most desirable of all experiences, the romantic adventure. Some day I would have great romantic adventures, but in the meantime I would have to content myself with any small incidents of this nature which might occur during my holidays. With the help of the imagination these could be made to resemble the genuine article.

But holidays were short and few, for the medical curriculum was such an exacting one that it allowed me very little free time. Into every day at the hospital was crammed the maximum of work; lectures occupied a large part of the morning and they were followed by attendance in the wards and the out-patient departments, and by demonstrations in the laboratories and the medical museum. We were like chickens on some intensive poultry-farm being stuffed to the beaks with food for our sprouting feathers, our wings and our growth into fully-fledged fowls. The medical school of St. Bartholomew's was famed for its teaching, and like an industrious chick I gorged myself with facts, retiring to my rooms in the evening, stuporous with over-feeding. The belief to which I had come at Cambridge, namely that science was the only reliable guide to living and that in time it would give me answers to all my questions grew stronger. I even dreamt of a day when I myself, borne on the wings of research, would rise into the air and make great discoveries. Poor little chicken, fed on grains of scientific knowledge and dreaming of being an eagle soaring towards the sun! Little did you guess how short were your wings and how limited was their range of flight. If I had examined it more carefully I would have found that the food on which I was being reared contained as much chaff as it contained grain. A great deal of it was only words, empty husks that contained no kernel of true knowledge. Doctors are particularly clever at covering up gaps in their knowledge by means of high-sounding words derived from the dead languages. Some people show a tendency to develop gout, so we term their unknown weakness 'the gouty diathesis', and having done so, we feel more comfortable and wiser. Other patients, for no apparent reason, develop jaundice, so we label their yellowness 'idiopathic'. The Greek language provides us with an impressive curtain of classical terms behind which ignorance can be discreetly hidden, and the medical lecturers at the hospital made full use of it.

Suspicious now of all conclusions that did not rest on a scientific basis, I was inclined to dismiss as illusory those strange experiences when for a moment the world with its 'loud trafficking' retired into the distance and I seemed to catch a glimpse of things that had been hidden from me before. Such moments were of a religious nature and not to be encouraged, for psychologists had clearly shown that religion was a retreat from reality, a compensatory illusion sought by men who found life too difficult to face. I had made up my mind to have no more dealings with false guides to knowledge, but to follow reason, that clear light that had led man slowly upwards from the level of the beasts to the exalted height on which he now stood. Religion was therefore sewn up in a dust-sheet, labelled 'Not wanted during the voyage', and thrown into the hold, where it remained for a great many years.

My holidays were not so much planned as accidental. Every now and then Selous would take charge of me and would carry me off willy-nilly in search of adventure. One of these periodic rebellions of his was now about to occur. Roof-climbing at Cambridge had given me a taste for mountaineering, and later I had had experience of the real thing amongst the Cumberland hills. There, with my companions and primed by Owen

Glyn-Jones' invaluable book on rock climbing, I had learnt to cling to steep slabs of rock and to wriggle my way up chimneys. The crannies and footholds of the Eagle's Nest arrete, the Hand-Traverse, the Stomach-Traverse, Slingsby's chimney and Kern Knott's Crack had been so carefully mapped out by Glyn-Jones that we were familiar with them long before we had actually met them. His book was our bible and the fact that he had met his death later on the slopes of the Dent Blanche conferred on his words a kind of sanctity. The passion for mountaineering grew and in my Bloomsbury lodgings of an evening I made practice circuits of my room. I learnt to scramble from the mantelpiece on to the top of the bookcase, and thence, hanging perilously from the picture rail, to struggle by means of various pieces of furniture back again to the mantelpiece. By this means I could make a complete circuit of the room without ever touching the floor. Poor Mrs. Weeks, our landlady, must often have pondered deeply in her home in the basement over the strange behaviour of her lodgers, with Mr. Wilkinson studying Chinese in an exotic garment on the first floor and Mr. Walker on the second balancing himself for no apparent reason on the mantelpiece. Unknown to herself, she supplied by her unexpected entry into my room that incalculable element which exists in all serious climbing, the falling of stones down 'couloirs', or the sudden noise of an avalanche. She and her overworked maid, Eliza, rendered the circuit of my room far more exciting.

An unexpected letter now arrived from my cousin Osborne telling me that he was spending a climbing holiday in Switzerland and inviting me to join him there. I was due for a short summer holiday and I sent him a wire gladly accepting his invitation. A few days later I was in the Alps, to be more precise at Zermatt. The mighty pyramid of the Matterhorn towered above our little village, a challenge to any climber. We must get into training. This we did by tying ourselves together with a rope — the special rope supplied by the Alpine Club was easily recognized by the strand of red wool interwoven with its hemp — and climbing for hours over scree, moraines, escarpments, glaciers and all the other hindrances to progress we could find. My cousin was a far more experienced climber than I was, but he seemed to me to be unnecessarily assertive. Sometimes his dogmatism on the subject of the correct route was such that I would untie myself from his company and assert my right as a free man to find my own way across the glacier. It was almost always the wrong one, but after two hours of wandering amid bergschrunds and crevasses, Black Hawk, who never had much to say, was reduced to silence and he would rarely admit his mistake. To have done so would, after all, only have encouraged Osborne's pigheadedness. Having finished the preliminary part of our training we climbed the Riffelhorn by a great variety of routes and then made an ascent of the Breithorn. Here Selous had his first experience of a night in an Alpine hut. We shared it with a man whom I was told was a well-known climber, a certain Mr. Martin Conway, who was taking his two daughters up the long tedious snow promenade of the Breithorn. At last the great day arrived for the ascent of the mighty giant at whose foot we had been living for the last ten days. In beautiful weather we ascended the Matterhorn and having conquered it we proceeded to belittle our achievement. Why had people made so much of a climb that we had found so easy? The very question conferred on us a feeling of superiority.

Now for the Rothhorn. This peak looked less imposing, but was said to be much more difficult, and in unfavourable weather it might even prove to be dangerous. We went to Zinal, where we were joined by Parkinson, a house-physician at Bart's. There we were forced to wait, for the fine weather had broken and in bad weather the Rothhorn is best avoided. Four days later the sky seemed to be clearing and, with two guides, we made our way towards the Zinal hut. We had it to ourselves, for the weather still looked threatening and under unfavourable conditions the Rothhorn was a mountain with a bad repute. The guides awakened us two hours before dawn with the news that things still looked so unsettled that it would be wiser for us to abandon the climb. Certainly it seemed that their advice was good, for looking up at the great peak towering into the darkness above us we could just make out that its summit was enshrouded in cloud. A low rumble of distant thunder spoke with even greater emphasis in support of our guides' opinion, but having waited so long we were not disposed to give up all hope. We would wait, we said, for a couple of hours and see then whether the weather had sufficiently improved to allow us to undertake the ascent. At the end of that time it seemed that we were to be rewarded for our persistence; the peak was now uncovered. My cousin had made up his mind. 'We will go,' he said; and we went.

Two hours' climbing brought us to the snow arrete that leads on to the rock knife-edge of the Rothhorn. But all was not well with the party, for Parkinson, who at the hut was feeling off colour, was now obviously ill. He was indeed in such distress that although he was as anxious as we were to make the first ascent of the Rothhorn that season, he was easily persuaded to return to the hut. A sick man on a rope is a danger to all, and if he had not given in it is doubtful, in view of what was to follow, whether this book would ever have been written. The party now advanced more quickly and in another half-hour we were on the rock, sometimes just below the skyline and at others *au cheval* on the ridge itself, with one leg pointing down to Zermatt and the other dangling above Zinal. It was a thrilling climb, and when at last we clambered into a tiny hollow that marked the summit of the Rothhorn, even the taciturn Black Hawk was induced to display signs of pleasure. We had done it, and we had done it under conditions that were none too favourable. Peering down towards Zermatt we could see far below us four tiny black dots moving slowly over a snowfield. It was another party of climbers tackling the Rothhorn from the Zermatt side and we watched them with interest.

'Why, they've given it up, and they're going back,' said my cousin a few minutes later, and we laughed the laugh of superior beings. 'The Zermatt people have given up', explained my cousin in French to our guides, who were looking in the opposite direction, 'they're going back.' But our guides seemed to be worried and when we followed the direction of their gaze we discovered the reason for this. Great black columns of cloud were advancing from Zinal in our direction, and as we watched them, first the valleys and then even the great neighbouring peaks were blotted out; a storm was brewing.

Four mosquitoes on a pinnacle of rock, we watched the preparations for such a storm as I had never before witnessed, even from the valley, let alone from the centre of the conflict. Suddenly we became aware of a low buzzing noise, like the whirr coming from an immense fly-wheel in motion. '*La foudre!*' shouted our guides, and looking at our ice-axes stuck in the snow behind us I saw a ghostly blue light playing around their steel heads. '*La foudre! Nous sommes perdus!*' moaned the guides and scrambling to their feet they began squeezing themselves into a crevice in the rock. From this refuge came later a torrent of *Ave Marias, Pater*

Nosters and invocations of their favourite saints. My hair stood on end and crackled and when I looked at my cousin I saw him as a newly canonized saint with the beginning of a halo. The atmosphere was literally electric. 'We can't wait here to be struck by lightning,' shouted my cousin, Osborne. 'We must make a dash for it.' There followed an abrupt interruption of the guides' prayers, a short and angry altercation in bad French, and then we were off. The rope was in a muddle, and I could not see where I was going, for a sudden gust of wind had wrapped my muffler round my eyes. When I unwound it, blinding snow struck me in the face. Black Hawk clenched his jaws and said nothing. His hour had come; he could suffer the ordeal by fire without flinching and he could, if need be, suffer a similar ordeal by ice.

But where were the guides taking us? This was clearly not the way back towards Zinal, for we were facing in the opposite direction. Salvos of thunder deafened us, lightning played round us and snow blinded us. 'Down there quickly,' shouted the rear guide in my ear, and he braced his feet against a rock, so that he could better take the strain of the rope. Down, slithering, falling, struggling to one's feet again and then once more downwards. What a strange way we were going, right over the face of the mountain sloping downwards towards Zermatt. Now we had reached a tiny snowfield, caught up between two immense buttresses of rock. What was happening? Comedy had got mixed up with tragedy, and I felt strangely elated and inclined to giggle. I was moving too quickly for my cousin and from time to time the rope between us tightened and jerked him forward so that he looked like a doll being dragged along the pavement by a careless child. As a result he was, not unnaturally, hot and angry. There was nothing of the saint about him now and the halo he had worn had been discarded. But what was going to happen? Would we manage to get through, or were we fated to perish on the Rothhorn as the great Owen Glyn-Jones had perished on a neighbouring peak? That sort of thing was picturesque and romantic only when viewed from the distance and it would be unpleasant to be blotted out like a fly swatted on a wall. How would my mother take the news and what would all my friends have to say about it? I found myself reviewing the situation adversely, just as one becomes critical of the plot of a story which has begun to be displeasing. Little had I thought when I had accepted my cousin's invitation to join him in Switzerland that it would all end like this. My soliloquy was suddenly interrupted. A crack as though from the whip of a Brobdingnagian giant swept the party off its feet and we found ourselves in the snow, quivering like a string of galvanized frogs. I was conscious of having received a blow on the right arm and back, although there was nobody near me to deliver it. 'Throw away your ice-axe', shouted a voice, 'the metal tips attract...' On again. 'Damn it,' cursed my cousin, and taking a penknife from his pocket, he hurled it away from him down the slope. Steel was a dangerous possession and it was wisest to get rid of it. But as we hurried on the noise of the thunder began to grow less and the wind seemed to be dropping. In another twenty minutes we were out of the worst of the storm and it was possible to rest for a minute.

'It's lucky we were struck while we were crossing that snowfield and not whilst we were on the rocks. It was soft enough to prevent us from rattling down to Zermatt,' said Osborne, when he had got his breath.

'Damned lucky,' I answered, in a tone of authority, as though I knew all about snow and about lightning. 'But where are we going?'

'Our guides have done splendidly. They've found an absolutely new route and we're making for Zermatt. Look, you can make out the Monte Rosa Hotel.'

The storm by now had nearly blown itself out and the clouds that still raced across the sky were high above our heads. Below us lay Zermatt, with its big hotels full of tourists who were probably standing outside the doors looking up at the storm in the mountains. 'A storm', they had been saying, 'what a magnificent spectacle it makes, with the lightning playing round the peaks.' They did not know what it was like to be a fly caught on a lightning conductor, a tiny human being surrounded by the deafening orchestra of the skies. We resumed our journey and, making good speed, we could soon see some of the tourists in Zermatt watching our progress through a telescope.

Thrusting our way through the crowd in front of the hotel we found the manager and asked for rooms. The fronts of my trousers were still intact, but the rear portions were hanging in shreds on the rocks of the Rothhorn. 'Keep your hat behind you,' whispered my cousin, who always subscribed dutifully to the proprieties. I did what was expected of me and my hat remained on guard until the manager had conducted us to our bedroom. Then I retired to bed until he had procured a new pair of breeches from a Zermatt outfitter to guides.

In bed that night four people reviewed the events of the day and then went into committee. To the Personage the matter on the agenda was only of secondary importance. A great person might climb a mountain and be struck by lightning, and again he might not. Such incidents were entirely immaterial to his greatness. It was the other three who had more decided opinions on this subject. 'How wonderful I was', muttered Black Hawk, 'I never turned a hair even when things were at their darkest. Now for Kinchinjunga and Everest.' Selous, strange as it may seem, showed an enthusiasm very much tempered with prudence. 'Danger is danger', he said, 'and nobody enjoys it more than I do. But there must be a limit to everything. A good spice of danger is what I want, not uncontrollable storms, lightning and avalanches. These forces of nature are apt to get out of hand and if one is not careful they may ruin everything. Better give up climbing and try something else.' Knight-Paton was inclined to agree with him. Martyrdom was all very well, but not martyrdom on a lonely mountain with nobody there to witness it. Besides, no cause would be served by death on a mountain, and martyrdom must be in the service of some cause. Mountaineering was really not in his line of country.

In this manner was it all decided. Next morning we climbed up the side of the Rothhorn, recovered four ice-axes lying abandoned on the snow, and made our way back, by an easy path, to Zinal. It was my last real climb.

CHAPTER VI

THE SPHINX

My father never lived to know whether the advice given to him by his friend in Welbeck Street was good or not. His death was almost instantaneous. On returning home one evening from business, he picked up a letter which was lying on the hall table, read it and exclaimed: 'Oh, why do they worry me so.' Then he fell to the floor and died within a few minutes, most probably from cerebral haemorrhage.

His death made a great impression on me. It was not only that he had died that troubled me, but that he had died in this particular way. Why had he worried so about matters that seemed to me to be of very little importance, and why did everyone worry? When I walked down the street and looked at the faces that passed me, the expression most frequently seen on them was one of deep concern. What was everybody so agitated about? If one could see behind the outer coverings and could read the thoughts that troubled these people what would one find them to be? Usually it was some entirely trivial matter that was causing so much friction — anxiety about the kitchen boiler, the way that Smith had spoken at the office, the gas-bill, James' chicken-pox and a hundred things that had happened, or that might happen, but that in all probability would never happen. Why had all these trifling happenings been given such importance that they now had the power to kill us? Boilers, gas-bills, Smith's way of talking were not in themselves lethal, but they had been made so. Because a friend had written to say that he did not like the hotel at which my father had engaged rooms for the party that was going down for a week's holiday at Eastbourne, my father had fallen down dead. If it were not so tragic, it would be absurd.

I thought a great deal about the problem of death as I stood there alone in that silent bedroom. Hitherto death and I had met only professionally, at the hospital, generally as rivals, but often as colleagues. Sometimes the machinery of life had been so badly damaged by accident or disease that nothing could be done to repair it, and in such a case death provided the only answer to an otherwise insoluble problem. Death was often a friend, but now, for the first time it had come too near me, and I resented its intrusion into my home. The body lying there on that bed was not that of a stranger or even of a friend, but that of the man to whom I owed my very existence. Why had my father been cut off in his prime when so many people needed him, not only here in this house, but in the slums of Poplar, where the poor men and women lived to whom he had given so many of his evenings. The man they had welcomed in their homes as their friend was my father, but perhaps I had never really known him as well as they had done. When we had talked, we had been like two people seated on different sides of a table at a conference, and the table had been too wide for either of us to lean across and grasp the other's hand. Now he had slipped away, leaving me with so many things unsaid, with so much I would have liked to have talked to him about. Why had I waited until it was too late?

False sentiment and display are mingled with genuine sorrow and suffering at every funeral, and as I drove back from the cemetery I was swept by alternating waves of anger and gratitude. How irritating were all those pious words and pretentious platitudes to which I had been forced to listen at the cemetery. And yet there had been something more than empty words — that unbidden crowd from the East End, those utterly unknown people standing at the service in their shiny black clothes and poor cotton gloves, and that queer old charlady who had furtively dropped her bunch of violets into the grave — that wasn't just a pious pretence. Yes, that was something which I would always remember, the sight of those unbidden friends of his from Poplar standing round the open grave.

But the current of life carries us swiftly onwards and the death even of a father is quickly forgotten. The finals of my examination soon took all my attention. So far I had escaped the small oblongs of pink paper that were handed to unsuccessful candidates, requesting them to present themselves again for re-examination in three or in six months' time in accordance with the extent of their failure. Now I was making what I hoped would prove to be my last visit to the examination hall on the Embankment. Again things went favourably and a batch of twenty candidates who had completed all that was expected of them, was lined up before representatives of the College of Physicians in order to be handed the fragments of parchment that informed the world that they were entitled to practise the art of medicine. A similar scene was afterwards enacted at the College of Surgeons in Lincoln's Inn Fields, and, with a more impressive ritual, again at the Senate House when I took my Cambridge degree.

Qualification removes some difficulties and introduces others; in other words, it substitutes for the problem of examinations the greater problem of earning a living. Hardwick, that veteran of the examination hall who had collected more pink slips than anybody living, pointed this out to me when we had returned from the ceremony at the College of Physicians and were standing talking together in the hospital square. 'What on earth am I to do?' he grumbled. 'Here have I been going down to the Embankment for over ten years and now the whole business has come to an end. Now that I'm qualified I'm a man without any mission.' There was something in what he had said, and as I myself, though much his junior, was in a similar position I could find no words of comfort for him. I also was called upon to decide what I was going to do. Probably the best plan would be to apply for the post of house-physician or house-surgeon. After thinking the matter carefully over I decided that medicine was the more cultured and the more gentlemanly of these two branches of my profession, and this being so, I made up my mind to approach the medical chief for whom I had recently clerked, Dr. Wilmot Herringham.

'Certainly you may apply for my house job,' that formidable man answered when I had screwed up my courage sufficiently to tackle him. Herringham had a big chin and a square black beard which waggled when he talked and this with his dark slanting eyes and his high cheek-bones gave him the appearance of a Babylonian priest. 'But you must remember,' he added, 'that I always expect those who are to become my house-physicians to do three months' preliminary work cutting sections for me in the laboratory.'

'I'm damned if I will,' exploded Selous within me. 'Spend three months of my valuable life cutting pickled meat for an old physician — what nonsense!' Outwardly I merely murmured that I quite understood Dr. Herringham's requirements and that I would think the matter over.

So, with the full approval of the inner chorus, I gave up all idea of becoming a physician, and veered violently in the direction of surgery. After all surgery was much more dramatic than medicine and demanded of those who practised it a greater degree of resolution and courage.

Before my eyes passed a vision of the lighted theatre, of the quiet and business-like preparations being made by the staff for an operation, of the shining instruments lying there ready on sterilized towels, of the patient waiting in the ante-room wrapped up in red blankets, and then, of the climax to this dramatic scene, the arrival of the great surgeon from Harley Street. All this made a great appeal to the romantic actors within me, although the drama of the operating theatre was perhaps less impressive than the desert scenes previously pictured by Selous. One day I stopped Sir Anthony Bowlby as he was crossing the square, and told him of my desire to become his house-surgeon. Unlike Herringham he demanded no conditions from me.

'Delighted, my boy,' he answered cheerfully, 'send in your application, and I will give it my careful consideration.' His consideration was not only careful, but it was favourable. I was nominated to become his house-surgeon in six months' time. Six months — what would I do with them? I would employ them in getting more experience. This I actually did, but it was not the experience that I had planned to obtain, for Selous had his own ideas about the meaning of that word.

As will already have become apparent the great hunter was an unscrupulous opportunist and a moment that was favourable to his plans came quite unexpectedly a few weeks later whilst I was standing on the platform of Finsbury Park Station. Sammy Dixon and I had been playing golf at Highgate — a finicky game, more suited to the requirements of retired colonels than to those of the romantic trio within me — and we were waiting for our train back to Farringdon Street.

'Do you happen to know of anybody who wants to walk from Uganda to Khartoum?' asked Sammy, just as I was wondering whether I should go by underground or take a 'bus to Oxford Circus, where I had a dinner appointment with a friend. Before there was time to think I heard a voice within me say: 'I do.' There was no need to inquire who had spoken.

'Well, if you know of someone I can put him in touch with a friend of mine who is anxious to make this journey. I know that he is on the lookout for a companion.'

'Introduce me. There is nothing I would like better than to walk from Uganda to Khartoum.' I was in the position of a listener, and of a listener who must not interfere. Everything was being arranged between Selous and Sammy Dixon.

'You? But I thought you were going on for Bowlby,' said Sammy in surprise.

'Yes, but not for at least six months.'

The friend turned out to be one of Sammy's old Cambridge friends, a Mr. Harold Beale, the secretary of the Varsity Swimming Club. After having been introduced to him in the square of St. Bartholomew's we arranged to meet together for a talk in an underground teashop somewhere near St. Paul's. It seemed absurd to be discussing in such a place camels, the load that a Swahili porter could carry on his head, and the equipment that would be needed for a two months' trek through Equatorial Africa; but then, life itself was absurd, so that this talk in an underground teashop was quite in keeping with it. Of greater importance to me than the amount that a Swahili could carry on his head was the amount of money that I could carry in my pocket. Big-game shooting was obviously an expensive sport and American millionaires and Austrian Archdukes had converted East Africa into a very costly playground. My father had left me a hundred a year and here was I discussing the details of an expedition the total cost of which might well amount to five or six times that figure. But Beale above all wanted a companion and these financial difficulties were eventually adjusted; I would pay whatever I could manage and he would be responsible for the rest. He was a big, good-natured man who talked very fast about elephant-guns and sporting Lee-Metford rifles, and as he made many digressions and was liable to break off in the middle of what he was saying to give vent to an unexpectedly high-pitched laugh, I had some difficulty in following him. Before us, spread out on the marble-topped table, lay a map of British East Africa, and on this he traced a variety of possible routes with the point of his penknife. As Beale could not leave England for at least another month, a journey from Uganda to Khartoum might be too late in starting, for it would bring us to the neighbourhood of Khartoum at the peak of the sandstorm season. This being so, it would probably be better to give up all idea of this trek and to dedicate ourselves solely to the pursuit of game. We could either go south in the direction of Kilimanjaro and German East Africa or work north towards the Abyssinian border. He was particularly anxious to get elephant and that would of course partly determine our route. Selous' heart glowed with pleasure, for not only was the elephant the lord of the forest, but two or three good pairs of tusks would almost pay for the whole expedition. It was soon decided that elephant would be our chief aim, and that Beale would let me know as soon as it was possible for him to do so the date of his sailing. We parted with mutual expressions of goodwill, he making his way to Lloyd's, where he did some leisurely work two days a week, and I back to St. Bartholomew's.

During the walk to the hospital I did a great deal of thinking, or perhaps it would be more accurate to say that a great deal of thinking occurred in me. Why should I wait about in London doing odd jobs at the hospital for four weeks? Why shouldn't I start straight away and have a holiday in Egypt before sailing down the Red Sea? Egypt was the home of romance and mystery and Romer lived in Egypt. Last time he was home on leave he had invited me to pay him a visit. I could do so now, but with all those camels and porters to be paid for, I would have to travel like a true Scot, looking at every sixpence before I parted from it. Egypt had the reputation of being expensive, but I was sure that somehow I could manage both Egypt and British East Africa. If I had done that Iceland trip on ten pounds, surely I could manage Egypt on say twenty and have enough left to reach East Africa and make my contribution to the expenses of the African expedition. Anyhow, it was worth trying. The following day I visited various shipping offices in the city and discovered that I could get to Port Said very cheaply on a Brocklebank freighter that carried also a few passengers. I telephoned to Beale telling him of the change in my plans, arranged to meet his ship when it called at Port Said and sailed from Liverpool five days later.

Even the seasoned traveller feels the thrill of those first few dramatic minutes in a voyage when a great ship slowly draws away from the quay and, trusting to her own engines, casts off her attendant tugs, swings into the middle of the river and makes for the open sea. I would have been stirred by what I saw from the deck of the Brocklebank freighter had I been bound only for Boulogne or Hamburg, but I was not bound for any ordinary port, but for a place which was far more wonderful than anything to be found in Europe. If anyone had any doubts about the nature of this voyage of mine, these would be rapidly dispelled by a visit below to my cabin. There, as part of my luggage, was a new Browning pistol, a camp bed, a sleeping bag, mosquito curtains, a new pair of Zeiss glasses and a good supply of quinine. Personally I was in no need of any of these new possessions to remind me of what lay ahead, for at that very moment I could feel the rub of a rough canvas belt against my skin, a belt the pockets of which were literally bulging with golden sovereigns. I had decided that I would be independent of such dull things as letters of credit and banks, and that, like the old explorers, I would carry all my wealth on my own person, between my shirt and my skin. Only later, while shopping in Cairo, did I discover the disadvantage of this ancient method of carrying money. It was awkward to have to strip in public whenever it became necessary to pay for purchases, and alarming to discover, as I sometimes did, that I had left all my money behind me in the hotel through having omitted that morning to remove it from its nightly position under my pillow.

Emotions, like gases under pressure, seek a vent, and for lack of any other method of releasing them, I took to writing verse. When this proved to be worse even than I had expected it to be, I started a journal in which in due course were recorded the rounding of Cap Finisterre, the call at Gibraltar, the first glimpse of the North African coast and our arrival at Port Said. There I waved good-bye from the quay to the half-dozen or so fellow passengers who were continuing their voyage further east and then turned in the direction of the railway station.

Unfamiliar sights are apt to appear to be unreal, and as I gazed out of the window of the Port Said to Cairo train, I had the feeling that I was not actually in Egypt, but was visiting an Egyptian exhibition at Earl's Court. The Arab villages, the fellahin ploughing with their oxen, the tiny mosques and the clumps of palm trees had been constructed out of canvas and plaster, and the figures I saw in the village streets were not what they pretended to be, but were only employees of the company dressed up in Arab garb. It was only after I had said to myself several times, 'This is Egypt, and actually I am here,' that they became a little more genuine, and that Earl's Court receded into the background.

On reaching Cairo I called at the address from which Romer had last written to me. After a long wait the door was opened by such a genuine Arab that my English was as incomprehensible to him as his Arabic was to me. From his expression and his gestures I at length grasped that his master was not at home. Further efforts to find out his whereabouts at last produced two words that I understood: 'Jockey Club'. So to the Jockey Club I went, only to find that again Romer was not where I hoped him to be. He was engaged in surveying the Libyan desert and from what the porter at the Jockey Club said I gathered that his camp was pitched on the western edge of the Delta near a place called Wahed. 'Then I will survey the desert with him,' said a voice within me, and off I went, bag in hand, to Wahed.

I arrived late in the evening and on making inquiries I learnt that the encampment of the Egyptian Survey would be found at a short distance from the railway-siding and the melancholy huddle of houses around it which constituted the village of Wahed. Half an hour's walk brought me to a collection of tents on the edge of the desert and when I entered Romer's tent I found him seated on a packing case and writing on that particular brand of dirty paper which is favoured by all government offices. If one has lightheartedly invited a friend who lives at the safe distance of a thousand odd miles away to drop in and see one, and if two years later that friend actually arrives carrying with him a Gladstone bag, the moment of his entry into one's tent must inevitably be a startling one. But whatever thoughts were crowding into Romer's head, outwardly he remained calm. 'I'm delighted to see you,' he said, 'and you must stay as long as you can. Have you had supper? Very well, but at any rate you'll have a drink or some coffee and I'll tell Hassan to pitch a tent for you. By the way, I hope that you don't mind snakes.'

Now, if there is one subject on which Black Hawk, Selous and Knight-Paton and the Personage were heartily agreed, it was on the subject of snakes. It was our secret shame. We did not talk about this, but we all knew that the mere thought of coils slowly unwinding themselves caused a wave of horror to pass over us. My father had once told me a story which had curdled my blood when I was a boy. While travelling in Ceylon he had been kept awake one night by noises coming from a large tin trunk under his bed. Next morning he had discovered that it was full of his host's pet cobras. I apparently was about to spend a similar night but without the comfort of knowing that the cobras were inside a trunk.

'They crawl through the holes,' explained Romer two hours later, as he was showing me my tent. 'We found three of them in one of the tents this morning. This place seems to be stiff with them but they are quite harmless unless you attack them or tread on them, so it doesn't really matter. Good night, and I hope you'll sleep well.'

'So this is Wahed,' I murmured to myself when I was alone. 'I must cork up all those damned holes.' But the whole contents of my bag were insufficient to close more than a fraction of the innumerable gaps between my tent and the desert sands, and I soon gave up the attempt to make myself cobra-proof. As there was nothing else I could do I retired to bed, blew out the candle and eventually fell asleep, but not for very long, for Wahed had thrills to offer its visitors other than snakes. Three hours after retiring I became vaguely aware of shouts that were growing in volume and when I opened my eyes, I found that the interior of my tent was illuminated by light from a lantern shining through its canvas walls. Tumbling heavy-eyed out of my bed I peered through the door-flap. 'A sandstorm', yelled Romer. 'Look after that tent of yours and grab hold of anything you can find. You had better . . .' The remainder of his warning was cut short by the arrival of the storm. Snap went the ropes and the tent sailed into the air like a mad ballet-dancer twirling her skirts. I was no longer alone but in the open air and the desert was alive with white-robed Arabs, clutching at canvas, and filled with a frenzy of twitchings and whirlings and of dervishes howling — mad pandemonium. Then it all stopped as suddenly as it had begun and sad little bundles of canvas lay strewn across the desert, as though a laundry van had been driving round throwing out washing. 'So this is Wahed', I repeated to myself, as I began to dig for my trousers buried under a heap of sand.

'Sorry you've had such a bad night,' apologized Romer when he had time to pay me a fleeting visit.

'Oh, I don't mind sandstorms,' I answered truthfully, 'they're part of the desert, and anyhow, it seems to be morning.'

'Well, slip on your things quickly and I'll tell them to brew us some coffee. It'll be in my tent over there — when they've managed to put it up again.'

Dressing after one's bedroom has been visited by a sandstorm is no simple matter. I'm not exactly a tidy person, but I can generally count on my clothes being in the room and somewhere approximately where I left them. On this occasion they were not where I had left them. They were somewhere in the Libyan Desert, and the finding of a collar-stud in so much sand demands time and patience. It was not surprising therefore that Romer's phrase 'slip on your things quickly' seemed to me to be an inaccurate description of my morning toilet, or that the coffee was cold when I eventually swallowed it.

The work of the day now began. According to the *Oxford Dictionary* to survey is to 'let the eyes pass over and take a general view of the chief features of something'. In the case of the desert this is a simple matter, for the chief feature is clearly sand. We, however, were doing something quite different from this; we were triangulating and making a map of it. It was Selous' first piece of desert work and although he would have preferred galloping across the sands with that little black bag of his tied to the saddle, he thoroughly enjoyed galloping across them with theodolites, chains, water-levels and long striped poles clutched to his chest. The air, except in the middle of the day, was keen and invigorating; the sun shone with just the right degree of fervour and my Arab horse moved under me with the speed and ease of a swallow's flight. It was all very delightful and I spent some of the best days of my life helping to draw imaginary triangles on miles of featureless sand and taking a tiny part in the production of maps to be used some forty years later in a famous desert campaign. It was only because it was essential that I should be in touch with the Cairo shipping offices and be available as soon as Beale's ship was signalled off Port Said that I left this desert life and made my way back to Cairo. One of the few consolations for changing Wahed for Cairo was that while there I would be able to visit the famous Pyramids.

They were impressive, for no man can stand in front of that great mountain of stone, the Pyramid of Cheops, or trudge round its immense base without feeling his own insignificance in comparison with the size, the age and the dignity of this vast monument. But I had seen so many photographs of the Pyramids that now that I was in their presence I was slightly disappointed. They were impressive but not so awe-inspiring as I had expected them to be. There was also the Sphinx to be seen and, disinclined as I was for more sight-seeing, I felt that it would be a mistake to depart without even looking at it. The Sphinx was the subject of even more picture postcards than the Pyramids were, but it had to be seen and I strolled across to where they told me it would be found. I caught sight of it quite suddenly, and it looked at me out of the hollow in the desert in which it lay, no, not at me, but at something which lay beyond me, further than I could ever see. I was of no account to this mysterious being at which so many generations of men had looked for a fleeting moment and then disappeared, and as I stood there, gazing at the Sphinx, there arose in me a feeling of discomfort which grew steadily stronger. Suddenly I became angry with the crowd that had collected round me to ask for alms or to try to sell me spurious scarabs. Why would they not let me alone? I shouted at them and then turned to examine again the face which looked across the sands, the face of which Arabs and Turks had made a target. The strange thing was that although it was badly mutilated, it had in some incomprehensible way remained whole. What was even more remarkable was that the Sphinx had the countenance of a living being, and of a being who knew more than ordinary men. Small wonder that it was surrounded with such an aura of mystery and that the legend of the secret of the Sphinx had arisen. I returned silent and dispirited to Cairo, and experienced a sense of relief when I seated myself on the terrace of my hotel to drink coffee and smoke cigarettes and to watch the chattering crowd passing along the street. The presence of all that animation gave me back my sense of personal existence again and restored to me my peace of mind. I was no longer what I had been an hour previously, a wraith, a being with such an evanescent existence that the Sphinx had not even noticed it; I was a young Englishman taking his ease and dreaming about the valiant things he was about to do in East Africa. Slightly ashamed of what had happened, I decided that it was all that mystery-mongering about the Sphinx and its secret that had had such a strong suggestive action on me and, having come to this satisfactory conclusion, I did my best to dismiss the whole matter from my mind. More than twenty years later I found a book that gave me the formulation for which I had searched in vain in the presence of the Sphinx. Ouspensky's description in *The New Model of the Universe* told me what I had felt, but could not describe.

'At first I saw only that the Sphinx looked beyond me into the distance. But I soon began to have a kind of vague, then a growing uneasiness. Another moment, and I felt that the Sphinx was not seeing me, and not only was it not seeing me, it could not see me, and not because I was too small in comparison with it, or too insignificant in comparison with the profundity of wisdom it contained and guarded. Not at all. That would have been natural and comprehensible. The sense of annihilation and the terror of vanishing came from feeling myself in some way too transient for the Sphinx to be able to notice me. I felt that not only did these fleeting moments or hours which I could pass before it not exist for it, but that if I could stay under its gaze from birth to death the whole of my life would flash by so swiftly for it that it could not see me. Its glance was fixed on something else. It was the glance of a being who thinks in centuries and millenniums. I did not exist and could not exist for it. And I could not answer my own questions — do I exist for myself? Do I, indeed, exist in any sort of sense, in any sort of relation? And in this thought, in this feeling, under the strange glance, there was an icy coldness. We are so accustomed to feel that we are, that we exist. Yet all at once, I felt that I did not exist, that there was no I, that I could not be so much as perceived.'

There was a great deal to see in Cairo, but it all cost money and the belt round my waist was noticeably lighter. I had economized as rigidly as I could, but the prices in Cairo were very high. Now there are two ways of travelling cheaply, the direct and the indirect. The direct method is obvious — it means travelling third class, staying at small hotels, doing without a complete set of meals and observing a hundred small economies of this sort. The indirect method is much more subtle and has to be discovered and developed by experience. One example will suffice. Suppose that you find yourself in a foreign town and in need of a meal, the maximum fill at the minimum cost. For a small sum you can purchase at a restaurant a cup of café-au-lait and rolls and butter. For the same sum by the use of the indirect method you can buy rolls and butter, a cup of coffee and one or two cups of warm milk. It is quite simple. Order the coffee and the rolls and butter in the ordinary way and after adding all the milk and drinking half of the coffee, call the waiter. 'Waiter,' you complain, 'this coffee is far too strong. Would you mind making it weaker.' The waiter reappears, fills up your cup to the brim with warm milk and departs. You drink half the coffee and again summon him. 'I'm sorry, waiter, to be so fussy, but my doctor has forbidden me to drink any but the weakest coffee. Could you oblige me?' 'Certainly, sir,' he answers, if he is a satisfactory waiter, and fills up the cup again to the brim. Sometimes you can do it a third time, but usually, if more milk is required it is better to catch the eye of a new waiter. But there are limits to the employment of these rather niggardly methods of living, and it was with a certain sense of relief that I learnt that the ship in which Beale had sailed was due next day at Port Said. I hastened to meet him. Having made my way on board, I caught sight of a portly figure on the upper deck leaning over the rail and watching the derricks unloading some of the cargo. It was with considerable excitement that I made my presence known to the man who was to be my companion in the great adventures that were soon to unfold themselves.

'Good heavens!' he said after he had returned my greeting, 'I had forgotten all about you. But let's land, find somewhere we can lunch and talk things over.'

By the time that he was due to sail everything had been arranged. There was no room on his ship, but I was to follow him down the Red Sea by the first boat available. I would land in Mombasa, take one of the trains on the newly opened Uganda Railway and join him at Nakuru. By that time he would have got together a *safari* and would be ready to start. Beale talked at great speed and in the two hours we had been together so much had been said that I felt a trifle exhausted as I waved him good-bye from the quay. But it had all been very satisfactory. I discovered that a German liner was due to sail for Mombasa within a week, so it would not be long before I rejoined him. In a comparatively short time I would be experiencing all the wonderful things I had read about in that big yellow book of Selous' in the dining-room bookcase at home, camp fires, African nights and *boomahs* built against wild beasts. I would be following the spoor of elephants through forests, and would be listening to the distant roar of lions. How glorious it was to be alive and to be taking one's full share of life's great adventure.

CHAPTER VII

SELOUS' HOMECOMING

I⊤ is unnecessary to describe the voyage from Suez to East Africa, for however thrilling they may be to the novice, ships, porpoises, flying-fish,
palm trees and tropical coastlines are much the same wherever one happens
to encounter them for the first time. I had sailed from Egypt late in Decem-
ber and New Year's Eve was celebrated on board S.S. *Feldmarschall* with
Teutonic thoroughness and with unlimited supplies of Munich beer. We
were on a German ship which carried many German passengers, but the
unchallenged leader in the second-class saloon was Clara, the English maid
of one of the first-class passengers. It was she who organized all our games
and dances and, long after I had retired to my berth on the first morning
of the New Year, I could distinguish her voice leading the roystering
choruses which were still being sung on deck. Five days later we steamed
into the harbour of Kilindini, the port of Mombasa, and before the throb
of the engines had stopped dozens of little boats could be seen putting out
from the shore. The ship was soon encircled by them, so that she resembled a dignified old hen surrounded by a clutch of importunate chicks.
The majority of the boats were crowded with noisy and gesticulating
Swahilis, selling fruit or clamouring to take passengers on shore. After
the health and the other port officials had concluded their business and
we were at liberty to land, I made my way, with my luggage, down the
gangway, to be captured immediately by an enormous negro who carried
me off in triumph to his boat. I had inadvertently left my spare trousers
behind me in the cabin, but even though at this moment I remembered
them it was too late for me to salvage them. My captor would never have
allowed it and in any case Selous was in almost as great a hurry for me to
land as was the gigantic Swahili.

The moment when the great hunter threw his leg over the gunnel of
the boat and planted his foot again on the soil of Africa was a dramatic
one. The long pilgrimage that had started in that tiny hunting-ground
behind the bicycle shed some twenty years ago had ended and Selous, the
great explorer, the tracker of elephants, had at last returned home to the

wide open spaces and the great forests of the Dark Continent! When I looked around me it would seem that nature herself recognized the greatness of this event and was celebrating it. Gay coloured birds were engaged in ceremonial flights overhead, frogs croaked welcoming choruses in the rushes, flowers bedecked the trees and gay streamers of bougainvillea were swaying in the breeze. It was a gala day and my journey from Kilindini to Mombasa, seated on a wheeled chair and pushed along a light railway by perspiring negroes, was for me an ever memorable event. No Roman triumphal procession to celebrate a great victory could have been more impressive than Selous' entry of Mombasa. The day ended with an excellent dinner at the Mombasa hotel, in the company of a pale Italian count who was wearing an eyeglass. After dining together we both partook of prophylactic doses of quinine, the count demonstrating how this nauseous drug was best swallowed by inserting it into a small hole dug in a banana.

Next morning I dressed up in khaki, purchased a pith sun-helmet at an Indian store, sauntered up and down the stifling streets of Mombasa during the heat of the day, inspected the native quarters of the town and, by a fraction of a second, escaped being bitten by a camel. From time to time I returned to the hotel for copious drinks and for the purpose of anointing new mosquito bites with fresh applications of witch-hazel. On the following day I caught one of the rare trains running on the Uganda Railway to Victoria Nyanza.

Trains are, as a class, impersonal and austere beings. Like collectors of inland revenue they live in an atmosphere of forms and regulations, schedules and time-tables, and, oblivious to all human weaknesses they remorselessly pursue their stern official aim. But this train in which I was now seated was utterly different from any I had previously met. It was a humane train which seemed to be more concerned with the private needs and desires of its passengers than with the demands of the time-table. Were we beginning to feel hungry and in need of a rest? We were. Very well then, the guard would telephone ahead for dinner to be ready for fifteen guests, and the train would stop at the next station and we could all get out and have a nice meal. Had we had enough, or would we like to wait a little longer and take a little coffee? Certainly; the train would be delighted to remain as long as we liked. After all, it was there for our convenience and there was no need for anybody to hurry.

In this manner, and with many stops, we sauntered across plains full of scampering antelopes, and over bridges spanning dried up streams in the direction of Victoria Nyanza. On the following night we reached my destination, Nakuru. There, with mutual regret and with many parting messages from the whistle, the train and I parted company. But I had little leisure for sentimental musings on the subject of this train, for Beale, illuminated by a lantern held aloft by a black servant wearing a tarbuch, was shaking me warmly by the hand.

'Glad you've turned up. Have you had a good journey? Now then, Sardi, look alive and get together the new B'wama's kit. We've only a short distance to go. Hope you've fed, but we can soon get something together if you haven't.' A stream of words, interrupted occasionally by that high-pitched laugh, poured into my ears. Dazed, but conscious that I was in competent hands, I followed the two rather incongruous figures — the big florid Englishman and the small negro boy — through an impenetrable African darkness to the camp. In such company it was not necessary for me to speak; it was not even essential that I should listen. I was dusty and tired, and as we were to make an early start next morning I retired as soon as possible to bed. The mournful howling of jackals in the distance was a novelty, but it had no power to disturb my slumber.

After what seemed but a very short interval Sardi, the youth with the tarbuch, appeared in my tent still carrying his lantern. Surely it was not time yet to get up? The hour before dawn is for me an hour of pessimism, and for a few minutes I wondered whether I would not prefer to sleep on rather than to start on this journey into the unknown. In any case there seemed to be no pressing need to start so early. I was on a holiday, and holidays were designed for one's comfort. I had no liking for early rising but Selous had views of his own and after a short struggle he got me out of bed and into the clothes of an African explorer. Breakfast was eaten in passover fashion, with staves and girded loins, and it lasted only as long as it took time for our caravan to load up. Then Mahomet, the chief man, having at last realized the drift of the big Englishman's many instructions, the advance was sounded and we turned our backs on Nakuru. The morning was fine, the sun was rising into an unclouded sky and as the light grew stronger we could see that the plain was literally teeming with game. Gazelles galloped away in hundreds, flocks of zebra turned round and gazed at us and a large inquisitive wart-hog, after sizing us up from the cover of the long grass, decided to trot in the wake of our caravan.

Our plan was to trek through the Rift Valley and, turning north across the lower slopes of Mount Kenya, to make a circuit of Lake Baringo. It was believed that we would have less difficulty in finding water by going in this direction than by making South, towards Kilimanjaro. All this I learned from Beale as I walked with him and the two gun-bearers at the head of our safari. Suddenly the caravan came to a halt and a whisper of 'simba' (lion) spread along the line. Mahomet reported that the cook had seen a lion slink into that clump of bushes there in front of us. Hassan and Fara, our two Somali gun-bearers, immediately approached this thicket and out of it leapt a leopard, which sailed through the air in one magnificent bound. Beale's rifle cracked, but the bullet went too high and the hunted escaped over the brow of the hill hotly pursued by the hunters. I felt secretly glad that such grace and beauty had escaped. How much better it was that the leopard should continue those wonderful movements than lie at our feet a splendid but motionless corpse. I wondered whether it was not a little bit disloyal for me to harbour such thoughts.

As we made our way up the long Rift Valley the country became more parched and, in places where the grass had obviously been burnt, the ground was strewn thick with cinders. I learnt later that it was the practice of the Masai to set a light to the vegetation in order to improve the quality of the grass on which their wandering herds of cattle browsed. The bare patches burnt in the tawny grass gave the land over which we were walking the appearance of the hide of some mangy lion. In Egypt I had found difficulty in believing that what I saw was real, but here the whole country was so lion-like that had one of these noble beasts actually appeared I would have accepted it as being genuine without question. Again the safari had stopped. This time it was because Hassan and Fara had seen, clearly outlined in a circle of cinders, the mighty spoor of elephant. They bent over it, told us that a three-quarters grown bull and three cow-elephants had passed that way, and then they shook their heads. The tracks were at least three days old and there were signs that the quartet had been travelling very fast in search of a new feeding-ground. By now they might be anywhere, for elephants, unlike Uganda trains, may travel for sixty miles without a stop. It was a pity, but in spite of the Somalis' disappointing verdict I remained thrilled. Until that moment I had never appreciated the immense size of an African elephant, and I looked at the gigantic spoor with amazement. Later I was to find even bigger foot-prints, so large that if one of them had been filled with water it would have provided me with an excellent sitz-bath. And these were not the only signs of the strength and prodigious size of the quarry we were to follow. Sometimes we came across great boughs that had been torn from the trees and then tossed aside, strong saplings bodily uprooted and wide lanes trampled flat through the tall elephant-grass as though a number of steam-rollers had driven through it. For weeks we were fated to pursue these great lords of the animal world but without ever having the good fortune to overtake them. One night we were so near to our quarry that we could hear them feeding in the neighbouring forest, but before dawn they had gone. It was a gigantic game of blind-man's-buff in which the elephants, who had far more to lose than we had, defeated us.

An African trek is full of incidental excitements, but when looked at in retrospect it is seen to be made up of days of a somewhat monotonous pattern. Up an hour before dawn for a hurried meal while the porters were striking camp, we would then shoulder our guns and set out on the march as soon as Mahomet brought news that all was ready. At the start the sun was low on the horizon and it was so bitterly cold, especially when we had reached the lower slopes of Mount Kenya, that we buttoned up the collars of our coats and walked with our hands deeply buried in their pockets. By ten o'clock it was blazing hot, jerseys and coats had been peeled off, shirt-buttons undone and we were panting along like dogs following a butcher's cart on a steamy summer day. In a few hours a halt would be called for a hurried lunch, and then on we would go again. Those were days when big game was not yet slaughtered from aeroplanes and from lorries and before cinema experts, seated in well-equipped vans, made films of Equatorial Africa. At the start we had taken with us three camels, but as these were continually stumbling and falling over with their loads, we sent them back home with their Somali owner. Our only transport therefore was human transport and our only guide to finding water a small inaccurate map. Late in the afternoon Hassan and Mahomet would usually be summoned to a conference on this all important subject of water, a conference which was conducted in a mixture of Swahili, Arabic and English. Contrary opinions would be expressed as to where it would be found and then we would be on the march again. At last, as the sun was setting, a glorious discovery would be made and in some small hollow we would find — a pool of green froth from which arose an abominable stench. Water! Now we could camp and relax; the day was finished and we could enjoy our evening meal.

It is interesting to see how quickly what at first appears to be a nameless and featureless crowd breaks up into a number of distinctive and easily recognizable individuals. At the start I appeared to be travelling with Beale, with a black boy who wore a tarbuch and who was called Sardi, and with a crowd of negroes so alike that it was impossible to distinguish one from the other. Very soon I discovered in the crowd the presence of the two Somali gun-bearers, Hassan and Fara. A few days later I realized the existence of the two Askaris, men who were armed with ancient fire-arms with which they were supposed to guard the camp. Then Mahomet, the leader of the porters, made himself known to me chiefly because it was he who got into trouble whenever anything went wrong. I next learnt to pick out the gay Misharibu, that light-hearted man who was always singing and who invariably started the marching songs whenever the other porters were beginning to feel tired. The choruses they sang generally ended in shouts of laughter, for the lyrics were improvised and highly topical. 'Who is the big fat man with the pink face who sweats so freely?' Misharibu would sing, and to this question would come the answering refrain: 'It is Mafoota, who is like one elephant seeking for another elephant and is unable to catch him.' 'And who is the smaller man who walks beside him with his head on one side and looking at the ground?' 'It is Kejunga, the man who hopes one day to shoot a rhinoceros with a child's pistol.' Later I discovered a man who had the features of my Aunt Maggie at Highgate and another who was the counterpart in ebony of Mellor, the head prefect at school. In this way, one by one, there slowly emerged from a homogeneous black crowd a number of characters whose white prototypes I had known well in previous years.

How strange it was to find myself travelling in Africa in such company, for even Beale, my only white companion, was an acquaintance rather than a friend. I had spent an hour in his company in a London teashop, had lunched with him at Port Said, and now here we were living together in the tiny world of our camp, as isolated from the rest of the world as if we had been living on a desert island. We were like two swimmers who had happened to have climbed on to the same raft and because they had been thus accidentally thrown together had decided that it was necessary to become better acquainted. If dissimilarity and the possession of complementary vices and virtues provide a satisfactory foundation for friendship, then we had undoubtedly started with these advantages. Mafoota — I still think of him by this name — enjoyed doing and talking, whilst I by temperament was inclined to watch and to listen. He was big and very impressive to all the natives, whilst I, by comparison with him, was small and of very little account. But the fact that he was the undoubted leader of the expedition freed me from all sense of responsibility and gave me far more freedom and leisure than I would otherwise have had. At first sight this might appear to be an unfair arrangement, that he should have been saddled with most of the work and I be allowed to enjoy all the play. The arrangement was actually to our mutual advantage. Your active businesslike man dislikes interference and gets pleasure from the fact that he alone is directing affairs and Mafoota obviously enjoyed his paramount position. He and I were therefore very well matched and, like strange stable companions, we took pleasure in each other's company. Over meals we discussed sport, the habits of game, the small events of the day, the many failings of our cook and our chances of eventually coming on elephant. The ground on which we met was always safe ground and as we both had been brought up in the same environment, namely that of the 'varsity and the public school, there was little chance of our falling out.

Although elephants were scarce rhinoceros were plentiful and, three days after we had left Nakuru, Hassan and Fara discovered the fresh imprints of a cloven-hoof on the high ground above our encampment. We followed hot on the spoor and came to a place where the rhinoceros had evidently indulged recently in a dust bath. As we traced the tracks onwards through the thick undergrowth I suddenly looked up and saw what appeared to me to be a large dining-room table, on its side, moving rapidly across the gap between two thorn trees. Simultaneously came the report of Mafoota's rifle, and a splash of claret spilled over the table. Then it slid still more quickly down the hill and was lost to view. We hurried in its wake and in the valley we found an angry rhinoceros tossing its head under a large thorn tree. Its nose moved rhythmically up and down as it drew in the air and sniffed for our scent, and its small malicious eyes were red with hate. Suddenly the great beast stiffened and tossing its horn it made a bee-line for Hassan. Craft and brute force were now matched and Selous stood like a child at a circus, his eyes glued to the ring. Opposite me was Mafoota, with his rifle at his shoulder and swinging from side to side like a weathercock. He was anxious to intervene but it was impossible for him to do so without running a risk of wounding Hassan. Crack again went his rifle as the pair raced broadside past the sights and the rhino stopped for a moment to regain its breath. Whom would it next choose to chase in this exciting game of tig? I looked at the small nickel-plated revolver in my hand and then up at the trees. How uninviting they looked, covered with their two-inch thorns, and how difficult and painful it would be to climb them. But the rhinoceros had again chosen Hassan, and off the two of them went twisting and turning, snorting and panting, as though a mischievous guttersnipe was being chased by a fat policeman. Good, the guttersnipe was keeping his head and was contriving to bring the policeman again broadside on to Mafoota's rifle. Clever guttersnipe. Mafoota fired twice, and the rhino came heavily down on its knees, made an unsuccessful effort to rise and then, when the rifle had spoken once more, it rolled on to its side. The tail passed into my possession, and that night and the next and the following one we ate rhinoceros steaks. When hammered for two hours on a board and dried in the sun, they were still tough, but, at any rate, possible to eat.

Stopping a few days in districts where game was plentiful and then again advancing, our safari wriggled its way along the great Rift Valley, and then climbed the lower slopes of Mount Kenya. Here the nights were so cold that in the morning the men's blankets were covered with hoar frost. Then having circled the grand peak we turned north in the direction of Lake Baringo. During the whole trip we met very few people, some Masai families travelling with their flocks in search of new feeding grounds, a fierce-looking Tirkhana warrior pursuing two escaped slave-boys, a band of Masai on a marauding expedition, and on three occasions only, white men. Two of these were British government officials and two were Italian explorers nosing around the southern approaches to Abyssinia. History was in the making.

There could be no doubt now that we had made an unfortunate choice in deciding to travel north. Large tracts of the countryside had been set on fire by the Masai and as I stood at the door of my tent of an evening and gazed into the distance I seemed to be looking at a land at war. In front of me was a long irregular line of crimson advancing to the attack;

to the right was a hill that had surrendered and was now well behind the line of battle, whilst there on the left the columns of smoke rising from the valley showed where the conflict was still in progress. Mafoota cursed this mimic warfare, for by driving the game far to the north, it was seriously interfering with our sport. Elephant fear only two things, fire and terrier dogs. Of terriers we were free, but with all these conflagrations around us we would have to travel far and with great speed if we were to overtake the great lords of the forest. The disappointment was bitterer for Mafoota than it was for me, for even though elephants were lacking, there were plenty of other animals to be watched. And it was the living beast and not the sporting trophy which interested me most. I would lie quiet for hours behind some bush watching the uncouth and stilted gait of the hartebeeste, the wonderful leaps of the impala, the skittishness and curiosity of the zebra and the immense strides of the giraffe as they helter-skeltered across the plain with their heads moving up and down like the china mandarin in my mother's drawing-room. On other days I would wander through the scrub by myself and make useful contributions to the larder in the way of wild geese, partridges, guineafowl and pigeons. And besides this game what strange and exotic birds were to be found everywhere. At a few yards distance from the camp kitchen there were always congregated a number of marabout storks that with hunched shoulders and heads on one side, gravely observed every movement of the cook. They looked and behaved exactly like an assembly of black-coated elders in a Scottish kirk. Half a mile away from one of our camps was also a clump of trees under which I sat for a whole morning watching clouds of vivid colour sweeping from tree to tree. First would come a cascade of crimson, to be followed in turn by successive waves of vivid green, light-blue and orange, jewelled flights of birds which circled above my head and then suddenly wheeled and settled on the branches. To have fired at such loveliness and brought it tumbling to the ground would have been impossible for me. Like Sindbad in the cave of treasure I sat there spellbound.

Black Hawk and Selous were finding in the expedition all that they needed: Black Hawk, sore feet and stifling heat; Selous, camp fires, charging rhinoceros, lions snuffling round the tents at night or roaring at the dawn, buffalo skulking in long grass, and innumerable animals that were no longer figments of the imagination, but living, impetuously moving creatures The external world no longer contradicted inner imagination and, delighted with this real scenery, the actors within me postured and strutted to their hearts' content. There was no longer anybody there to gainsay them, nobody to ask awkward questions or point to inconsistencies, nobody to oppose them; they had the stage to themselves.

Although Selous was now relieved of all necessity for devising adventures, he still used his imagination as a means of maintaining them at an adequate level. By the exercise of a little ingenuity he could convert what was only a trifling incident into a daring exploit, thereby obtaining the maximum of thrill at a minimum of cost. As an example of this may be quoted the morning on which I arose from my bed in the dark in order to visit the corpse of a rhinoceros that Mafoota had shot on the previous day. Lions had been frequently heard at night and they often left a circle of spoor around our tents, but up till now I had not actually seen one. This I felt ought to be remedied as quickly as possible, and I was seeking now the body of the rhinoceros, just after dawn, in the hope of surprising some lingering marauders at their feast. In the faint light of the coming day I could make out that the mighty corpse was surrounded by revellers, not those that I had hoped to see, but a ring of greedy vultures, so gorged with meat that they could barely stand, let alone fly. It was disappointing and I was on the point of starting for home when I caught sight of them — a troop of lion advancing on me at the double. Dropping quickly to the ground I clutched my rifle. Selous had asked for one, but nature had been over-generous and approaching me were six or seven. The light was so poor that I could scarcely see my sights, so I bided my time. Two minutes later not lions but a family of wart-hogs trotted up, caught sight of somebody staring at them along the barrel of a rifle, swerved aside and scampered off in the direction of home. When Selous returned to camp he expressed bitter disappointment, but it must be confessed that his words were not always to be trusted.

Only once did he err on the side of underestimating the importance of the game he had marked down. When stalking antelope I had occasionally spotted ostriches, but the ostriches had at the same time invariably spotted me. Now, although in England it is a crime to shoot at a sitting bird, in Africa there was nobody to object to this departure from good sportsmanship. I kept my eyes open therefore for the chance of a sitting shot, and at last that chance came. There on the plain, three hundred yards away, was a magnificent male bird sitting with his great neck right up in the air. Was he taking his turn in squatting on eggs, or was he merely enjoying a siesta in the heat of the day? I did not care, for eggs were only eggs, and even if they had hatched I was only robbing young birds of an unessential father. I fell prone on the ground and started on my long stalk. It was no easy task, this that I had undertaken, to get near to an ostrich squatting on a plain utterly devoid of cover. Flat on my stomach, wriggling sideways like a worm, dragging my rifle behind me and scraping my face on the earth, I made good progress. How would it look through the sights? I raised my rifle slowly and peered along the barrel. Too far; I must get fifty yards nearer before I dared fire. Little by little, wriggling, perspiring, with aching muscles and with eyes full of sweat, I gained on my bird. Another look; should I, or should I not, pull the trigger? No, better make sure, the silly thing had not seen me. Another thirty yards and it would be impossible for me to miss. I had done it — the sights were in line — and the bird was mine. Already I pictured myself presenting those magnificent tail feathers to my sister and telling her of the pains I had taken to get them. What would she do with them? Would she make them into a hat, a fan, a boa, or — he had risen to his feet and he was not a bird, but a *man*, a good-looking Masai with a girdle of feathers and with a spear with its broad shining head high in the air. Heavens, what was to be done? Here was I on my stomach pointing a rifle at a gentlemanly warrior who, however fierce he might look, had done me no harm. Think quickly. Out of the corner of my eye I spied to the left of me a gazelle browsing on the grass. I made a sudden flank turn, continued my stalk, got the gazelle well sighted and fired. What luck, it had dropped. Springing to my feet I ran to the fallen gazelle, summoned up all my strength, threw it across my shoulder, staggered up to the ostrich and laid it at his feet. 'A peace offering', I panted, pointing to the scapegoat. He smiled. 'The ways of the white man are incomprehensible', he seemed to say, but knowing no Masai I was probably mistaken. He was evidently pleased, and that was all I wanted, so I left him flaying the antelope with the broad blade of his spear. Had he really been taken in by that sudden flanking movement of mine? I very much doubted it, but of one thing I was sure, namely, that he little knew how nearly I had pulled that trigger.

I suppose that the most important incident in our trip, from the point of view of what journalists call copy and what Selous means by adventure, was the incident that finally deprived us of our cook. I am always suspicious of cooks, not necessarily on the score of their cooking, but of their moral integrity. I do not, of course, refer to superior cooks, that is to say, to highly paid chefs, or to women known as treasures, but to the ordinary native cook. I have indeed a theory that it is the native servant with an eye to his own profit who becomes a cook, not because he enjoys cooking, but because he hopes to find in the kitchen a richer field for making a number of little extras. When he later discovers that these opportunities for unofficial profiting are few, he often becomes entirely unscrupulous. This at any rate is my theoretical justification for my mistrust of native cooks. Like many others of his class our cook was fat, but this was a point in his favour, for if a cook does not thrive on his own cooking, there must be something wrong with it. The only vice that actually appeared on the surface in the case of our cook was his fondness for gambling. He it was who encouraged those surreptitious card parties — carried on in the light of the camp fires far into the night and finally dispersed when he could stand the chattering no longer by Mafoota's angry dash from his tent. And he it was who vanished so completely towards the end of a long march that after sending out search-parties and firing many guns, we had sorrowfully concluded that our poor cook had been the victim of a lion, only to discover, ten days later, that all the time he had been enjoying a stolen holiday at a neighbouring village. In other words, our cook was a pleasant enough rogue with an eye for his own profit.

On the particular night on which occurred the event which is about to be described there was no card party, for the men were tired after a long march and were lying asleep, five in each tent and as tightly packed as dates in a box. Mafoota and I were taking a short stroll together in the dark before we also turned in, Mafoota carrying a rifle, and I a lantern. Suddenly the quiet of the night was broken by a piercing shriek. We stopped abruptly and turned to face the camp.

'Another rhinoceros', said Mafoota. In the early hours of the previous morning a rhinoceros had stumbled into our camp and had caused a considerable uproar. So the same thing had happened again. We stood there straining our ears and the noise of snapping branches warned us that some big animal was coming in our direction.

'It's not a rhino,' I said, but without conviction.

Whatever animal it was that was advancing, it had now stopped, and so close to us that we could hear its breathing. Then came a low growl.

'A lion,' whispered Mafoota, 'hold the lantern behind me.' I tilted it so that the sectors of light passed over the line of bushes in front of us and then leapt down on to the tufty grass at our feet. How artificial and theatrical bushes and trees appear by lantern light, as though they had been cut out of painted cardboard or wood. The scenery revealed by the lantern was so unconvincing that I had difficulty in believing that anything that might happen against such a background could be real. Mafoota had raised his rifle, but the night was without a moon and the feeble gleam of the lantern showed us nothing except the dark mass of the bushes and the make-believe grass at our feet. We stood still and listened. Heavy thuds, gradually becoming fainter, told us that the lion was now moving away from us. The noise in the camp was increasing.

'Better get back quickly,' said Mafoota, 'it sounds as though something's wrong there.'

We found the camp in an uproar. There were shouts of 'B'wama! (Master). Bunduki! (guns). Simba! (lion)', and we caught glimpses of figures perched high up on branches or in process of scrambling up trees. The Askaris, who should have been on guard, were nowhere to be found, and the only people I could discover on the ground were the four Kikuyu guides who were to escort me back to civilization in a few weeks' time when I was due to leave Mafoota. Their naked bodies were thrown into strong relief by the firelight and they were stooping occasionally to seize a blazing faggot and to hurl it in the direction of the bushes. Slowly we learnt what had happened. The lion had crept along the line of scrub that fringed the encampment and had raided one of the tents. In it he had found four porters and the cook, who, being the cook, naturally enjoyed the privilege of sleeping with his hand nearest to the door. He was now missing and there was no time to be lost. We seized all the firearms we could lay hands on and Hassan, Fara, the two penitent Askaris, Mafoota and myself formed a line of guns as though we were a party of men starting on a partridge drive. Then we advanced in the direction of the bushes, keeping as good touch with each other as was possible in such darkness. It was where Mafoota and I had met the lion on his way out of the camp that the search-party would be most likely to find his victim. Clutching my shotgun and loosening the revolver in my belt — Selous fancied himself with a revolver ever since by a fluke he had brought down that partridge on the wing — I stumbled along in the darkness, to fall down a few minutes later on something soft and warm.

'The cook!' I shouted, and Mafoota was soon at my side.

'What a pity,' Mafoota sighed, 'dear, dear, what a shame!' His voice sounded like that of a housewife who has come across a broken jug on the floor, and who, on examining it better, finds that it is beyond repair.

'What a pity, yes, but what a story,' said somebody within me. 'Callous, horrid and selfish,' snapped someone else in angry protest. How could anyone think of stories in the presence of such tragedy! Yet there had been a part of me that had been going over the events of the night and that had found them thrilling — the darkness, the sudden scream, the growl from the bushes, the search-party, and now, the dead man on the ground. Surely he must be dead, with his head rolling like that when one touched it and with those marks of great teeth in his neck, but the others were looking at me, as though they expected me to take some action. The words 'a case for a doctor' were clearly written on their faces and for the good name of my profession I felt that however useless it might be something must be done. The title of a handbill that I had once seen came suddenly into my head, 'The resuscitation of the apparently dead from drowning'. It was not particularly appropriate, but it would be as good as anything else, and solemnly and deliberately I enacted a windmill with the dead cook's arms. Round me stood the laity, both coloured and white, impressed by the resourcefulness of doctors. 'I am afraid it's no good,' I said, after a decent interval, 'it's useless to go on with this, for the man is dead.' It was enough, the verdict of medicine had been given, and with a feeling that everything right and proper had been done, we lifted up our heavy burden and carried it back with us to the camp.

Life pays no heed to the rules of art or to the requirements of drama, and the scene which Selous had recently found so stimulating suddenly lost all interest and meaning. Having deposited the body in the middle of the camp and covered it with a blanket, there seemed to be nothing left for us to do, except go to bed. Well, there was something to be said for going to bed when one had done a long trek under a tropical sun.

I was in bed, but I was not allowed to go to sleep, for the insatiable

Selous insisted on re-enacting the whole drama, adding here and there the few touches required to make it perfect; the dark night, the sleeping man oblivious of his doom, the lion creeping along the line of bushes, the snapping twigs . . . Hello, what was that? A branch had snapped outside, somewhere on my side of the tent. I could have sworn that there had been the noise of a breaking twig and that it was not just the product of my imagination. Mafoota was beginning to snore, and a snore is very like the noise made by a hunting lion, but I was sure that there was something moving outside the tent. 'Nonsense, Selous, you are romancing, you are embellishing your story.' Suddenly, there was a shout followed by a rifle shot. Mafoota and I burst out of the tent and a bullet whinnied past us at the same moment that we heard the report of the rifle that discharged it. 'Don't shoot, you fool. Put that sanguinary gun down, or I'll . . .' The uproar had increased and the end of Mafoota's speech was lost to me. The drama of the night had not yet finished, and clearly we had gone to bed too soon.

'Where is he?' yelled Mafoota.

'There in the bushes, B'wama,' answered Hassan.

'Get hold of Fara,' shouted Mafoota to me, 'and see that he collects all the guns.'

Again the line was formed and again we advanced like men walking down partridges, but this time we drew a blank. Only one thing was certain, and that was that the lion had knocked down the tent next to ours. But if he was not in the bushes, where the hell was he? How can one find a cat in a garden when there is no moon and the night is as dark as pitch? It was useless to speculate and still more useless to go on searching for a lion in all that blackness. We retired, but not this time to bed. The lion was hankering after meat, we had deprived him of his kill and he would almost certainly return. It would be wiser therefore to remain up and on the look-out for him. We spent the three hours that separated us from sunrise huddled round a fire, peering into the night and doing our best to decide whether the dark mass we could just make out, twenty yards away from us, was a bush or a crouching lion. In all probability it was a bush, but both Selous and Mafoota thought that it had moved and once Fara was sure that he had seen two glowing eyes.

The group round the fire would have made a good subject for an artist with a genius for lighting effects. On each side of me crouched my

Kikuyu, their spears reflecting the firelight and their gaze seldom shifting from the outer circle of darkness. Occasionally they moved, generally for the purpose of taking snuff, but unlike my old friend Mr. Magnuson they carried it, not in a snuff-box, but in an old cartridge-case conveniently stuck in a slit cut in the lobe of the ear. I was confident that if a lion did charge out of the darkness I would be perfectly safe, for those long spears, sharp as razors, would prove far more efficient at close quarters than Mafoota's elephant gun. Next to the Kikuyu sat Fara, his magnificent teeth gleaming between his parted lips, his face lit with pleasure. Somalis were always brave, but he was the bravest of all Somalis. To demonstrate his courage to us he offered to find a teapot, a kettle and tea, and without waiting for our permission he crept away from the firelight to the place where the cook's box of tricks lay abandoned near the bushes. On the opposite side of the fire Hassan was sitting on his haunches, his body as lean and as hard as that of any fakir. Hassan had no need to demonstrate to anybody his bravery, for nobody would ever have dreamt of doubting it. Had he not already told us how once he had crept into the body of a dead zebra and had waited alone in that warmth and stench for the arrival of a lion. We heard that night a great deal about lions, but even more about Hassan. Bigger than anyone, and unusually silent for him, sat Mafoota, his great figure wrapped in a blanket, his hand grasping his elephant gun. He looked absurdly like a fat gipsy woman warming her hands by the fire and waiting for her husband's belated return.

As the hours wore on expectancy gave way to listlessness and weariness, and from the direction of the other fires, around which our porters had been gathered, came an increasing volume of snoring. But we had not long to wait, for Jupiter was climbing up the eastern sky and already the darkness was lessening. Quick on the heels of his planet came the sun himself, and as his first rays fell on the white tents we heard the distant roar of a lion. The long wait was over and something within me told me that it was high time for breakfast. I looked in the direction of the cook's fallen tent, and I noted with pleasure that Sardi had already taken on his work. A billy-can was suspended over a fire, and I could just catch a faint aroma of coffee.

We buried the victim of the night and, to prevent the interference of marauding beasts, we piled stones and branches of thorn over the grave. It was all we could do, for the religion of the cook was unknown to us, and to erect a rough wooden cross might well have been out of place. Then a chastened safari set out again on the march and for once Misharibu, the singer, was silent. Our way led us through a forest which was as dark and as awe-inspiring as is the interior of some great cathedral. Above our heads towered the mighty arches of the trees and as the morning breezes stirred their topmost branches there reached our ears a sound like the music of a distant organ. Every now and then this music was broken by the scuffling of unseen monkeys and by a noise as though made by someone striking a hammer on brass. It was the metallic call of the anvil-bird.

During that silent march I enacted the part of Kejunga, the man who walked with his eyes to the ground, for excitement had given place to despondency. I was thinking of the event of the night before, and more particularly of that moment when I had fallen over the dead body of the cook. 'What a pity,' Mafoota had said, and then, as though someone else were speaking, I had heard myself say, 'What a pity, yes — but what a story!' These different voices which spoke in me, these strange people who came and went, these warring sides of my nature, what did it all mean? Was I nothing but a shabby lodging-house in which irresponsible boarders lounged and talked, with no thought for anybody but themselves? Who was I, and where was I going, not only on this trail, but on the bigger journey of life? What did I expect to find when I had gone a little further, and would it be worth having when I had found it? Of this nature were my thoughts as I walked through the cool and the gloom of that forest, as conscious of the obscurity within as of the darkness which lay without. Mystery was afoot; yes, the mystery of my existence and of truths at one time almost within reach, and then rapidly receding into the distance.

The days of camp life and safari were now numbered and the morning soon arrived on which I was to take my farewell of Mafoota and, with my four Kikuyu, to make my way back to the railway. I would just have time to pay a fleeting visit to Victoria Nyanza and then I would return to Mombasa, en route for home. How far away that old life seemed, and all that old routine which I must take up again where I had laid it down. Having collected together my few belongings, said good-bye to Mafoota, given small presents to Sardi and the two Somalis, I turned my back on the camp and started out for Naivasha, the nearest station on the Uganda Railway. I see when I refer to my old diary that the thought of my return to civilization was not altogether unpleasing to me. In it is this entry. 'After all, a civilized life is not wanting in certain minor advantages, as for example, the advantages of a nicely cooked dinner and of a well-made, comfortable bed.' These I was soon to enjoy again but by the time I reached London the pockets of my belt were all empty and I had just enough money left to pay for my ticket on the Hampstead tube. It was a strange figure that entered the railway compartment, for my luggage was strapped to my back, and precariously balanced on top of it all were a leopard skin, two pairs of oryx horn, some dried fish purchased in Aden and an old pair of boots. 'That's the worst of travelling,' said the tube attendant, as he shut the sliding doors behind me, but exactly what he meant by this enigmatical remark was more than I could tell. Did he imply that the greatest disadvantage of travelling was the risk of having to carry one's luggage on one's back, or was he merely sympathizing with me because all holidays must end? I do not know, but he was a nice man with an alert intelligent face, and I am sure that his words were well intended. There was something after all to be said for civilization and beds and nicely cooked dinners, yes, and even for tubes and tube attendants. I was glad to be back again.

CHAPTER VIII

BEDSIDE MANNERS

I WAS now Bowlby's junior house-surgeon, working in the surgery most of the day and, if my 'firm' happened to be on duty, what seemed to me to be most of the night. 'Wanted in the surgery, sir, a bad accident case,' the burly hospital porter would announce, and the house-surgeon responsible for the admission of new cases would turn out of his bed and make his way to the ill-lit room in which the city ambulances deposited their cargoes of human wreckage. Accidents, attempted suicides, drunks, bruised and screaming wives, paupers fainting for lack of food, fat men attacked by apoplexy and thin men in diabetic coma, all of these were brought to this room. Kneeling by the side of the stretcher, with a huge city constable standing in the background, the house-surgeon on duty would have to decide whether the case must be admitted, whether it was a medical or surgical emergency, whether place would have to be found for it in some neighbouring infirmary, or whether by lying for a time on the stretcher in front of the casualty room fire, the patient would recover sufficiently to allow him to stagger back to that particular slum in which was situated his home. It was difficult work, and more especially so when the patient was unconscious and therefore could give no history of his illness, utter no complaints, lift no limbs and show no tongue. What was going on inside that head? Was the brain soused with alcohol, or put out of action by a drug procured by guile from a chemist, or was it being poisoned by some toxins elaborated in the patient's own body? Was haemorrhage taking place within the skull, so that it would have to be opened immediately, or was this merely a case of concussion, from which the patient would recover sooner or later if he were kept quiet and warm?

These were the kind of questions to which we had to find an answer, calling in the help of our corresponding house-physician whenever we were particularly worried in order that he might share our responsibility. All the time the tall city constable stood in the background lending to the scene an atmosphere of dignity and law and order. Often Sister Surgery, a lean figure in blue, with a competent-looking face and hair turning grey, would put in an appearance and offer some valuable suggestion. 'If you want a stomach-pump I will send nurse to get one . . .' 'He can lie there for an hour or two and I will get nurse Hawkins to record an hourly pulse . . .' Then she would disappear again to another corner of her kingdom to procure crutches for a child, to stop the noise made by an excited patient recovering from gas, to instruct a young mother how to give the medicine to her baby, or to tell an aged man exactly what to do with the recommendation he had been given to an infirmary. Sister Surgery's advice was well worth having and I soon got rid of the prejudice that so often prevents a newly-fledged doctor from profiting from advice coming from unqualified sources. These old sisters had something more than an immense store of experience, something even more than knowledge; they often had wisdom. Even the old-time porters, through long experience, had acquired a knowledge of practical medicine that might come in handy. 'A fracture has just arrived, sir. It looks to me like a Collis.' 'Better be quick, sir,' another had said to a colleague of mine, asleep after a heavy day on duty in the surgery, 'Mr. Jones, your new dresser, is about to open an aneurysm. He thinks it's an abscess.' The porter was right, and Mr. Jones' inopportune operation in the surgery was stopped in the nick of time.

At the end of six months the junior house-surgeon becomes a senior and, leaving the turmoil and noise of the casualty department, he takes on the quieter but even more responsible work of the wards. Sir Anthony's two wards were Stanley and Darker, each under the charge of its Sister. With Sister Darker I soon came to terms, but Sister Stanley caused my heart to beat faster every time I turned the handle of the door leading to her domain. It was the first time that my gallant band of actors had been forced to have dealings with what is known as a difficult woman. Women always disconcerted me, but this one was to prove quite impossible. The truth is that the inner quartet had little knowledge of, or little use for, the opposite sex. Ever since Selous had been dragged in from the back of the bicycle shed to have his hands and face washed before being presented to the callers taking tea in the drawing-room, he had been convinced that women's chief function in this world was to interfere with the legitimate activities of men. Sometimes they did this directly, as was the case when they deliberately interfered with his play, but sometimes they achieved their object indirectly by marrying a man and demanding all his attention. For this reason anyone who wanted to get on comfortably with his work must avoid them. Black Hawk was inclined to agree with Selous, but he was less explicit in his protests. Braves were braves and squaws were squaws, creatures of an inferior breed; that was all that could be usefully said about it. Knight-Paton's views were divided, for he subscribed to the laws of chivalry and had an affection for women of a rather helpless, male-worshipping type. He had even on occasion lost his heart to small flaxen-haired blue-eyed maidens, so that he was not disposed to exclude all femininity from his world. The fact that there were women amongst the crowd that watched the triumphal progress of the Personage through that crowded hall shows that he also was inclined to tolerate the existence of females, provided of course that they did not make nuisances of themselves.

After a few brave but ineffective gestures Selous, Knight-Paton and the Personage retired to the wings, discomforted and nursing their grievances whenever Stanley Ward was entered. There they remained sulking for the rest of my term of office, so that it was Black Hawk who generally took charge in Stanley, Black Hawk who outwardly maintained his calm, but inwardly seethed with rage. Now that I look back on the past from the more detached vantage point of the present I am bound to confess that Black Hawk's seeming indifference was a sham. Had the mask been lifted behind it would have been found an indignant, frightened and impotent brave, and it is quite likely that the world was less successfully deceived by his serene exterior than he believed it to be. Sister Stanley was by no means an uncommon type of woman. To the world she was hard, with cold grey eyes and a lean aquiline face. She treated her nurses, many of her patients and her house-surgeons with an icy coldness, but surreptitiously and in whispers would often give out comfort from some secret store of warmth within her. All her good was done by stealth, as though it shamed her to show to others what inwardly she felt. Nor was her secret charity confined to patients in her ward. Unlike the great majority of nurses, she possessed a private income and, quite unknown to us, she used it as a means of supporting in the country a number of crippled and destitute children. What a puzzle she presented to me. Even though I knew nothing about the clandestine home for children, I had noted her untiring devotion to some of her patients; to Maud, for example, that pale, querulous girl who was suffering from tubercle of the spine. So much did Maud irritate the rest of us that we only went near her bed when something definite had to be done, such as an abscess to be dressed or the notes to be written up. Yet Sister looked after her, month in and month out, with all the devotion that a mother shows for her own ailing child.

During the six months of being senior house-surgeon I absorbed a vast amount of knowledge, not only knowledge of surgery but of the ancillary subjects of my profession. From my able chief I learnt much that I have never forgotten: how to stand with my hands behind my back at the moment of giving a medical verdict and how to make this verdict seem convincing and weighty; the right method of touching an anxious relative lightly on the shoulder and of giving him the comfort of knowing that everything that could be done was being done and that he must now wait patiently for the result of the treatment; the best way to lift the eyebrows slightly and to shake the head when that relative ventures an opinion that perhaps it is not really necessary to operate; and that most useful of accomplishments, the best method of breaking off profitless conversations with garrulous patients. Anthony Bowlby was not only a good surgeon, but he was also a wise man and he would have made a name in any profession or business he had cared to take up. He became my model and I have borrowed from him so many movements, mannerisms, inflexions of the voice and methods of speech that I fear I should stand awkward and mute in my consulting room if by some magic all that I learnt from Bowlby were suddenly to be removed. It is Bowlby who now greets patients entering my room, Bowlby who bids them be seated and Bowlby who waves them good-bye. But there was one item in his professional equipment which I have never been able to emulate, not because I did not wish or attempt to acquire it, but because the material given to me at birth seems incapable of receiving its imprint. I refer to Bowlby's wonderful capacity for remembering names. 'How are you, Blenkinsop?' he would say, when a strange face unexpectedly appeared in the crowd that followed him round the wards during his afternoon visits. 'Let me see, I last met you fifteen years ago at the B.M.A. meeting in Huddersfield.' He could recall equally well the names of patients who had been in the wards many years ago. 'There was a patient in that bed by the window, a man named Smithers, whom I operated on for similar symptoms and they turned out to be due to an aneurysm of the renal artery. You remember him, Sister?' This name-memory seemed to be a magical gift, the secret of which was known to Bowlby and to a few of the more successful kings, or perhaps only to their official remembrancers.

Whilst Sir Anthony gave me so much out of his store of riches, he at the same time produced for me new difficulties. Up till now I had looked upon this house-surgeonship as a kind of stopgap in my career, or at most, as a finishing school in the profession into which Selous and Knight-Paton had thrust me. My medical work in London was never regarded as being important in itself, but it was the path which I must tread if I were to acquire that galloping horse and that small black bag tied to the saddle. But Bowlby was upsetting my plans. He had made such a strong impression on the Personage that the latter recalled the thoughts which had stirred in his mind that time when he had inspected Sir Dyce Duckworth's and Sir Lauder Brunton's smart broughams drawn up in the hospital square. Deserts and horses and Arab sheiks were all very well in their way, but did they lead to fame? He was sure now that they did not, and that greatness lay, not in deserts, but in Harley Street. He therefore missed no opportunity of impressing on me the importance of the honorary staff and he was continually reminding me of the celebrated names associated with the past history of the hospital. Honourable medical appointments were whispered in my ear. 'Fellow of the Royal College of Surgeons, President of the College, Surgeon to the Royal Household, Surgeon to the King, Paget, Percival Potts, Lawrence, Savory, Bowlby,' he droned on, repeating a dozen famous names in my ear and conducting me round the Great Hall of the hospital in which the portraits of many eminent surgeons hung. Selous and Knight-Paton were frankly alarmed, for they saw their mounts disappearing into the distance, and they had no desire to become tame demonstrators of anatomy and pathology, or to climb on to any other of the preliminary rungs of the ladder that led to the Personage's new conception of greatness. The mere idea of staying on in London and of sacrificing adventure and romance in favour of long hours of duty in the surgery appalled them. 'With a little hard work and a little good luck you can become surgeon-in-ordinary to His Majesty the King,' said the Personage, with the assurance of a card-player who knows that he is about to take a trick. He was right. Selous and Knight-Paton looked dejectedly at the cards lying on the table, realized that they had lost and left the room. I was now definitely committed to an entirely new direction in life. I would remain in London, work like a nigger, wait patiently for the senior members of the staff to retire or to die and I would then become Assistant Surgeon to the hospital. There would be no more travel for me. Romance and adventure would have to be sacrificed.

Can anything that is real and enduring arise only out of the imagination? My father had once dreamt of a band of children that played music and sang hymns at street corners and out of this dream eventually materialized the Shaftesbury Hall Children's Band. It was very dear to him, that band, and once a year it came down to Bealings for its annual outing. But unless the desire to bring new influences into the shabby lives of the people of Poplar had already existed, unless he had had at heart the welfare of the Shaftesbury Mission, the dream would soon have been forgotten. So was it, in all probability, with the dreams of Selous and Knight-Paton. When on that fateful day they gave the casting vote in favour of my becoming a doctor, they were making use of a desire incompletely formulated, perhaps, which was already there. As a boy I had been curious about the physical machinery of life and on the lawn at Bealings were often to be seen the bones of various domestic animals bleaching in the sun. I loved to fit them together and to see how in some joints the movements were free and how in others the bones were permitted to move only in certain directions. Still more thrilling was the interior of a rabbit, with each organ wrapped in its own glistening membrane, and with that long tube along which the food had to pass in the wonderful process of digestion. It was therefore not entirely a hardship for me to have to follow the Personage's new lead and to devote myself whole-heartedly to surgery. A part of me welcomed this change in my plans. The first step was to make an intensive study of anatomy and to sit for the preliminary examination for that essential qualification, the Fellowship of the Royal College of Surgeons. When this and the final examination had been successfully passed two new steps had to be taken: the first, to begin research on the special subject chosen by the College for those competing for the Jacksonian Prize, and the second, to send in an application for the next vacancy at the hospital, which would almost certainly be that of Junior Demonstrator of Pathology. My life was soon so fully occupied with medical work that there was no time to think about anything else. I was now convinced that there was only one road worth travelling by, namely, that along which I was hurrying, the road that eventually led to a consultant practice in Harley Street.

The advertisement for the post of demonstrator in pathology was now pinned up on the hospital notice board and I sent in my application. It was successful and I was informed that I could begin work as soon as the new laboratories in process of construction were completed. So far as could be seen it would probably be another five or six months before the builders had finished their work. On hearing this news Selous and Knight-Paton returned to the card table that they had previously left. All might not be lost, and they would at any rate play another rubber. 'Six months,' they said, 'six months, and with nothing at all to do.' The Personage looked up and realized that another game had now begun. 'With more than enough to do,' he commented, 'there's the Jacksonian essay to be got on with, not to mention your work in coaching Jones for his L.S.A.' But the two allies were not to be browbeaten. 'Jones will fail in any case,' they said, 'he's come down in that examination five times already, and *your* coaching will make no difference.' The Personage's face assumed an expression of incorruptibility. 'It's a matter of principle,' he answered. 'You've promised him special attention and you can't let him down.' The two allies, Knight-Paton and Selous, exchanged glances. They would play another suit. 'Wilson is a much better coach than you are, and why shouldn't Jones join his class? He's far more likely to pass his examination with Wilson to help him than with you as his coach.' The Personage abandoned the use of Jones for the partners had clearly won that trick. 'Well, anyhow, quite apart from Jones, there's the work for the Jacksonian prize to be considered. Essays are to be submitted in May and that means only another ten months in which to finish it.' The allies now produced another good card. 'You've already done all the actual research needed for it and it will only take a couple of months to write the essay.' The Personage saw that he had lost. 'Nothing will induce me to leave my work,' he said, flinging down a weak card and hurriedly leaving the table. Knight-Paton and Selous had won, but the details of their expedition — they invariably went on an expedition — had yet to be settled.

These details were decided on the following Sunday in the parlour of the White Horse Inn at Shere. I had gone down there in order to escape from the atmosphere of the hospital and to decide what part of the world I should next explore. Selous and Knight-Paron had been busy meanwhile in visiting many of the shipping offices in the city. They now placed on the floor a number of brightly coloured pamphlets with illustrations of magnificent liners sailing into palm-fringed harbours in various quarters of the globe. The Personage looked on at these preliminaries, haughty and censorious. 'You've had your fling,' he said, 'and rolling stones never gather any moss. You've decided to go to Harley Street, and if you're to succeed in doing so, you can't afford to travel.' Selous was not in the least disturbed. 'Why should a stone collect moss?' he said. 'Moss doesn't improve it. A stone is a stone and moss is moss. In any case there are six months with nothing to do, and we shall go abroad. That was settled long ago and we've only come down to Shere to decide *where* to go.' Henceforth Selous took no further notice of the Personage, but stooped and picked up from the floor one of the sailing lists with a bright picture of the Pacific Ocean on the front page. 'The South Sea Islands,' he said, turning over the page. 'Let me see — coral, coconuts, hibiscus flowers and maidens, surf-riding and sharks.' He held the sailing list in his hand and looked round to see what effect his words had had before replacing it on the floor. Knight-Paton was gazing into the distance, as though some old memories were stirring in his mind of missionary days in the Pacific, and he said nothing. The Personage protested. 'It's too far,' he snapped, 'I insist on being back in time.' Selous admitted that he might be right, and stooped to pick up another pamphlet. 'China and Japan — rickshaws, chopsticks, temples, dragons and mandarins.' Nobody showed any interest, so the Orient Line was discarded in favour of the Royal Mail Steam Packet. 'South America — green tea, Inca remains, gauchos, tangos, armadillos and jaguars. There are also Aconcagua and the Andes.' Selous had made a mistake in mentioning mountains, for all had agreed to abandon climbing. 'India — temple-bells, indigo, snakes, yogis, elephants and tigers.' Selous uttered the last two words with relish and slurred over the word 'snakes'. He had made an impression and he spread the last pamphlet not on the floor but on the table. He then opened a small atlas which had been brought down specially to Shere and turned to the map of Asia on which he traced a long line with his finger, a line which started at Port Said, travelled down the Red Sea and then swept across the Indian Ocean, past

Ceylon to end at Calcutta. 'It's only three weeks' sailing from here,' he said, looking up. There was a pause during which he consulted a list. 'And,' he added, 'an excellent ship leaves Liverpool the day after to-morrow.' His tone indicated that everything had been settled and that the discussion was at an end. The Personage realized that he had lost and that it would be useless to offer any more resistance.

I had just time to buy a few necessities, to arrange with Ball that he should send me a cable whenever the date was known at which work in the new laboratories was to start, and to tell Jones that I thought that he had had enough coaching from me and that if he wanted any more he should join Wilson's excellent class. I also sent two cables to India, one to my cousin in the I.C.S. and the other to Major Rait of the I.M.S. Then I left overland for Genoa to catch the S.S. *City of Glasgow* on its way to India. It was obvious that this would be my last chance of seeing something more of the world, for when I had taken up my work in the laboratory I would have to remain a prisoner in London. It was therefore almost a sacred duty for me to make the best of my few remaining months of liberty.

CHAPTER IX

THE PERSONAGE FINDS INDIA MORE
THAN TOLERABLE

How can I write about India, that vast continent of a hundred different races, different creeds, different climates and different ages? What did I see there, equipped as I was with so little understanding, with such scant knowledge of her ancient literature, her philosophy and her religion. I took with me to India the outlook and the ideas of an Englishman and I brought back only what I had taken. How seldom do we realize the limitations of our understanding and how little are we aware of the poverty of our thinking. We peer at the world through a tiny chink and then come away from our peep-hole with the belief that we have seen everything, whereas we have seen little or nothing. Jalau'ddin, the Persian Sufi poet, has made the subjectiveness of our knowledge the theme of one of his poems in that masterpiece of his, the *Mathnawi*:

'Since thou art a part of the world, whosoever thou art thou deemst all to be of the same description as thyself, misguided man.

'If thou whirl round and thy head whirl round, thy organ of sight sees the house whirling round;

'And if thou art narrow at heart thou deemest the whole world to be narrow; and if thou art happy, as thy friend would desire, this world seems to thee like a garden of roses.

'How many a one has gone as far as Syria and Iraq and seen nothing but unbelief and hypocrisy; and how many a one has gone as far as India and Herat and seen nothing but selling and buying.'

Only twice in the four months I was there did I see anything more in India than 'selling and buying'. The first occasion was when I was standing on the steps of the Scindia Ghat at Benares, one of the forty-seven places at which pilgrims to Holy Ganges wash away their sins. Around me swarmed a crowd so mixed, so strange, so seemingly mad, that I felt like someone who had inadvertently strayed into one of the circles of Dante's Inferno and who, because he possessed no clue to the meaning of what was happening there, looked on it with consternation and amazement. Near by me was a gaunt naked man, his body smeared with ashes and his locks plastered with mud. Fanaticism blazed in his sunken eyes, and his lips moved as he repeated and repeated again a string of words. His 'chela' had laid an empty gourd at my feet and was apparently waiting for my alms, but the man for whom he begged repelled me and no alms were forthcoming. Further away an emaciated youth was standing like a stork, one foot firmly planted on the ground and the other tucked away in his groin. Next to him was another youth who was pointing a wasted and ankylosed arm to the skies. And all the time a crowd of bathers, children, young girls and boys, old crones, cripples and monstrosities were swarming down the steps towards the river. Some of those who bathed were beautiful and were wearing chaplets of flowers, whilst others were hideous and clothed in rags. Youth and age, beauty and ugliness, health and disease, sanity and madness pushed their way past me down the steps which led to the water.

Heavy-hearted and tired of the dirt, the smell, the squalor and the useless suffering around me, I at last turned in the direction of home, stopping only as I reached the top of the steps to look at a motionless figure beneath an awning. My eyes rested on a middle-aged man who was sitting in the now-familiar attitude of the Buddha, as still and as silent as a statue of the great teacher he followed. How different was that calm face, that body in which every muscle was not only motionless but also relaxed, how different was everything about him from all that I had found so distasteful in the crowd that surged around me. How he towered above them — he was seated on a raised and shaded platform — not only physically, but mentally and spiritually. His countenance was serene and he had the innate dignity of a saint, whilst they — yes, they were like the maimed and stricken patients of a vast out-patient department, the casualties of some remorseless industry that in pursuit of its own ends pays no attention to human life. That was it, they actually were casualties. Before me was seated the one who had succeeded, the man who had striven long and in the end had attained what he had been looking for, but those who swarmed round him were the failures, the false prophets, the fanatics, the imitators, and the people who had fallen by the way. They had failed, but could one blame them? Some of them had been so heavily handicapped from the start that it was impossible that they should ever succeed, and others had begun well and then wandered from the path. 'Straight is the gate and narrow is the way which leadeth unto life, and few there be that find it.' These words suddenly came into my mind as I looked at the crowd making its way down the steps which led to the river. In speaking thus surely Christ had meant to lay emphasis not only on the difficulty of finding the gate, but also of avoiding missing the way after the gate had been passed. And heaven knew that the journey on which this great multitude of India had started was a perilous one, for they were not seeking the easy Western ideal of worldly success but the far more difficult goal of spiritual enlightenment. It takes courage to turn one's back on the familiar everyday world, as these people had done, and to seek an unknown and unseen world of a higher order. They had hoped in the end to attain serenity and peace, but the path along which they travelled was a treacherous one and they had only found superstition and fanaticism. I turned away from the motionless figure and made my way slowly back to the small hotel at which I was staying.

India is a continent and one cannot describe a continent. It has left me with memories of arid plains over which black buck flash, of old red-bricked cities crumbling into dust, of temples built on the site of temples still more ancient, of cupolas rising above tamarind trees, and of narrow streets filled with beggars, wailing lepers, fat merchants, thin fakirs, almond-eyed girls, impudent youths, priests, babus and wandering, sad-eyed cows. Hawks and pigeons glided above the roofs, whilst underfoot was a carpet of dust littered with garbage and filth.

I had found awaiting me in Calcutta a letter from Major Rait inviting me to visit him at Purneah, a once prosperous station in northern Bengal, but now, on account of the failure of the indigo trade, a station of dwindling importance. I was glad of this opportunity to escape from the heat and the smells of Calcutta and I made my way as quickly as possible to Purneah. It was a typical Indian station, that is to say, it consisted of a sprinkling of well-built bungalows in which dwelt the European residents, an English club and a straggling native town. It did not take long to realize that the club was the hub around which everything else in Purneah revolved. It was to the club that every European went when at the end of the day's work he wished to forget for a few hours India and her troubles. A dance was actually in progress at the moment when I entered the club, and a rather stout man with grey hair trod on my toe and then stopped to apologize. Having received my reassurance that no harm had been done he seized his partner by the waist and whirled back into the *mêlée* of dancers. 'He seems rather a strenuous dancer,' I said, as soon as he was out of hearing. 'Yes, that's old Kendal, the judge,' answered Rait. 'He's as keen as mustard; he never misses a dance and puts in about two hours' exercise a day. He says that there's nothing like dancing for giving one a good sweat and for shaking up the liver. He has scarcely ever been known to speak to his partner, but changes her for another as soon as she's blown. Would you like to dance?' As I did not suffer from a sluggish liver and had sweated as much as seemed necessary, I did not avail myself of Rait's offer to find me a partner.

We retired instead to the smoke-room where, seated in one of its comfortable chairs, I was initiated into the art of drinking pegs and smoking cheroots. By listening to the conversation I learnt a great deal about the curious habits of the natives, their utter unreliability and their lack of appreciation of the schemes which the government had evolved for their benefit. I was also given some useful advice on the subject of servants. There were apparently two alternatives: I could either engage a boy who spoke no English and was comparatively honest, or else obtain one who had been to a mission school and had learnt there both English and dishonesty. Having discovered in East Africa how easily one could get on with the universal language of signs, I chose the former.

When my servant arrived he turned out to be an exact replica in brown of Stanley Anderton, the master who had been so severe with me at my preparatory school. But now it was I who held the upper hand and who was not going to tolerate any nonsense. I had purchased a Hindustani grammar before leaving England and during the voyage I had learnt from it a few nouns and adverbs and the second person imperative of as many of the verbs as I could carry in my head: 'Thou shalt go, thou shalt pack, thou shalt come, thou shalt bring.' It was remarkably simple and I had been assured that all that it was necessary for the visitor travelling in India to know was the second singular of the imperative and the first plural of the indicative: 'Thou shalt prepare quickly. We depart at noon.' I learnt these parts of the verbs in my grammar and paid no attention to the rest.

At dinner a few evenings later my host told me that in a few days time he was going to Ghatia to attend a camel fair. Would I care to accompany him on what was for him an official visit? Never having been either to Ghatia or to a camel fair I gladly availed myself of his offer. 'Thou shalt prepare — camel — Ghatia,' I announced to Ahmed, my servant, at the end of dinner. He had been standing to attention behind my chair as I had often had to stand to attention in front of Stanley Anderton's desk. Ahmed bowed and thereby intimated that he had understood his master's command. How much better it was to have a boy who knew no English and had never learnt to steal. I was gratified by my rapid progress in the universal language of India and inwardly commended Ahmed for his intelligence and honesty.

Ghatia was a small neighbouring principality ruled over by a Nawab and, as we were bound to meet this ruler at the fair, my host thought that it would be as well for me to know something about him. The present ruler was still a boy when his father had died, and his up-bringing as well as that of his younger brother was entrusted to his mother and a tutor. The latter was one of those people who are usually described as being 'live wires', and from the very start the tutor had decided to make the most out of his position. By ingratiating himself with the widow he quickly gained her confidence and within a short time had obtained complete control over the two boys. The scheme that he intended to put into practice was to ruin economically the elder of his charges, now the Nawab of Ghatia, in the hope that he would be called in afterwards to deal with the resultant chaos in the state finances. In this case he would become the virtual master of Ghatia. Fortune favoured him, for the young Nawab was by temperament extravagant; and, what was still more welcome, he had met, fallen in love with and married the daughter of an English photographer in Calcutta. This was a good beginning, for the Nawab's subjects hated mixed marriages and they would never tolerate a future half-breed ruler. Not only had the marriage made the Nawab unpopular, but his subjects would probably take steps to poison the child and possibly also the mother as the best means of preventing the birth of any more Eurasian offspring. The tutor was now encouraging his charge to exceed his revenue, but he was not having it all his own way. A new and unforseen power had intervened in the shape of the Nawab's mother-in-law, an astute old lady, who having quickly sized up the position, was now out to defeat the tutor's nefarious schemes. The story was an interesting one and I looked forward to meeting some of its characters.

We arrived at the fair and found there about three hundred grumbling camels and one very morose cow-elephant tied by her leg to a stake. She was obviously in a bad humour and was looking with disdainful eyes at the vulgar herd of camels into whose company she had been thrust. But after all this was not an elephant fair but a camel fair, and it was they who had the right to resent her presence here and not she theirs. There was very little time to inspect the animals, for a gala performance, at which we were expected to be present, was about to start in the improvised theatre. At that very moment a salaaming native was announcing that the procession to the theatre, headed by a band, was on the point of moving off. He waved his hand in the direction of an ox-cart in which were seated eight native musicians all carrying brass instruments. As soon as the master of ceremonies had obtained our gracious permission to form the procession he hurried off to do so. It was led by an old bearded man in a scarlet turban who carried an ancient sabre. This he held upright at the salute and then, as his arms got tired and he lapsed into forgetfulness, the sabre slowly drooped until it ended by pointing at his yellow shoes. Behind this leader marched a company of native police, whose duty it was to keep off the crowd. The police were followed by the ox-cart, its musicians now producing such a noise out of their cornets and trombones that the camels were in danger of stampeding. At the tail of the procession and the cynosure of all eyes, walked Major Rait and the Personage, the latter calm and dignified, but unbending from time to time to acknowledge the huzzahs of the crowd.

The procession was such a success that two complete circles of the fair were made in case some late-comer should have been cheated of the sight. Then we moved off in the direction of the theatre and, passing through the open doors, entered the building in which the play was about to take place. The transition from the bright sunlight outside to the gloom within was so abrupt that at first I could see nothing, but gradually I realized that the building was filled to its utmost capacity with waiting people. 'A hush fell upon the multitude as the Great One made his way with slow and dignified steps to the dais that had been erected at the far end of the hall, and a sea of faces turned in his direction.' No, it was not a dais to which the Personage was being led, but a sofa covered in Cambridge blue silk spotted with pale pink nosegays. How touching, Cambridge blue. But there was no time for sentimentality, for a slightly-built young man, in an amber silk robe and wearing a necklace of jewels, was holding out towards me a delicate hand, coffee-coloured on the back and pink on the palm. He was obviously the young Nawab and I was glad to see that I had been placed next him. The band struck up 'God Save the King', the crowd rose to its feet, the Personage stood rigidly to attention, and then we all sat down.

On the other side of the Nawab was a dispirited-looking girl, the bright colour of whose jewels served to enhance the pallor of her face. The national anthem had apparently upset the thin little boy whose hand she had been holding, and in order to comfort him she now took him on to her knee. He looked a very unwholesome child, and although I was on the side of the Nawab I was forced to agree with his subjects that this product of a mixed marriage would never make a really satis-factory ruler. The other leading actors in this pathetic family drama, namely the villainous tutor and the clever mother-in-law, did not seem to be present, for when I looked round behind me I could see nobody there except servants, guards and officials. My own private bodyguard, Ahmed, had joined Nawab's retinue, wearing, as was his custom, his shirt outside his trousers. As the Nawab's servants had received him with-out any signs of surprise I presumed that this peculiarity of Ahmed's was not so *outré* as I had formerly imagined it to be. In front of us was the stage, already lit by footlights although the curtains had not yet been drawn. The members of our brass band had melted into the audience and a gentler kind of music was now being produced by two players of stringed instruments who were seated one at each end of the stage. Although their melody was monotonous, it was infinitely preferable to that which had come from our brass band. Realizing that I was sitting next to an Indian ruler I began to search in my mind for suitable themes for conversation. When I passed in review the topics in which a young ruler ought to be interested they did not seem to be very stimulating to talk; the ways of state elephants, the fatigues of a levee, the assessment of taxes; I turned all these down as too difficult to handle and continued my search for a more promising subject.

'Do you believe in many cylinders, or do you think that four are enough?' suddenly asked the Nawab, who had evidently been engaged in a similar hunt and had run down his quarry first.

Cylinders. Good gracious, I must switch on to another part of my brain for he was talking about cars, a subject about which I knew very little. 'I think that four are sufficient,' I answered, 'for it means fewer plugs to clean.'

The Nawab gave my words far more consideration than I felt they deserved, so much consideration, indeed, that I began to feel alarmed. At last he broke the silence, but not before it had become acutely uncomfortable. 'I have several old cars, but now I want to buy a completely new and up-to-date automobile.' (What a strange word!) 'But I have not yet decided on the make. My tutor advises a six-cylinder Bentley, but my wife's mother tells me that in her country Morris-Cowleys are all the rage.'

I scented the smell of gunpowder and heard the rumble of a distant battle. I was on the side of the stout-hearted lady. 'Undoubtedly she is right,' I answered with emphasis, 'everybody in England is now buying Morris-Cowleys. You could not do better than follow her advice.'

The curtains were now being drawn and the conversation for the time being was abandoned. A man with a sword was addressing a woman (obviously a boy in female garments) whom he appeared to be about to behead, but before doing so he was apparently justifying to her what he was about to do. His speech went on for at least half an hour and I realized that the murder was a very leisurely affair and that, consequently, there was no urgency for the lady to make an effort to escape. Meanwhile the musicians continued to twang their instruments and the Nawab to converse with me. He had got well into his stride and was now talking about gramophones, cinematographs, a new patent corkscrew which he had bought when he was last in Calcutta, and the favourite for the Grand National. As I was not keenly interested in any of these subjects I made a determined effort to bring the conversation back to India. I therefore inquired about the play, explaining that my Hindustani, although improving, was too limited to allow me to catch the drift of the actor's speech.

'He's speaking in Urdu,' explained the Nawab, 'but there's no hurry about that for it will go on for five or six hours.'

'What, that speech?'

'No, the play. Perhaps you would prefer to come to my palace. It's not far from here.' He had detected a slight droop in my voice following his announcement that an Urdu play might only finish in time for breakfast.

'That would be very nice,' I said. We rose and, following our example, the rest of the sofa and armchair party rose also. The Nawab's guard, with its veteran commander dressed in a uniform that certainly must have belonged at one time to the East India Company, fell in behind us and escorted us out of the theatre. I walked with the Nawab in the vanguard of the procession, and as conversation had flagged my mind was picturing the palace we were about to enter. I had always wanted to sit cross-legged on a silken cushion, eating fruit or sweetmeats out of a golden dish, and watching the nautch-girls dance. This would be infinitely preferable to listening to that interminable play, and perhaps at the end of the evening the Nawab would send me home on an elephant with a garland of flowers round my neck. Here we were at the palace and it was not exactly the palace of my dreams.

We entered a hall remarkable chiefly for its chandeliers. They were suspended from innumerable hooks in the ceiling and, because the area of the ceiling was limited and the Nawab's appetite for glittering glass was very great, a string of lustres had been tacked to the bannisters. Conducting me straight to his favourite den, so that I had no time to see whether the lustres ran the whole way up the staircase or stopped at the first landing, the Nawab opened a door and I entered a room furnished with three lounge chairs, of the kind patronized by Indian colonels, a collection of gilt, cane-bottomed benches, a few crimson plush stools and two slender bamboo tables. The windows were draped with lace curtains from Nottingham, and on the walls were two oleographs, one of a very solid Queen Victoria in full regalia and the other of a man with Dundreary whiskers and a sun-helmet who was pushing the muzzle of his gun down the throat of a tiger clinging to the hind quarters of his elephant. My heart sank through the bottom of the cane chair on which I seated myself. Whether the Nawab noted my sudden listlessness or not I do not know, but he clapped his hands and a servant in a none-too-clean white robe appeared.

'Bring the sahibs whisky and soda.'

A bottle of White Horse, a syphon and three glasses were placed on the bamboo table at my side, and pouring myself out a peg — I have little taste for whisky — I began to drink languidly.

'And now if you would like it my wife and I will show you the new dance,' the Nawab suggested with his charming smile. 'I have a good gramophone and some excellent, quite up-to-date records.'

I felt some surprise and looked inquiringly at Major Rait, for I had been under the impression that in India only professionals danced and that no high-caste Hindu would ever think of displaying his limbs before guests.

'The Nawab is very English in his ways,' explained Major Rait, 'and we should like to see him dance.'

'What is the new dance?' I inquired.

'The cake-walk. It has just arrived here from Broadway.'

What did it matter? What did anything matter now that my picture of the mysterious East had been shattered? So I lay back in the pattern of chair approved of by Anglo-Indian colonels, placed my glass in the hole cut in the arm of it, pulled moodily at my cheroot and watched an Indian ruler and his wife going through the steps of the new American cake-walk. For me the evening was finished and the sooner I could make my escape from these surroundings, the better for me. Even the Personage felt that a day that had begun with a triumphal procession and 'God save the King' should have ended with something better than a gramophone and a cake-walk.

An hour later our host, who had insisted on ordering one of his carriages to take us home, came to the hall to see us off. As none of the many chandeliers provided any light a servant preceded us into the hall carrying an oil lantern. We stepped into the Nawab's carriage, waved good-bye, swept round a curve in the drive and then, more abruptly, round a corner. We swept too fast, there was a sudden jolt, the noise of snapping traces and we were all but shot into a heap of rubbish lying at the side of the road. Our coachman alone showed no surprise at what had happened but climbed off his box and with an impassive face examined the broken traces. His nimble fingers soon retied the string with which the traces had been previously mended and we proceeded again on our way.

The time had now come for me to leave Northern Bengal and to see something more of India. Rait had given me an introduction to the Rajah of Japati in the hope that he would invite me to a tiger shoot, but when I visited him it was clear that the Rajah's tigers were not for me. They were to be reserved for some government official to whom he wanted to do a good turn. An alternative fortunately presented itself. My cousin, a newly-appointed assistant commissioner in the Central Provinces, wrote to me telling me that he was about to start on a tour of his district for the purpose of assessing its taxes. He would be living under canvas for the next few weeks and as there was plenty of game in that neighbourhood he thought that I would perhaps care to join him. I gladly accepted this invitation and I took the opportunity on my way south of visiting the great show cities of India, Delhi, Agra, Lucknow and Cawnpore. Agra and Delhi were crowded with the wonderful remains of the great Mogul empire and at the end of ten days' sightseeing my eyes were so sated with what they had seen that they refused to take in any more new impressions. The palaces, mosques and courtyards through which I wandered were in such good preservation that they gave me the feeling that their inhabitants had left in a hurry and that as soon as the emergency had passed they would return to people again the palaces that they had temporarily deserted. To intrude into these rooms in the absence of their owners seemed to be almost an impertinence on my part and, weary of marble floors and inlaid walls, I made my way slowly towards the last of the show places that it was my duty, rather than my inclination, to see, the Taj Mahal. Picture postcards in India and magic lantern slides at home had made the tomb of Mumtaz Mahal so familiar to me that I had no relish for the visit I was about to pay.

The Taj Mahal is surrounded by a high wall so that only the tops of the four high minarets at the corners of it are visible until one has climbed up the steps leading to the gateway and passed through the gate itself. Absent-mindedly and with thoughts elsewhere, on the morrow's journey, on my meeting with my cousin, on anything except the object of my visit, I entered the garden in which stands the tomb of Mumtaz Mahal. Then I looked up. My first impulse was to kneel and to worship, for quicker than thought came the realization that I was standing in the presence of a beauty that was akin to the divine. Not as the result of a succession of impressions did this feeling arise in me, but rather as a sudden revelation born of a single impact. This was not a building with a central dome and four corner towers, but it was a message reaching me from another sphere; it was a clear assurance of the existence of a world of the spirit which at that moment seemed to be nearer to me than the world in which my body was moving! It was knowledge invested with a certainty that is never attached to the wavering thoughts of the intellect. At that moment I saw; at that moment I knew. Never had I felt such a compulsion to prostrate myself and to worship as when I stood there at the gateway to the Taj Mahal. The garden was full of brightly-robed Mohammedans passing up and down the broad path fringed by lines of cypress trees which led the eye gently forward until it rested on the platform on which stood the consummate work of Sufi builders. The Taj is a place of Mohammedan pilgrimage and I was conscious of a growing sense of companionship with the brightly-robed people who were passing backwards and forwards along that pathway. Differences of race, upbringing and language disappeared and in silent communion with these others who had come there to do homage I began to worship and to show gratitude for the message we had been given. Then slowly, and at peace with all things and all people, I made my way towards the building. How rich was the carving, how wonderful the inlaid work on the walls and how superb the whole design. But none of these details really mattered; what mattered was that the Taj Mahal existed. To analyse it and to think about it seemed as irrelevant as to count the number of commas occurring in the Gospels.

I remembered the Sphinx and I recalled how, when I had looked at it, its age and its preoccupation with things beyond my ken had had such an effect on me that I had been overwhelmed by the feeling of my own insignificance. But, unlike the Sphinx, the Taj had an intimate and personal message for me, and it was peace and not fear that dwelt in this beautiful garden. Yet although they differed, both of these experiences brought with them the same feeling that I had caught a glimpse of something which was real, something which made the ordinary events of my life seem tawdry and utterly insignificant. How strangely did these rare moments of heightened existence and of greater understanding seem to flow together. The rest of my life was like a number of pillars, separate and isolated structures, but high above them, like the converging lines of an arch, these moments of understanding came together in the zenith of the dome. The first glimpse of the Taj and of the Sphinx, those few minutes of self-revelation under the light of the Arctic sky at Thingvellir, that earliest experience of 'coming to' on the Sussex Road, those rare moments, and others not here recorded, seemed to merge, each adding some new understanding but all with the same message for me. At those moments alone could I be said to exist, at those moments alone was I in the presence of the more real. Viewed in contrast with them the rest of my life was like a puppet show, a meaningless masquerade, a fantasia, a medley of dreams.

Next morning I left Agra for the Central Provinces with the feeling that I was on my homeward journey and that everything that might happen now was incidental and of no importance. What did all this coming and going, these small personal affairs of mine really matter? But my cousin expected me, so I would go to Banda and join him for a time in his camp. Automatic reactions soon re-established their hold on one and in a few days the things which for a short time had been seen to be utterly insignificant closed round me, imprisoned me and shut out all else from my eyes. The actors were again in control.

Living under canvas with a district commissioner was obviously something very different from anything I had previously known in the way of camping out. It was more like attending a wedding than being under canvas. Each of us had a Delhi Durbar tent for his bedroom and we met together for meals in a still larger marquee tastefully decorated with muslin hangings and palms. At the end of an excellent four-course dinner my cousin would announce, between puffs at his cigar, that on the morrow we would be on the move again and that we would lunch together near some village with an unpronounceable name. But this move entailed no trouble, for during the night skilled servants would load the dining-room and the kitchen with all its equipment on to ox-carts and would transport them twenty miles so that luncheon would be ready by the time that we rode up. If I wanted sport during the journey I had only to take my rifle, commandeer the inhabitants of some neighbouring village as beaters and scour the hills for Sambur.

On the day about to be described I had decided to go off on my own and to join my cousin at the new camp about lunch time. During the previous night, while everybody was asleep, I had risen from my bed and had crept into the neighbouring jungle. There, lying on the ground, alone and in pitch darkness, I had listened to the noises of an Indian night, to scurryings and tiny squeaks in the darkness, to rustling in the grass and occasionally to the noise made by some larger animal moving through the undergrowth. What intense activity began when humanity went to sleep. To-day I would wander through India in the sunlight and would try to see some of the animals that I had only heard on the previous night. I set off alone in the direction of the village near to which our new camp was to be pitched, dressed in a pair of well-worn khaki shorts, a collarless grey shirt and a white coat, the pockets of which were filled with cartridges. The site of our next camp was to be near a village the name of which began with 'Chand', and I felt that if I could only remember this prefix I would have no difficulty in finding it.

There was very little game to be seen, but Selous was content, for he was exploring India and there was plenty to interest him even if he shot nothing. Mile after mile I walked, keeping some sort of direction, as I moved through the trees and undergrowth, by means of a hill ahead of me, shaped like a camel's hump. At last, rather tired and thirsty, I reached open country, and with a clearer view, I started to cross a dusty plain bare of all vegetation. What was that in the distance, just to the right of the hump-like hill? It was a city surrounded by a wall in which was a great gate flanked by two watch-towers. Yes, there were men in the towers and now I could see a small group of people issuing from the gate. Knight-Paton was carried back to the Middle Ages and was en- thralled. Oh, for the good old days when all cities were walled like this one and when brave men manned the battlements or rode out of the gates to battle for some noble cause. But what were those people doing and why were they all coming in my direction? Good heavens, they were coming to meet *me*.

We met in the middle of the plain and the six *zemindars* (native land- owners) who made up the party immediately prostrated themselves before me in the dust. Then, with a dignity that had suffered nothing from this obeisance, they rose and conducted me towards the city. Oh, why had I omitted to put on a collar, why had I not shaved more carefully that morning, and why had I forgotten to slip a pocket-comb into my pocket? But these regrets were useless for my escort was obviously far too polite to notice any deficiencies in my toilet. These were the thoughts that were passing through my mind as with leisurely steps I accompanied the *zemindars*, my new escort of friends, towards the walled town. 'Not friends,' corrected the Personage, 'adherents, rather, or perhaps subjects,' and noting their deferential manner I felt sure that he was right.

We had now reached the city and the Personage, walking along the lane left by the crowd, entered what I took to be the town hall. 'A hush fell upon the waiting multitude and as he made his way with slow and dignified steps to the dais that had been erected at the far end of the hall, a sea of . . .' No, again it was a little different. The hall was nearly empty, but at the far end of it there most certainly was a dais and on the dais was a large chair like a throne, with smaller ones on each side of it. The Personage had by now forgotten the deficiencies of his toilet and he seated himself upon this comfortable throne. After obtaining permission to sit in his presence the *zemindars* ranged themselves on each side of him. There was a long silence which was broken at last by the *zemindar* who spoke the best English.

'May food be prepared for your excellency?'

No, his excellency would not eat. Although hungry and still more thirsty, the Personage knew by now that in India a great man must not eat in the presence of a small one. By doing so he loses caste. Again there was a long silence.

'Has your excellency had good sport?'

'No. I have found but little game.'

'What particular game does your excellency want?'

'Everything,' said Selous, 'sambur, panthers, tigers, elephant' (he had forgotten that in India elephants are only ridden and not shot).

'There are many panthers in this neighbourhood,' answered the interpreter after a short conference with the others. 'A kid shall be selected and tied to a tree just outside the city near a great rock where panthers are always to be found. The city is indeed poor on account of the very bad harvest, but it will be honoured to provide your excellency with a kid.'

'You've had a bad harvest?' I asked in the tone of a benevolent king unbending to his subjects.

'The worst for fifty years,' hastily answered the chief *zemindar*. 'Money is now so scarce that we are hard put to it to pay our heavy taxes.' And the five others, catching the drift of the talk, all moaned in unison and wrung their hands.

'It shall be considered,' I answered, suddenly seeing daylight. By Jove, how surprised they must be at the uniform worn by their new district commissioner! I turned up the collar of my jacket while the *zemindars* were not looking. The really important thing had been said and the conversation now began to flag. The *zemindar* who had borne the brunt of it tactfully brought it to a close.

'A mount has been prepared,' he announced. 'Does your excellency often travel on foot?'

'No, not very often,' I answered briefly, as I led the way down the hall. Outside the door stood a beautiful white arab horse with a red saddle, red saddle-cloth and bridle. The design of these trappings carried my mind back to the Mogul empire, for the bit was made of silver and a feathery plume waved above the horse's head. So many friends were anxious to assist me up into the saddle that they raised me too high and I nearly fell over on the other side. Meanwhile the stoutest of the *zemindars* held on to the stirrup-leather and he continued to do so even when I began to move off. From a walk I broke into a trot and the stout gentleman still remained attached to me so that I was reminded of that well-known engraving of the Greys and the Gordons charging into battle, each Gordon holding a Grey's stirrup. We had left the gates and a clear plain stretched before us but it was obvious that he would never stand the pace and I pulled up. The English-speaking *zemindar*, having seen that some hitch had occurred sprinted up and rejoined us. 'The *Talikdar* (mayor),' he said, 'is short of breath' (a fact that was so obvious that I deemed no reply to be necessary). 'He is hopeful, your excellency, that you will excuse him from further attendance.'

'Certainly,' I said. The mayor let go the bridle with evident relief and salaamed. 'And what about the horse?'

'The horse is your excellency's,' was the answer. 'Our harvest has been so disastrous that we have no corn with which to feed him.'

'I'll see what can be done about it,' I said, and gave the horse his head. We made good going and in half an hour I was cantering up a gentle slope towards our camp hidden behind a clump of trees. In a few minutes more I had reached it, to find that my cousin was just on the point of starting lunch.

'Hello,' he said, 'where on earth have you been and who gave you that fine palfrey?'

'Never mind,' I answered, 'I have my own adventures, but before I speak about them, how's business?'

'What business do you mean?'

'Why, the assessment of taxes.'

'Oh, that's all right,' he answered. 'We assess them on harvests and they seem to have had a mighty fine harvest around here.'

'That's what I suspected,' I said as I helped myself to the curry. 'By the way, why are you so smartly dressed?'

'Well, you see, the people expect it of me. Even an assistant commissioner is a *burra sahib* to them, and they'd be amazed if I were to turn up dressed as a tramp like you. Why, you're not even wearing a collar.'

'I suppose they would be surprised,' I answered thoughtfully.

That evening the Personage took the air in front of his tent, walking up and down with his hands in his pockets and his eyes on the ground. Yes, there was a great deal to be said for life as a government official in India. Twice during this trip he had been forced to rein up because a *ryot* had prostrated himself in front of his horse in order to present him with a petition. What a pathetic faith these simple people had in the power of the British Raj to put things right. Well, he had seen that those petitions were forwarded to the proper quarters where doubtless they would be carefully considered. My thoughts were interrupted by the sight of five natives approaching my tent and carrying on their heads trays heaped with dried fruit and with those sticky sweets which are so dear to the palate of the Indian. They placed these trays on the ground and salaamed. I had not expected visitors, but the Personage, who had noted with pleasure their respectful behaviour, immediately took charge. One of the men now stepped forward and, after bowing three times to the ground, delivered a speech. Unwilling to miss anything on account of his ignorance of the language the Personage hurriedly summoned my cousin's servant to act as interpreter.

'What's he saying?' he asked.

'He says this, sahib. "We Hindus would have it known that it is the custom in our country to make gifts to honoured guests. We therefore now make this humble offering to you of the royal blood".'

The Personage drew himself up to his full stature and then stroked his chin thoughtfully. He had a good opinion of himself and had pictured himself in all sorts of important roles, but this idea of being of royal blood was one that in his wildest moments he had never entertained. My cousin's servant waited for a moment and then asked, 'What message shall I give them, sahib?'

'Tell them,' answered the Personage, 'that we thank them from the bottom — from the bottoms of our hearts. Tell them that we are very pleased and let them take away the white horse I rode to-day and return it to its rightful owner.'

The Personage had spoken truly when he had expressed his pleasure, for India to him had now become more than tolerable. It was a land of adventure and romance in which almost anything might happen. To its glitter and its splendour he had taken as naturally as an actress takes to presents of pearls, and he was far too grateful to it for its gifts ever to suspect that some of the pearls might be of the Woolworth variety. In any case that would not have mattered much for on that ill-lit stage on which my actors moved Woolworth pearls and paper crowns were quite as convincing as real ones.

A few days later, as though to set a seal on all that had gone before, an important looking envelope arrived for me, the back of which was adorned by a golden crest supported on each side by rampant elephants. Within was a letter in which the Maharajah of Charkaris intimated that he intended shortly to celebrate the anniversary of his accession to the throne and that he would be very pleased if I would grace the festivities with my appearance. The Personage had no difficulty in reaching a decision, for the Maharajah's palace was one of the show residences of India and, situated as it was on an island in the middle of a lake, it looked like a splendid wedding-cake resting on a mirror. This time he would really sit on cushions and watch the nautch-girls dance, and a chaplet of flowers would undoubtedly be hung around his neck on his arrival at the Maharajah's palace. But he had forgotten that in England there stood an ancient hospital that cared nothing for his plans. That hospital was now in need of a new demonstrator of pathology and twenty hours later a cable arrived from Ball informing me that the hospital laboratories were now finished and that as work in them was about to begin I must return immediately. There was a brief struggle, and then I left for Calcutta to catch the first ship of the City Line that sailed from there for home.

CHANGED VIEWS ON GREATNESS

INDIA was not the only place in which the caste system survived. It existed also in a modified form at St. Bartholomew's, and on my return to the hospital I was elevated to a higher caste than that to which I had formerly belonged. Its distinctive garb was different and the short white coats which I had previously worn as a house-surgeon were no longer of any use to me. A demonstrator of pathology required a coat that reached down to the ankles and with a breast pocket that provided room for three fountain pens, one containing black ink, one red and one green. The manner of walking across the square used by the two castes was also different. I could no longer stroll arm in arm around the fountain with a friend, for demonstrators must give an appearance of bustle and hurry and must be seen hastening across the square carrying a rack of culture tubes or disappearing up staircases with the tails of their long coats flapping in the breeze. The text 'Whatsoever thy hand findeth, do with all thy might' was carved over the doorway to the medical school and a demonstrator had to live up to this and to set a good example to the students. Even senior students now called me 'sir', and those who had just arrived at the hospital occasionally mistook me for a member of the honorary staff. The honorary staff — what a long way off that seemed? It was true that its members would now on occasion take me by the arm and, walking slowly across the square with me, would discuss the bacteriology of a particularly difficult case. Some of the more junior members of the honorary staff talked to me sometimes in terms almost of equality, but all the time I knew that the distance between them and me was the distance that separated the Brahmin and the Vaisya. Only an epidemic of death amongst these Brahmins or an unlikely decision to retire before the retiring age arrived could cut down the many years that must pass before I could become a member of the honorary staff and I calculated that it would be at least nine years before I had any hope of becoming an assistant surgeon. For nine long years I would probably be cutting sections, peering down microscopes, growing cultures in incubators, preparing vaccines and groping amongst unpleasant organs in the post-mortem room for the cause of a patient's death. It was a depressing thought and I dwelt on it as little as possible.

Besides the routine work of the laboratory there was also my special research on the Jacksonian subject to be done — Selous and Knight-Paton had lied in making out that it was completed — and three mornings every week I attended the City of London Truss Society. I had been elected an assistant surgeon to this institution, a post I had applied for chiefly because it would bring me in an income of one hundred pounds a year. Now, a hundred pounds is a hundred pounds even if one has to be at Finsbury Square by half-past eight in the morning in order to gain them, but after six months' work I came to the conclusion that the money was earned too dearly. A truss is a serviceable appliance, but there are limits to its powers, and here in the City of London Truss Society's waiting room were to be found all of London's worst rupture cases, old men who were falling to pieces and bursting asunder like worn-out sacks of meal. 'It takes ten years to learn to fit a truss properly,' said Mr. Gask, the senior surgeon to the Society, while instructing me in my work, and more than once I wondered what I would be like at the end of those ten years. By then I might be capable of fitting a truss — but would I be able to do anything else? Selous and Knight-Paton began to loathe Finsbury Square, with its gloomy windows looking out on to a soot-begrimed garden. As I hurried across the square, five minutes late, I could see young men arriving at their offices and seating themselves at their desks to brood over their invoice books and ledgers. By no effort of the imagination could Finsbury Square be regarded as being anything else than it was, a cell in a forbidding prison of industry and finance.

Selous and Knight-Paton began to give trouble. 'What a life for anyone who calls himself a man', they would say as I was crossing the square. 'Look at those pale young clerks imprisoned in their offices and take warning from them. Bowlby may be all right but what about old man Phipps — do you want to become like him, with no interest in anything except some crackbrained idea that appendicitis comes from cooking in enamel saucepans? It's a mug's game, this idea of waiting on in London for dead men's shoes, if you ask us.' I had not asked them, and it was they who were forcing their opinions on me. I would not allow their craving for adventure and romance again to ruin all my plans. I had made up my mind to get on to the Bart's Staff and, having done so, there must be no looking back. Everything would be ruined if I were to give way to this innate craving in me for travel, adventure and romance. I had had one lucky escape already but I could not count on being so fortunate next time. Three months previously I had called on my old school friend Flitch and he had told me that he had been commissioned to write up an expedition which was about to trek right through Central Asia from the Caspian to the Pacific. Apparently one of the Kaiser's sons had fallen in love with an English girl and, because his Imperial father had forbidden the match, the young princeling had decided to disappear for two years into the wilds. An English Guards' officer was to lead the expedition and Flitch was to write a book about it. I had immediately applied for the post of doctor but the Kaiser's son changed his mind and the whole expedition fell through. It had been a fortunate ending for me and I realized now how stupid I had been to have jeopardized my whole career to so little purpose.

Strange to say it was not Selous and Knight-Paton, those insatiable seekers after romance and adventure, but the Personage who in the end was responsible for uprooting me from London and for driving me for five long years into the spiritual wilderness of the River Plate. His action was particularly reprehensible since it was he who had been originally responsible for my decision to remain in London and to qualify for election to the hospital staff. But the visit to India had proved unsettling to the Personage and ever since then he had been examining and re-examining the subject of greatness. He was now troubled with serious doubts whether the path he had chosen, namely the one that led to Harley Street, was actually the best one for an aspirant to greatness to follow. In the hope of resolving these doubts and of arriving at a final decision on this matter he began to use the Socratic method of argument. 'What is the prerogative of the great?' he would ask, putting down the morning paper and looking around at the occupants of the third class carriage in which I was making my daily journey to Farringdon Street. Obviously, none of those people were great; one had only to look at their faces to see that. 'The great', the Personage answered, after a moment's reflection, 'the great enjoy the prerogative of exercising power. Has the consulting surgeon any real power over anybody other than his patients — and of course the nurses and a few of his juniors? No. Then he cannot be considered great, and I see no reason to become one.' I resumed the reading of the morning paper and on that particular morning I happened to arrive at the City of London Truss Society just as Mr. Gask was entering the front door. It would be a good opportunity for a few words with him.

'Good morning. I suppose, Gask, that it is really important to know all there is to know about trusses?'

Gask smiled. 'Undoubtedly, if you're to become a really efficient surgeon.'

'And I suppose that it's important to become a really efficient surgeon?'

'Walker, there's something about you I don't understand. You do your work at the Truss Society very well, but you have never seemed to me to be as serious about it as I would like you to be. What is on your mind and what makes you ask me these queer questions?'

'I don't know, I was just wondering.'

Gask would be utterly incapable of understanding the doubts that were troubling me and I felt the uselessness of taking him into my confidence. In any case there was no time for talking, for the waiting room was over-flowing with patients. In another minute we became legislators in irre-concilable quarrels between trusses and ruptures, peace-makers who were often unable to promote peace. But all the time Gask's words were ring-ing in my head. 'It takes ten years to learn to fit a truss.' Ten years of this, Heaven preserve me!

It was obvious that the Personage would not remain for long satisfied with such an incomplete definition of greatness as the simple assertion that it entailed the exercise of power. Within a few days he put to himself the question, 'Who then exercises power? Kings, royal courtesans, grand viziers, prime ministers and their wives, generals, demagogues and fash-ionable preachers,' came the answer. After going through this list it became obvious to him that the most hopeful line for him to take was that of becoming prime minister. 'That means money, standing for par-liament, being elected, doing useful work in the committee-rooms, obey-ing the Whips, becoming an under-secretary, reaching the cabinet and then number 10 Downing Street. The first step is money, and in the laboratory and at the City of London Truss Society money simply does not exist.'

Now it is not to be supposed that the Personage formulated his new aim so clearly as this, or that if he had done so he would not have been conscious of some element of absurdity in his thinking. Conscious is indeed a word which can never be used in connection with him or with any of his colleagues, for consciousness was an attribute in which they were singularly lacking. If at that moment he had been asked what he intended to do, he would probably have answered that he meant to make money as quickly as possible so that he could retire from medicine at an early age and take up a political career. He would have said nothing about becoming prime minister although, in the words of current psychology, this idea was undoubtedly lurking somewhere in the realm of his sub-conscious. But the ideas of current psychology are very misleading, for it is a mistake for us to picture ourselves as icebergs with one-seventh of our mind projecting into the clear daylight and the remaining six-sevenths plunged in the dark depths of the ocean. Our thinking is not sharply divided, in the way many psychologists would have us believe it to be, into the brilliantly lit, or conscious, and the dark, or subconscious. We live rather in a state of perpetual twilight in which there is neither bright sunshine nor dark shadow to break the monotony of the scene. Gradations of light there are, but not sharply defined regions as psychologists, in their desire for some method of classifying the mind, have pictured. When I look back on this theatrical performance which represents my life I do not see my actors at one moment in the obscurity of the wings and at the next moment in the full glare of the limelight but rather as figures moving about on an ill-lit stage on which is neither highlight nor shadow. This being so, the Personage must be forgiven for appearing to be so presump-tuous. He is not so much an arrogant fool as a poor actor groping in the dusk.

The biographers of great men are fond of putting on record some trifling incident which proved to be the first step in the long chain of events ending in their final triumph, and what is true of the great is equally true of the obscure. An unimportant event was now to occur which had the effect of changing the whole course of my life and of carry-ing me in what afterwards proved to be an utterly wrong direction. It was my accidental discovery of a notice in the advertisement columns of the *Lancet* headed 'The River Plate' that was responsible for this. For no other reason than that this was an unusual beginning to a medical adver-tisement I continued to read it.

'Wanted, a resident medical officer to the British Hospital in Buenos

Aires. Salary £300 per ann. with board, laundry and lodging. Applications to be sent to Dr. Colbourne, The Laurels, Beckenham.'

It was obvious that nobody could save enough on three hundred a year to retire from medicine at an early age and take up politics, but it was equally obvious that the Spaniards had not called that South American river, on the banks of which Buenos Aires had been built, the River of Silver to no purpose. It was given this name, because its discoverers were treasure seekers who believed, and believed rightly, that they had found a land which would satisfy their hearts' desires. Buenos Aires was the place all those multi-millionaires came from, the millionaires who spent their money so lavishly in the luxury hotels of Europe, and this advertisement was well worth looking into. I tore it out of the *Lancet* and placed it carefully in my wallet. That evening, after a great deal of thought, I sent in an application to Dr. Colbourne, together with a list of my qualifications and past appointments. By doing this I had not, of course, committed myself, for in the end I could always refuse to go. For the next few days I was aware all the time of an undercurrent of excitement, an excitement which reached its height when a week later a letter arrived, the envelope of which bore a Beckenham postmark. I tore it open with the feeling that it was the most fateful letter I had ever received, a letter which would determine my whole future. It merely stated that Dr. Colbourne would like to see me and that he would be very pleased if I would dine with him at his house on Thursday evening.

I arrived at 'The Laurels' at the stated time in a dinner-jacket, and when I met my host I was thankful that I had taken this precaution of dressing. Dr. Colbourne was a man who would no more have thought of dining in anything but a stiff shirt, even when alone, than he would have thought of leaving his house in the morning without a collar and tie. That at least was clear, but otherwise he rather puzzled me, and I had the greatest difficulty in placing him. His manner was half-way between that of a Spanish grandee and that of an old-time Virginian planter and his speech was in keeping with this mixture for somehow he managed to mingle in his voice the rich tones of Spain and the softness of the speech of the Southern States. After less than half an hour's conversation with him it became apparent that he was on terms of intimacy with aristocratic people in all quarters of the globe, and on realizing this the Personage hastened to mention some of his own grand friends and acquaintances. It was only after the neat parlourmaid had filled up our glasses with port and retired from the room that the real business of the evening was mentioned. Colonel Colbourne — I could never think of him as an ordinary doctor — had apparently been so favourably impressed with the good report I had sent him of my capacities that he had chosen me, out of several hundred applicants, for the post of resident medical officer to the British Hospital in Buenos Aires. If, therefore, I was prepared to go — and the Colonel's smile indicated that he had used this conditional clause in jest rather than seriously — the job was mine. Having made this announcement he sat back in his chair with an expression on his face that clearly indicated that I was a very fortunate young man, and that he, Colonel Colbourne, had conferred on me an outstanding honour.

The news may not have produced on me the effect that the Colonel had expected for the very simple reason that not for a single moment had I considered the possibility of my application proving unsuccessful. It was therefore impossible for me to display the surprise and gratification which the Colonel evidently expected to read on my face. My chief desire now was to obtain from the Colonel more precise information about the work of the resident medical officer at the British Hospital and about the prospects of practice in Buenos Aires. It would be interesting to know, for example, what had happened to those who had previously held this post. Had they been very successful and been able to retire from medicine at an early age? The answer to this question would help me to make up my mind whether to accept or not the post I had been offered. I inquired of the Colonel what had happened to previous resident officers of the British Hospital in Buenos Aires.

'Well, let me see,' he said, stroking a smartly trimmed Vandyke beard. 'There was Hargreaves, yes, Hargreaves — he returned home.'

'Why?' I asked.

'Didn't like it. Quarrelled with the committee, or something. Anyhow, he came back.'

'And the man before him?'

'Oh, that was Hopkins. He took to drink. Bad case, that. So far as I can remember he married some devoted woman soon after leaving the hospital, went up the Amazon as far as he could get and then died of fever complicated by alcoholism.'

'And his predecessor?' I asked, hoping for brighter news.

'That was young Elliott. He wasn't much good, and he ought never to have gone out there. I didn't choose him, and the man who did made a bad mistake. You see, he was the sort of fellow that's keen on poetry and painting and all that sort of thing, and after he'd been there a few months he said he didn't like the place, and complained to the committee. They wouldn't let him go, but they had to ship him home in the end with a nervous breakdown, and in charge of a nurse.' The Colonel smiled at me as one man smiles at another over the weaknesses of humanity. Poor young Elliott. The Colonel and I could perhaps forgive him because, being medical men, we knew the tricks that the mind could play on one, but no man who was worth his salt would have to be sent home with a nervous breakdown. Elliott ought never to have been chosen. That at least was clear.

It seemed better not to go further into the history of the resident medical officers of the British Hospital, so the rest of the evening was spent in discussing such subjects as the regulations that governed medical practice in Buenos Aires, the best way of obtaining a local degree and the chances of making a career in Argentina. Of the last, of course, there could not be the slightest doubt, and the Colonel assured me that I was just the type of man who would do brilliantly in Buenos Aires. I left him with the impression that to all intents and purposes I had accepted the post, but I promised that in a few days' time I would send him an official confirmation of this.

My interview at Beckenham had given me much to think about. On the whole Dr. Colbourne had confirmed me in my idea that Buenos Aires would prove to be a veritable gold mine to a man with the English Fellowship and although he had emphasized the difficulty of obtaining the local qualifications necessary for practice outside the hospital, he had assured me that with hard work and a little diplomatic handling of the examiners it could be done. The only disquieting part of our talk had been that which referred to the fate of my predecessors. If the British Hospital in Buenos Aires was such a garden of roses — and Dr. Colbourne had said that he envied any young man going out to it — why had those who had previously walked in that garden collected nothing but thorns? Was there something wrong with the men who had formerly taken this job or was there something wrong with the job? A decision had to be reached and to be reached soon, so I made up my mind to retire to the quiet of a Turkish bath and there, wrapped in towels, my muscles relaxed and my mind very clear, I would settle my fate. I would examine every factor, weigh up every argument, put on one side all the 'pros' and on the other all the 'cons', and then, like an auditor with the figures before him, I would balance the account. A Turkish bath would provide exactly the right environment, for I had noticed that some of my brightest thoughts came to me in baths. Napoleon always lay in a hot bath when he had an important decision to make and I would do the same.

This was how I pictured it, but the picture was a misleading one. Only the first part of my programme went according to plan. I lay on my couch wrapped in towels, my body glowing and my mind relaxed, and the events of the evening at Beckenham passed before me as though they were being projected on to a screen from a lantern. First, Colonel Colbourne appeared, dressed in his well-fitting dinner jacket and stroking his tiny grey beard. Again I heard his gentlemanly voice telling me how much he envied a young man who was on the point of sailing to Buenos Aires. Then he disappeared, to give place to my version of Elliott, the weakly one, and this in turn to a portrait of myself, the future Argentine consultant, with an enormous and lucrative practice. Suddenly the sequence of my dreams was broken, and I was brought back with a jerk to the Turkish bath in which I was lying. The man who was sharing my cubicle had started to dress and he was fumbling for something he had apparently lost underneath his couch. What on earth was the fellow doing, making all that disturbance? Good heavens, he had found what he had lost and he was now adjusting it. The thought of the City of London Truss Society and of nine long years of waiting for a possible appointment on the hospital staff overwhelmed me. No, I could not stand it and I would go to the Argentine even although a hundred Elliotts warned me from the background against taking this step. It was in this way that the crucial decision which was to change the course of my life was taken. That evening I wrote to Colonel Colbourne to confirm my acceptance of the post of resident medical officer to the British Hospital in Buenos Aires.

The Royal Mail Packet *Asturias*, on which I sailed a few weeks later, catered chiefly for its Argentine and Brazilian passengers, by far the most important of the company's clientele. South Americans wanted heavy carvings covered with gilt, they needed music, not only while eating but during most of the day, they liked refreshments between their heavy meals, they required sweet champagne, so all of these things and many others were provided for them. It was indeed the ornate and heavily gilded saloon that gave me my first intimation that I had entered a new world, a world of which I knew very little, the great world of dollars. Facing me in this dining saloon were some of its most important inhabitants, people who were worth knowing, people whom indeed it was essential to know if one was to succeed in the new world I had chosen to live in. Sitting at my table was no less a person than Señor Gutierrez, whose Argentine estates were as large as a British county and the revenues he drew from them of prodigious dimensions. Opposite him, and dripping with diamonds, were his wife and two daughters, all of them so weighted with wealth and so glutted with food that they appeared to be utterly exhausted. On the other side of the saloon was the dark-skinned Fonseca family from Pera in Brazil. How like monkeys those little daughters of Señor Fonseca were, beautiful, soft-eyed, chattering monkeys that had been playing in a flour bin. Why had they chosen to powder their brown skins with 'pale naturel' when ground nutmeg or cinnamon would have been so much more appropriate. Nice animated little monkeys they were, with beautiful eyes and lovely teeth, sweet little scented playthings for those who could afford to keep them. And listen to the noise coming from that great parrot-house upstairs, that high-domed lounge in which these delicately nurtured creatures from South America spent so much of the day. I rose from my seat in the dining saloon and went slowly up the staircase to the chief glory of the ship, its palm-decorated, brocade-upholstered, golden aviary. Look at the parrots, gaudy feathered birds, Paris model parrots, and old grey duenna parrots with wrinkled eyes and piercing voices. What a cawing and a fluttering. The band was playing the Pilgrims' March from *Tannhäuser*, but these birds were making so much noise that it was impossible to hear it. Only the little parakeets sitting there in the corner were silent, those little love-birds sitting by themselves and talking only with their eyes. The noise was tiring, the air scented and overheated, and walking straight through the saloon I sought the freshness of the deck.

It was there that I met the Señora Susanna Torres de Castex. She was rich and she was Argentine, but she was different from the others if for no reason other than that sometimes she had taken notice of me as I walked around the deck. This time when I sat down in the vacant chair beside her, she put down her book and started to talk. She spoke to me of music, of the different races living in Buenos Aires, of travel in Europe and of her son, Mariano, a brilliant doctor now studying medicine in Paris. When I told her why I was emigrating to Buenos Aires she was sympathetic, inquired about my plans and asked about my Spanish. I must get on with this, she told me, and every day I must talk to her and practise it. No, I need have no fear that it would be a trouble to her; she liked my country and would enjoy her talks with me. Henceforth the Señora took me under her wing and a very warm and richly-feathered wing it proved to be. From her I learnt the ways of old Castille, for although she lived in Buenos Aires, she had never forgotten that she came of good old Spanish stock. She showed me how to talk as the Spaniards do, using their hands to emphasize their words, and the Personage, who had a liking for mannerisms, showed himself to be an apt pupil. In greeting her, or in leaving her, I would murmur, 'A los pies de Usted Señora', and then inclining my head and bowing from the waist, I would retire. Talking a foreign language, like dressing up, helps to free one from the limitations imposed on one by one's personality and, by speaking Spanish, I escaped for a while from the cramped and rigid forms of Anglo-Saxon life. I became more flexible and some of the warmth and vivacity of the Latin races got into my blood through using their words.

We stopped only for a few hours off Pernambuco, a town which from the deck was a thin line of low, white-walled houses with red roofs, a line which spread along the coast and shimmered in a haze of heat. Then the derricks having lowered the few passengers who wished to land there in a basket and deposited them safely in a boat, we sailed on towards Rio. What more beautiful gateway to South America could there have been than this, our first real port of call, Rio de Janeiro. Lovely by day, she was still lovelier by night with her lights dancing in the still waters of the harbour and the sugar-cane outline of her hills standing up against the luminous background of the tropical sky. As I drank in her beauty I recalled to mind the grime and ugliness of Finsbury Square and I felt that I had done well to barter its squalor for this splendour. How lovely and how gay was Rio and how sooty and stern was London. Henceforth some sparkling city like this was to be my home. Santos, our next port, did nothing to dispel my illusion, for although less queenly than Rio,

Santos was light-hearted and very like the brightly-dressed negresses who promenaded her streets and smiled as they passed. It was only at Montevideo that doubts began to assail me, for the weather had now turned colder and, although palms still raised their plumed heads and swayed in the rising wind, and although brilliant creepers climbed up the walls of the houses, these emblems of the tropics seemed to me to be more like visitors than actual natives. But what troubled me far more than the absence of anything strikingly beautiful on land was the fact that the Spaniards' 'river of silver' was in reality only a river of dross. We were now steaming up a forbidding brown sea across which was blowing such a bitterly cold wind that I hurried below in search of an overcoat.

We reached Buenos Aires only when it was dark and it was better that it should have been so. Any city situated on the banks of a river may appear beautiful at night, with its harbour lanterns winking a friendly welcome and its lights casting reflections on the water-front, and at night Buenos Aires was at its best. All was excitement and bustle on board, and as the great ship tied up to the quay the noise on the deck and on the land rose to a crescendo. The passengers and all the brightly-coloured birds from our gilded aviary were fluttering along the passages, twittering, chirping and cooing to their friends on the quay, or to those of them who had bribed the guardians of the gangways and had thereby managed to get on board. What a noise they were all making. I stood there alone on the deck, silent in a world of animation, a stranger in a strange land and a foreigner who stilled looked on the natives as being foreigners, whereas it was he who was now the foreigner.

Gradually it dawned on me that somebody was speaking to me. 'Are you Dr. Walker?' said a voice, and looking round I discovered a bashful and rather wan young man at my elbow. In a few words he explained that he was the secretary of the British Hospital and that he had come down to the quay to help me through the customs. After making this statement he lapsed into silence and whenever I questioned him, he seemed anxious not to commit himself, as though at some time he had been admonished for talking too freely. An hour later I was seated at his side in a horse-drawn vehicle which was clattering through the streets of Buenos Aires. How narrow, squalid and mean they were. The city was modern in so far as it had been built in a number of squares, but it was medieval in its odours. It looked as though its designers, having drawn up a general plan, had lost interest in their project and had allowed the builders to carry on as they pleased, placing, if they liked to do so, houses with imposing frontages and beautiful wrought iron gates side by side with mean taverns, flamboyant cinemas and slum-dwellings. Where, oh, where were the palaces of the millionaires of which I had heard so much? I turned and questioned my companion, and he told me that they were on the northern outskirts of the city near the great park of Palermo. Actually we were driving through the less fashionable parts of Buenos Aires in which the hospital happened to be situated. Well could I believe it, for dirty ragged children were standing at the doorways and playing in the streets, jeering at us as we passed and occasionally throwing stones as a mark of their disapproval. There were strange smells everywhere, as of a mixture of garlic and cheese, followed by drifts of the odour of decaying cabbages, as displeasing to the nostrils as what I saw was displeasing to the eye. I ceased to look out of the carriage and retired into an inner world of gloom and fatigue, in which I registered nothing.

Half an hour's drive brought us to a hospital standing in its own garden, but the garden had long ago been vanquished by building extensions, and it was now represented only by a few clusters of rather bedraggled palm trees. Tired and, I had to confess it, more than a little dispirited, I went to bed without troubling to see anything more of my new home than the entrance hall and the dark passage which led to my own room.

BUENOS AIRES

BUENOS AIRES, your name is as misleading as is that of the river on which you stand, for your air is good neither for the body nor the soul. It is like the air that broods over a swamp; it is heavy with fever, with the fever of avarice. Yet what right have I to complain, I who landed on your shore for no other reason than that of plundering your riches and bearing away with me all that I could carry. And as in certain stories the despoilers of treasure are caught in the vaults in which the trove is hidden, so was I entrapped in the land I had come to plunder, escaping only five years later, poorer in health and stricken in spirit.

I find it impossible to write of Buenos Aires and of its British Hospital without bitterness. Instinctively I turn away from that period of my life, prepared to write about anything rather than about that. 'Haec olim meminisse juvabit.' It is not always so and my distaste for recollection increases in intensity when I attempt to write about Dr. O'Sullivan, that bluff Irish surgeon who so completely dominated my life at the hospital. Beloved or hated, as the case might be, his name was never mentioned by anybody in tones of indifference but always with affection or hatred. He had come out to Buenos Aires, some ten years previously, with no special qualifications for surgery, and by sheer hard work and initiative he had made for himself a great reputation as an operator. Nor was this reputation without foundation, for his surgery was as forceful as was his personality, as bold and as uncompromising as his manner. Never have I seen a scalpel used with greater rapidity and never have I seen it achieve greater successes or be responsible for more spectacular disasters. O'Sullivan was the carnivorous type of surgeon. He had a poor opinion of medicine and an implicit faith in the power of the knife to cure the disorders of the body. Such a man as he would have been invaluable in the casualty clearing stations of France some five years later, where the maximum of work had to be done in the minimum of time, but here in the operating theatre of Buenos Aires his ruthlessness made me shudder. The human material on which he had gained his great experience was well suited to his purposes, for at the hospital he operated on the Italian employees of the railways, obscure and confiding men whose relatives were far too frightened to ask awkward questions or to complain if by any sad mishap an operation were to go wrong. His reputation had spread from Buenos Aires to the furthest regions of the great Argentine Republic and there were few Britishers who did not know his name.

His method of thinking was as inexorable and final as was his surgery; what he approved of he called common sense and all that he failed to understand or with which he disagreed he labelled 'cod!' Life for him was very simple but not for those who worked with him. The committee of management, honorary staff, matron, sisters and nurses were completely under his thumb and they knew it and resented it. On one thing only were they all agreed, namely, that whatever they might feel about him, it was wiser never to oppose him in the open.

It is no easy task to play second fiddle to a trombone, and not only was I playing a stringed instrument to his brass, but a muted instrument at that. If for example I ventured to remark that my old chief, Sir Anthony Bowlby, resorted to short-circuiting operations for duodenal ulcer only when all medical treatment had failed, his reply would be to raise his eyebrows and smile, thereby indicating that in Buenos Aires they knew better than to imagine that such cases as these would yield to anything but the knife. In Buenos Aires they had no use for all that 'cod' about anxiety neuroses and functional diseases. If a burly Italian knocked off work complaining of fatigue and of indigestion, there was only one right word for it — skrimshanking. 'Put him on my special treatment, Walker,' he would say, 'and the fellow will soon be asking to be allowed to get back to his work.' The treatment consisted of a diet of bread, weak tea and water, a purge at night and a foul-smelling mixture of valerian and asofoetida three times a day. 'That'll do him a world of good,' he would add, as I wrote down the instructions on the patient's board. Yet O'Sullivan had another side to him and there were hundreds who remembered his name in connection with some kindness, and even more who owed to him their very lives. He was as much loved as he was hated, but I realize now that I was one of those who hated him, hated him without knowing it, hated him if for no other reason than that my feeble muted sounds were lost in the bray of his brass.

The other members of the hospital staff were of no consequence. They retained their position only so long as they gave no trouble and, although outwardly they appeared to accept this, jealousy and resentment moved beneath the surface. Had I searched for a training ground for a political career, I could not have found a better one than the hospital in which I now found myself living. Nobody attempted to displace the great dictator, but discontented factions met together for whispered conversations in corners, and wires were pulled by cautious workers underground. It was obvious that if the resident medical officer was to have any peace he must rigorously keep clear of all these local politics, and remembering the fate of my predecessors, I did my utmost to suppress all personal opinions and feelings.

But I was not only resident at the hospital, I was also a new member of the University of Buenos Aires, compelled, if I wished to practise medicine outside of the hospital, to obtain an Argentine degree. It was strange to be a medical student again, and what was more, a student who was looked upon by his fellows as being something of a curiosity. The 'medico ingles' was soon surrounded by a circle of eager questioners at the Faculty of Medicine, and was asked whether he had been to Oxford or Cambridge, Eton or Harrow? 'To Eton and Cambridge', I answered briefly, straining the truth as little as possible, for no other public school appeared to be known except the two mentioned. Did I play football and did I know how to box? For the good name of England I answered: 'I do both.' My reply was received with enthusiasm. 'Then we'll arrange a great international boxing match between you and Rodriguez,' they shouted. 'He is our great fighter.' Fortunately for me the plan went no further, for Rodriguez would have had but a poor opinion of English boxing had it been represented by me.

At the end of four months my Spanish seemed sufficiently good to allow me to present myself for examination in botany and chemistry. All of the examinations at the Faculty of Medicine were oral and were held in public. According to my fellow students, written papers had been eliminated because no precautions that the authorities could have adopted would have been a match to their skill in the art of cribbing, and the examiners were well aware of this. So to the university I went for my hearing, to wait there in the examination hall, not for hours, but for days, until at last, when I had almost given up hope, my name was called by the usher. 'Doctor Macfarlani Voelca.' Clambering down many tiers of seats I made my way to a table, on the opposite side of which sat the four examiners.

'You are Italian?' asked one of them, adjusting his spectacles and examining me as though I were some strange new specimen that had just been added to the medical museum.

'No, señor, I am Scottish,' I protested.

'How very interesting.' He turned to his colleagues and communicated this news to those who had not yet heard it. It had a favourable effect, for as I afterwards gathered, Italian doctors had the reputation of knowing very little medicine, but of speaking Spanish fluently, whilst Englishmen were believed to be well qualified but to be poor linguists.

'Will you please turn the handle,' said the examiner, waving his hand in the direction of a machine that stood on the table and which had the appearance of a coffee-grinder. I did what I was told to do, and at the second turn of the handle a small wooden ball dropped out of the bottom of the grinder on to the table. The examiner picked it up, scrutinized it carefully and then referred to a syllabus in which the subject-matter of the examination was catalogued in numbered paragraphs. 'Number forty-two', he murmured, and this paragraph happened to be on the subject of ionization, the theme with which my speech must now deal. To a Britisher it is more than a little disconcerting to discourse in a crowded hall, and in a foreign tongue, on a subject which has been chosen for him by a gambling apparatus, but my speech on electrolysis appeared to have satisfied the listening quartette and I left the hall, an hour later, with the comforting knowledge that I had passed my examination in chemistry. Later I was told that this method of examining candidates had been instituted to avoid the possibility of any collusion between the examiner and the examinee, and that it dated from the days when presents of diamond rings and cases of champagne sometimes passed between the one and the other. But even if this were not true, the method was entirely in keeping with the customs of a country in which gambling was so widespread that children buying a pennyworth of sweets off a barrow enjoyed the thrill of roulette. After a child had placed a coin on his favourite number a wheel was turned and according to the position on which it came to rest he would receive five, ten or twenty lumps of coloured sugar. Lottery tickets filled shop windows, beggars sold winning numbers in the streets and in restaurants the fall of the dice decided who it was that should pay for the dinner and drinks. Chance decided everything in that country, everything from the game of shove-ha'penny played on the pavements to the vast fortunes daily changing hands in the business of the buying and selling of land.

Life is an unstable equilibrium, a ceaseless struggle on the part of an organism to adjust itself to changes in its environment and gradually I became accustomed to and took on the colour of my surroundings. I was living in a country in which people worshipped money and I learnt to bend the knee before the goddess of pecuniary success. And there could be no doubt of the wholeheartedness and the sincerity with which those who had come to Buenos Aires to make money followed their aim. Wealth in this country was a virtue and poverty a sin, and with the help of these two values the standing of everyone could readily be assessed. 'What sort of a man is Smith?' I would inquire about someone to whom I had recently been introduced. 'He's one of the best men in the country,' would be the answer, 'and he must be making at least a thousand dollars a week, even though he's only been out here a short time.' All that could be usefully said of Smith had been said and discussion about him was therefore at an end. In a short time I had been started along that treacherous path to prosperity known as 'buying shares on margin' and on the walls of my room at the hospital were pinned graphs, not of patient's temperatures or pulse rates, but of the movement of railway stocks and of the rise and fall in the value of land. Cordova Centrals had gone up two points and my spirits rose with them, but next week they had fallen three, and as I marked them down on the wall I felt that the foundations of my world were crumbling away. How strange and how alarming is the power which our environment has over us. Two years previously while standing at the gateway of the Taj Mahal I had been so conscious of the nearness of a spiritual world that all else sank into insignificance, but now I was completely absorbed in the rise and the fall of shares. And how in the name of sanity had all this happened? It had happened merely because on the ill-lit stage of my mind a feckless actor had imagined that greatness could be achieved by becoming rich and taking up a political career.

When work at the hospital was finished I would sometimes make my way into the centre of Buenos Aires and would dine at a restaurant much favoured by Englishmen, the Sportsman's Café. There in the same corner of the café were always to be seen the same trio of millionaires, Kendrew,

McConnell and Hawkins. Every night at eight they would lay down their cues at the English club and drive to the Sportsman's Café, where the table was awaiting them at which they had sat every evening for five years. On it, in its silver casket of ice, was the brand of champagne they always drank. The choice of a dinner required no thought, for Fernando, the waiter, knew better than they the dishes that would appeal to their jaded palates. Nor did topics of conversation need to be selected when they had settled themselves down to dinner, for they had talked on the same subjects ever since they had first met — the prospects for the harvest, the prices that land was fetching, the best breeders of pedigree stock, and the state of the cattle market. At half-past nine precisely they emptied their liqueur glasses, took another cigar out of the special box kept for them and lit it, stepped into the 'coche' awaiting them at the door and drove back to their club for a game of poker. Play closed at two, in order that each might get to bed and be ready again for a similar round of events on the following day. I watched these rich men with a pity that was so much wasted sympathy, for of what, after all, is life made up but of a sequence of habits. If our customary routine is disturbed we become uncomfortable and struggle to get back into the ruts in which the wheels of our being run so smoothly.

Mr. Craddock was well aware of this, and he was never able to adjust himself to the new experience of being a wealthy man. He was a supporter of the British Hospital, and I occasionally dined with him in his big home out at Palermo. Forty years previously he had started work on a small holding, or chacra, in the southern part of the Republic and, thanks to his industry and Scottish acumen, the chacra had eventually grown into two immense estancias. Now he was one of the richest Europeans in Buenos Aires, with a large house, many servants and a prominent position in Anglo-Argentine society. But none of these things appealed to Mr. Craddock and he seemed utterly out of place presiding over dinner parties at the head of the long dining table. But this was what his daughters wanted and he was prepared to fall in with their wishes. At the end of dinner, after the port had circulated twice round the table, Mr. Craddock would climb down from his chair — he was absurdly small and frail — and nervously tiptoeing along the carpet in my direction, he would whisper in my ear: 'I hope you'll excuse me, Dr. Walker, but I have business that must be attended to.' Then, like a man that has discharged a duty, he would hurry from the room. I wondered why a man who had worked so hard in the past and who was now a millionaire could still remain a slave to his business and it was not until my fourth visit to his house that I discovered Mr. Craddock's secret. Upstairs on the topmost floor was a shabby room which nobody who had not been specially invited was allowed to enter. In it stood an old kitchen table, three wooden chairs, a dresser, a clock with a broken hand and a box full of old ledgers. There, surrounded by the furniture with which he had started life, and often in the company of his faithful old wife, he would examine again the well-thumbed ledgers and would be at peace. The rich furniture downstairs, the servants, the guests and all the insignia of wealth were forgotten, and Mr. Craddock was back again where he really belonged, back in his old chacra. Leave him alone there, for the wheels of his being are running smoothly along the well-worn grooves of custom.

I was comparatively new to Buenos Aires but already I had settled down to my particular routine. My days were so completely filled with work at the hospital, lessons in Spanish, speculation on the Stock Exchange and efforts to obtain a hearing in the examination hall that I had no time to think of what I was doing, or why I was doing it. The most troublesome item in this full programme was undoubtedly the obtaining of my Argentine degree. My difficulty was not that the examiners were dissatisfied with my answers, but that they could not be bothered to question me. No Argentine ever thinks of turning up punctually to an appointment and more often than not he forgets that he has made one for *mañana* is a word as favoured in Buenos Aires as it is in Spain. I would make ten visits to the Faculty of Medicine before I would succeed in even sighting one of the four examiners whose duty it was to test my knowledge, and to collect four, at the same time, was as hard a task as to drive four pigs to market along an unfenced road. Even when three were eventually persuaded to meet me at the Faculty of Medicine the fourth was invariably missing, and on the next occasion, when by special efforts the presence of the defaulter had been secured, his three colleagues had not thought it worth their while to risk making another fruitless journey to the examination hall for so small a purpose as the examination of a foreign doctor. I sought my examiners in passages, tracked them to their private houses, wrote to them, searched out their friends in the hope of enlisting their influence, pled with their wives and, if an opportunity presented itself, I called them into medical consultation. Only after weeks of such efforts did I succeed in inducing them to meet me so that I might advance yet another step in this long journey of obtaining a degree. In all, there were some twenty-four subjects to be taken and some hundred elusive examiners to be shepherded into the examination. Small wonder that my predecessors had only collected thorns in this garden of roses in which resident officers at the British Hospital walked, and that one of them at least, had taken to drink.

Life in Buenos Aires was becoming very tedious, and when Mr. Muller, the accountant of an Argentine railway, suggested to me one day that I should accompany him on a journey to Paraguay, Selous jumped at it. I had almost forgotten the existence of the great explorer, so caught up had I been in the routine of the hospital, but Selous never missed his cue and before Muller had got half-way through his description of what he intended to do, Selous had assumed complete control. Somewhere in the middle of Paraguay was a large tract of land owned by a company to which Muller acted as accountant. Apparently, Macdonald, the new manager of the estate, was not proving to be a success, and the directors were dissatisfied with the reports he sent back to Buenos Aires. 'Between you and me, Walker,' whispered Muller, 'I think that he's cooking the accounts, and they've asked me to make this journey to see if I can get to the bottom of it. If I find that my suspicions are correct, I'm empowered to give him the sack. We will stay at the company's estancia for a couple of weeks and while I'm doing the auditing you can occupy your time with a little cattle-punching. Then, if there's time, we'll work our way up the River Parana beyond Asuncion and visit the Falls of Iquazo.'

The examinations were over for the time being, the house-surgeon could deputize for me at the hospital, I was feeling tired and I had earned a holiday. There was no reason therefore why I should not enjoy a brief respite from the noise and the heat of Buenos Aires. I gladly accepted Muller's offer. Even if obstacles had stood in the way of my being absent for a time it is doubtful whether Selous and Knight-Paton would have allowed me to pay any attention to them. They had had more than enough of that accursed city.

CHAPTER XII

PARAGUAYAN INTERLUDE

UNTIL we were settled in the train at Retiro, the terminus of the Entre Rios railway, I had had no opportunity of meeting Muller again and of finding out from him exactly where we were going. He was now seated opposite me, a stout middle-aged man, with a German name and head, but in all other respects aggressively British. I had even less in common with him than I had had with Mafoota, but I had a great respect for his financial ability and believed that he was a coming man. I was living in Buenos Aires and by a coming man I naturally meant a man who was bound to make money. He, on his part, felt that he owed me much for having steered his wife through a serious attack of typhoid at the British Hospital. The train pulled slowly out of Buenos Aires and, threading its way through the limbo of small chacras and decaying iron sheds that surround the city and through its more prosperous outlying suburbs, it was soon travelling across those rather desolate plains, the pampas, that provide the main scenery of Argentina. An occasional collection of low buildings under a clump of paraiso-trees, with a spidery galvanized iron windmill beside it, alone broke the monotony of the view from the windows. Muller put down his morning paper and began to talk.

'We shall arrive at Villa Rica on the Paraguayan Railway in about three days time. It is the nearest station to the estate. A couple of weeks' hard work should clear up all this muddle and then we'll make our way to Asuncion, steam up the river for a couple of hundred miles or so and visit the falls.' The programme seemed an excellent one and it was with a feeling of relief that I looked out of the window at the pasture lands of Entre Rios and realized that for the time being I had left Buenos Aires behind me. Late that afternoon we reached Ibicuy where the train crosses the river on a ferry. 'Some day this will be an important port,' said Muller, gazing through the window at the mud banks sloping down to the river. 'Brown, you know whom I mean, the late manager of the Northern Argentine, is convinced that the whole of this system of railways will eventually link up with those of Brazil and thus form a great central line passing from north to south. I advise you to buy land here. I shall do so myself.' Later I took his advice and nominally I still possess some ill-drained acres of desolate land on which browse the horses of settlers who have squatted there so long that by now they own my land. The great line that was to run north and south remained only in Mr. Brown's head and Mr. Brown is now dead.

A day later we reached Posadas, the end of the Argentine part of our journey and we left the train to cross the River Parana in a native canoe. Our ferryman was an attractive Paraguayan maiden, three-quarters Indian and one quarter Spanish, and she navigated our flimsy craft through the currents so skilfully and with such nonchalance that it was not even necessary for her to remove her cigar from her lips while doing so. From Concepcion, the Paraguayan town opposite to Posadas, we continued our journey by train until we reached our destination, Villa Rica, late in the afternoon. Muller's wire announcing the time of our expected arrival had apparently miscarried, for there was nobody on the platform except two Paraguayan youths, wearing wide-brimmed hats, shorts and large spurs strapped to bootless and stockingless feet. But soon a young cattle-man panted on to the platform and apologized for being late. It was the first time that I had met a cowboy outside the pages of *Chums* and *The Boy's Own Paper*, and I gazed with relish at his chaps, his cartridge belt and the two revolvers stuck in it. He introduced himself as Russell, the second-in-command of the estancia, and then blurted out suddenly that he was 'damned glad' that we had come.

'I'm having a hell of a time,' he said, 'Macdonald's drinking hard and he's out for my blood. Last night he chased me round the veranda with a revolver, and I'm damned if I can stand it much longer.'

Muller's eye caught mine, and although we said nothing, we knew what the other was thinking. Giving notice to a cook at home may not be pleasant, but it is at any rate devoid of danger. Discharging Macdonald from his job might not only be unpleasant, but an act of heroism.

'I've got six horses outside and I'll get your baggage loaded up on to one of them,' continued Russell. 'It's about nine leagues to the estancia.'

'Nine leagues on a horse,' exploded Muller, 'but I've never ridden one in my life. Can't you order a waggon?'

Russell smiled. 'Twenty draft of oxen couldn't pull wheels over those swamps,' he said. 'There's no way of travelling up here except in the saddle.'

'It's quite impossible,' protested Muller, with a look of German stolidity on his face. 'I couldn't do it.' But there was no alternative, and in the end my big companion was hoisted on to a guaranteed-quiet horse, and instructed how to hold on to the saddle. My own mount was an excellent one and as comfortable to ride as any arab. From the horn of my Mexican saddle hung a coiled fifty-foot lariat which brought back to my mind the exploits of the friends of my boyhood, Buffalo Bill and Black Gully Dick. With us rode Russell and the two Paraguayan cattle-hands, who wore over the left hip the long lasso apron used by all Argentine and Paraguayan cowboys. The remainder of their get-up included multi-coloured shirts, bright-hued handkerchiefs tied round the head, cartridge belts, six-shooters and long Paraguayan spurs. We were a tough looking lot — that is to say, all except Muller, who resembled some soft rich merchant who had been captured by bandits. The pained expression on his face as he bumped along on his saddle added to this resemblance, but deep within that big mass of soft flesh there was a hard kernel, for although he was obviously in discomfort, he seldom complained. Often when we rode towards what in the distance looked like lush meadowlands, it turned out to be, when we reached it, a shallow lake, with tall grass growing through the water. In places the lake deepened, so that the water reached to our saddles, and we were forced to draw our feet up to the level of our horses' necks to prevent them from getting wet. Mosquitoes and polverines, little midges so small as to be scarcely visible, rose in a cloud from the water and settled on our hands and faces. Usually I rode with Russell, but towards the end of the journey, in order to show sympathy for my companion, I dropped behind to talk to Muller.

'This fool, Macdonald,' he panted when our horses had dropped into a walk, 'we must be careful about him. A stitch in time saves nine. Have you got a revolver?'

Selous had never forgotten that day in East Africa when he had fired at two flying partridges and one of the birds had fallen, and since then he was convinced that he was a revolver shot. 'I've got one in my pocket,' I answered.

'Good,' said Muller, 'forewarned is forearmed, and it may be needed. Be as pleasant as you can to him, get him to show you round the estate and while you're out of the way, I'll go through the books. On no account pick a quarrel.'

This was about the last thing that any of the inner brotherhood intended to do. Selous' ideal was to permit just that degree of danger which imparted to events a pleasant thrill, but never to allow danger to get out of hand. He would be very pleasant with this man Macdonald, very pleasant, indeed. At the end of another hour we sighted the ranch, a long low 'adobe' house with a veranda, outbuildings for the cattlemen, a *corral* and a *laguna* fringed with lemon and acacia trees. We dismounted, turned over our horses to a boy who came running out to meet us, and climbed on to the veranda. As we entered what was obviously the main room of the house Macdonald rose from his chair and shook us warmly by the hand. Whether he guessed the real reason of our visit or not, I do not know, but I could detect no hostility in his manner.

I liked Paraguay and its people far better than I liked Buenos Aires and those that I had hitherto met there. The Paraguayans were a bloodthirsty but picturesque crowd, equally expert with the guitar, the lariat and the knife, but they possessed the simplicity and the directness which come from living close to nature. They had never left Mother Earth and having experience of her sternness they looked upon their lives as gifts that at any moment might suddenly be withdrawn. What they possessed was their own, something which they had won by hard experience and not merely borrowed from their neighbours. They had the honesty and frankness of children and like children they had discovered certain truths which were hidden from many of their more sophisticated elders. The very words with which so many of their remarks closed reflected a kind of childish wisdom and an acceptance of things as they were and as they had to be. *Quien sabe?* and *Que importa?* And when it comes to anything more complicated and abstract than the saddling of a horse, or the branding of a steer, who indeed amongst us can claim to know? What knowledge indeed have we of any of the things that really matter and of the things that we know, *Que importa?*

My share in the job in hand, namely the work of keeping on good terms with Macdonald, proved to be remarkably easy, for he seemed glad to find an excuse for getting away from an office which he clearly disliked and he readily agreed to show me round the estate. When, on our first morning together, a pony other than the one I had previously ridden, was brought up to the veranda for me I was outspoken enough to complain of the change.

'They ought never to have put you on that bronch and I've rated them soundly for it,' he answered; 'he's one of the worst buckers on the place, but bronchs are like that. One day as good as gold, and on another down go their heads, and they double up like a jacknife with a spring in it.'

'He tried to do that once,' I said, 'but I pulled his head up.'

'Then you did the right thing, but this pony's got none of those tricks. You'll like him.'

We cantered along together and eventually reached a line of trees marking the position of a shallow river. 'There are plenty of *jacaré* in that creek, and if you like, you can test your shooting on them. But look, there's a better target over there, two pigeons on the top of that tree. See whether you can bring one of them down with this Winchester.'

I dismounted, took the rifle which Macdonald had been carrying and knelt on the ground like a Bisley marksman, resting my elbow on my knee. I fired and the bird lifted up one of its wings. 'Near,' said Macdonald, 'but not quite near enough. Let's see if I can bring him down with my Colt.' Sitting firmly in his saddle he pulled out the long barrel from its holster, flicked it upwards towards the tree and fired. The bird dropped without a struggle, hitting the branches as it fell to the ground. Muller's words, 'Don't pick a quarrel with him', flashed through my mind. I wasn't such a fool as to go quarrelling with a man who could drop a pigeon at sixty yards without getting out of his saddle. Macdonald's Colt, like the forces of nature, could not be controlled and Macdonald must be treated with the same deference that Selous and Knight-Paton paid to lightning and avalanches.

On another day Macdonald introduced me to Paraguayan cattle work and I galloped round herds of steers swinging, but never quite daring to throw, my lariat. It would be ignominious to get tangled up in my own lasso and by error to catch, not a steer, but a cattleman. What an immense relief this was from the dreary routine of the British Hospital at Buenos Aires, and how grand it would be to spend the rest of one's life as a cowboy with a lasso in one's hand and with a saddlehorn there, nice and handy ready for grasping if one's mount suddenly swerved or bucked. Yet even as I galloped away to head off some wayward steers questions thrust themselves into my mind. What was I doing here, in Paraguay, dressed as a cowboy and pretending to be Black Gully Dick? These men who were with me were real and it was I alone who was masquerading. What was I doing, and, still more puzzling, what was this part of me that looked on and put all these awkward questions? Such thoughts were distracting in the middle of a round-up and, putting them away from me, I thrust my heels into the horse's flanks and galloped back again into my dreams.

The two weeks had passed so quickly that until Muller took me aside and told me that his work was completed I had not realized that our visit was nearly at an end. He had steadfastly refused to get up into the saddle again, and as it was too hot for walking, and no other method of transport was available, he remained most of the time alone and indoors. I only met him at meals and in the company of others, but on the last night of our stay he captured me as I was entering the house.

'Don't be surprised,' he whispered, 'at anything that happens to-night, and have all your things packed and ready before you go to bed.' It all sounded very mysterious but at the moment there was no opportunity for obtaining an explanation.

After dinner Muller and Macdonald retired as usual to the office, but, what was not usual, was that shortly afterwards the noise of laughter came through the wall. Still later I could hear snatches of a song. 'Good Lord, what's happening?' I asked Russell, who was sitting beside me on the veranda oiling his rifle.

'It sounds as if they were liquoring up,' he said, 'I know they've got two bottles of *caña* in there, as well as some whisky. I don't know about your friend, Muller, but once Macdonald has started, he never leaves off until he's completely logged. He's a buster, and not a boozer.'

I had had a long day, so I retired early to bed and soon fell asleep. In the middle of the night, as it seemed to me, although it was really just before dawn, I felt my arm being shaken. It was Muller, fully dressed and holding the dispatch-case in which he carried all his papers. 'Get up,' he whispered, 'and make as little noise as you can. The horses are waiting.'

More asleep than awake and too drowsy to ask questions I bundled into my clothes and followed him out of the house. Five horses were standing there in the dim light, in charge of two men who were evidently to act as our guides. Our luggage had already been corded on to a pack-saddle and in silence our small cavalcade rode away. Only when a mile separated us from the estancia did my mind fling off its blanket of sleep and allow me to ask a question. 'Where are we going, and have you given him the sack?'

'We're going to Villa Rica to catch a train to Asuncion.'

'So it's all right about those books,' I said, 'and he hasn't been cooking them? I like that fellow Macdonald and I'm sure that there can't be anything wrong.'

'It looks as though it was all wrong,' he answered briefly.

'Then you have fired him?'

'Discretion is the better part of valour, and a letter will do the work quite as well as a verbal dismissal.'

'If that's what you're going to do, I don't see why we've got to sneak away like a couple of burglars without any swag.'

'The swag is here,' said Muller, patting the leather case hanging from his saddle. 'He'd have smelt a rat if I'd openly taken away all the correspondence hidden under those old clothes in that chest-of-drawers of his.'

'So you made him drunk?'

'Exactly, and thereby saved a lot of unpleasantness.'

The idea that Macdonald was not straight displeased me and I disliked even more this ignominious getaway, so utterly out of keeping with the noble endings to the Wild West stories in *Chums* or the *Boy's Own Paper*. I felt heartily ashamed of our scurvy treatment of a man who had provided me with such an excellent holiday, but by the time that we reached Villa Rica I had come to the conclusion that perhaps after all Muller might be right. He had seen more than I had, and, as he would probably have put it, 'a living cur is better than a dead lion'. It was unpleasant to be a cur but, in these circumstances, perhaps justifiable. Macdonald seemed to be all right but a man was not a single person but a crowd, and in a crowd there was room for a defaulter of books as well as for an excellent companion, a crack shot, a kind host and a drunkard. Human beings were very queer.

CHAPTER XIII

THE PLAYHOUSE
NEARLY COMES TO GRIEF

RETURNING to Buenos Aires was like re-entering a crowded and ill-ventilated casino after enjoying an invigorating walk in the country. But the feeling that I was rejoining a number of people who were leading an entirely artificial life and who were dealing in false values was a passing one and I soon settled down again to my old routine.

It must be admitted that the picture I have painted of the great city of Buenos Aires is a prejudiced one and that I have projected on to the canvas some of the darkness which was gathering within me. I was unhappy and, as always happens, I was blaming my surroundings for this. Yet unfriendly though Buenos Aires was when compared with India, I made there a number of friends. My sister had married a wealthy estanciero and I spent many pleasant evenings at her house and in her box at the Colon Opera House. I also saw much of Dr. O'Malley, that wild and witty Irishman from whom later I was to receive so many kindnesses. It was he who introduced me to the Trevor family with its various ramifications living in a number of Buenos Aires suburbs. Young men who are tongue-tied and ill at ease with adults, and more especially with women, are often at their best with children, and I spent many happy hours playing in gardens with the younger members of the Trevor family. Sometimes O'Malley would take us all out for a sail in his yacht and peals of laughter would travel over the River Plate as we hoisted to the top of the mast, by means of a rope and a pulley, a series of young Trevors. No, life in Buenos Aires was not quite so grim as I have painted it. There were hours during which I deemed myself almost happy.

One by one the examinations were put behind me and now I had only five subjects in which to pass, five subjects which stood between me and freedom from O'Sullivan and the hospital. The first of these, clinical medicine, proved unexpectedly easy. I was allotted a patient lying in a ward of one of the large Argentine hospitals and told to diagnose the disease from which he was suffering. My patient happened to be a young

Italian, with a pale sensitive face and a carefully tended moustache. I bared his chest, tapped out his cardiac dullness, listened to his heart sounds and discovered a faint cardiac murmur. He was obviously a case of valvular disease, and it only remained for me to decide the exact nature of his cardiac lesion. 'Mitral regurgitation, fully compensated', he whispered in my ear as I bent over him. He had read the notes before they had been removed from above his bed and he knew precisely what the doctors had made of his case. 'Muchissimas gratias, señor!' I answered, 'que se mejore pronto.' ('May you get well quickly.') I grasped him warmly by the hand, as though counting his pulse and, when it was free, he took from beneath his pillow a visiting card which he handed to me. On it was printed a coronet and underneath it the name 'Il Conte de Cironcole'.

'You know Italy?' he asked, his eyes lighting as he spoke.

'A little,' I answered. 'But why are you here?'

'I left my country for this — ' he looked round the shabby fly-infested ward — 'in order to make money. That's why I'm here.'

'Are you fully compensated, like your heart?' I asked, but one of the waiting examiners called me before he had time to answer.

'What have you made of the case?' asked the professor of medicine, adjusting his tortoiseshell glasses.

'Mitral regurgitation. The heart is, at any rate, compensated, but I don't know about the rest of him.'

'Quite right. You needn't bother about the other organs,' he added, a trifle testily. 'Otherwise he's all right.'

I did not contradict him, but I had diagnosed better than had the professor the state of that man. 'I left my country for this,' he had said, 'in order to make money.' Would he succeed in his aim, and if he succeeded would it bring contentment?

Clinical surgery was not to be disposed of so easily as clinical medicine. I visited the Faculty of Medicine twenty-four times, on each occasion to discover that my examiners had again broken their promises and had failed to turn up. Months passed and a leaden weariness began to weigh me down. One cannot live for long in a bad atmosphere and in an environment which is out of keeping with all that is best in one without paying for it, and in the end I, like my friend Il Conte de Cironcole, paid for what I had done. Indigestion was now added to my other troubles and work at the hospital became so irksome that I had difficulty in struggling through my days. O'Sullivan noted my fatigue and my listlessness as I accompanied him on his tour round the wards.

'Champagne is what you want, my boy,' he said. 'Half a bottle of Pol Roger every day, and make sure that it is 1908 vintage.' To O'Sullivan champagne was the elixir of life and having exhausted its potentialities when given by the mouth, he prescribed it by all the avenues employed by doctors, by the bowel, intravenously and even subcutaneously. I had had the job of looking after one of the patients to whom it had been administered subcutaneously, mixed with saline, and had had some difficulty in explaining to her why her treatment had led to the development of abscesses in the leg. I had no faith in any of O'Sullivan's prescriptions, not even in champagne when given through the proper channel, and the last thing I was going to do was to spend my hard-earned money on Pol Roger 1908. No vintage could cure the wasting sickness of the soul from which I was suffering and I retained sufficient common sense to know this. But like many neurotics I blamed my surroundings for what had happened to me and felt that everything and everybody were banded together against me in hostile array. There was only one person's integrity which I never stopped to question, my own, only one being I never blamed, myself. It is strange that while walking along that thin crust that separated me from all the darkness and confusion that lay below, I never once thought that I might be responsible for my own condition. I felt that I was a tragic and ill-used man, but it never occurred to me that I was a man who had been maltreated by himself. It became more and more obvious to everybody that I was ill, and after examining me in my room one afternoon O'Sullivan came to the conclusion that I was suffering from a duodenal ulcer. He decided to make an exception of my case and to try the effect of rest, diet and medical treatment. 'We'll send him to the hills for a month,' he said to the medical colleague who was looking after me, 'and while there he must drink plenty of milk. It is obvious that the fellow needs a rest.'

I went to the hills of Cordoba, but took myself with me, and, encumbered with this, I had no rest. Cordoba was beautiful but I saw there only hostile mountains, a pitiless sun and an unfriendly sky. The milk seemed to be curdled even before I had time to drink it, the hotel was badly mismanaged and the general atmosphere of the hills unutterably oppressive. I returned to Buenos Aires in worse health than when I had left it, struggled to the examination hall, elicited the sympathy of the examiners and passed the last of my examinations. Then I went back to my bed in the hospital. 'Another month off,' said O'Sullivan, 'but this time we'd better send him to an estancia. The hills evidently did not suit him.'

Friends invited me to stay with them in their estancia at Epumer, a day's journey from Buenos Aires on the Southern railway. There, riding all day over the pampas, and enjoying the cheerful company of my host and hostess in the evening, my health began slowly to improve. Nobody could have worked harder than did Dr. and Mrs. Burr to restore my peace of mind and to free a spirit caught up in the coils of self-pity, but in the end they failed. I returned ill and despairing to O'Sullivan and the hospital in Buenos Aires.

'There is only one thing that will do it,' was O'Sullivan's verdict. 'We've waited long enough, too long if you ask me, and a gastro-enterostomy is clearly indicated.' I was by now resigned to anything, even to submission to O'Sullivan's scalpel. So in the theatre one hot morning a carnivorous surgeon, with clumsy nickelled tools, started off to discover and to repair a trouble that was not where he expected to find it. He opened the abdomen and searched amongst the organs of digestion for a spiritual illness, laying the blame on an innocent appendix and some inoffensive adhesions. Fortunately for me O'Sullivan had never heard of Descartes or of his belief that the seat of the soul is in the Pineal gland, that mysterious structure uncovered by deep dissection at the base of the brain, and it was equally fortunate that he decided that no short-circuiting operation was necessary.

'I could find nothing wrong with you,' he said, when I had convalesced sufficiently to hear the news, 'so I removed your appendix and then closed you up.' Nothing wrong! Everything was wrong. A brilliant young man, on the verge of success, was being cheated of his due. News had recently come from England that my essay had won the Jacksonian Prize, that I had been elected a Hunterian Professor of the Royal College of Surgeons, and at the bottom of my bed lay the parchment of my new Argentine degree. I had achieved all that I had set out to do only to be defrauded of my due. The removal of a blameless appendix would make no difference, and life for me no longer served any purpose. There was no such thing as justice in this world, no God in the heavens and no meaning in anything. What could I do? I could only wait for an answer to the letter I had written to M. a week or two before my operation. M. would not fail me. He was my only hope. .

The answer came a week later in the form of a cable. ON NO ACCOUNT LET ANY SURGEON NEAR YOU BUT COME HOME AT ONCE. M. It was from my closest friend. He had been with me both at Caius and at Bart's, and then, specializing in psychology, he had gone to Vienna to study under Freud and thence to Zurich, the home of Jung. I was his senior by a year, and as such had assumed the character of adviser and older friend when he had arrived as a freshman at the college and at the hospital. But somehow these roles had not worked, for what I considered to be of so much importance, namely, that one should take a prominent place in college affairs and games, appeared to him to be a mere bagatelle and a waste of time. Neither Caius nor St. Bartholomew's could swallow up M.; they remained merely part of his background, chance happenings in his journey through life. He was irreverent enough to laugh at the great people in the court and the square whom I so admired, looking upon them as adolescents who were slow in growing up, people who were amusing to meet perhaps, but who were not to be taken too seriously. So the relationship of senior and junior had been reversed, and it was I who now listened to M. and I who sought him out whenever life proved difficult. His wire was like a strong hand being stretched out towards me, and I grasped it firmly with the conviction that it would pull me out of the morass into which I had fallen. The cable had arrived too late to avert the operation but not too late to help me to decide what I must do.

A week later I was back on a Royal Mail boat bound for home, and as I walked up and down its broad decks, watching Buenos Aires dropping below the southern waters of the River Plate, words came back to me that had been spoken two years ago. 'That was young Elliott. They would not let him go, but in the end they had to ship him home in charge of a nurse, with a nervous breakdown.' Well, I was better than young Elliott for I could manage to get home without the help of a nurse. At Santos, the great coffee port of Brazil, I found a little tavern in the old part of the town and sat for two hours drinking cup after cup of black coffee, made from beans fresh from the hills on which they had been grown. As I made my way back to the ship I realized that I had got drunk on it, and that everything, both within and without, had suddenly changed. The gnawing at my vitals had stopped, a resplendent sun shone in the heavens above and colour had come back into the faded sky and the hills. The world that had been dead had now returned to life, and all because sitting in a dirty café I had drunk so much caffeine that my heart was dancing a wild fandango against my ribs. The exhilaration lasted until next day, and then the gnawing returned and the world began to fade. But I had learnt a lesson, for I knew now for certain that the trouble lay within me, and not in the things outside me. If caffeine could bring about this change it meant that the machinery of living within me was not actually broken, but was only running badly. All that was required was to find some means of tuning it up and M. would know how to do this.

He was waiting for me when I reached London. 'I'm glad you've come,' he said, 'and as I can manage to take a fortnight off we'll go straight out to Switzerland.' There was no reason for any delay, so as soon as we could book seats and reservations in an hotel we started for Adelboden. I breathed the pure air of the Alps and walked in the crystal-clear sunshine of Switzerland, hoping that they would bring about the longed-for change. But the great peaks and the sun were occupied with their own affairs and I existed for them as little as I did for the Sphinx. It was very disappointing. Surely by now I should have been feeling better, but the rat which had for so long gnawed at my vitals had not yet been expelled. One night I could stand it no longer, and leaving my room, I walked in the starlight and complained of my troubles to the Milky Way. No answer came, and filled to the brim with private tragedy, I returned to the hotel and went up to our room. M. was still up. Good, he at least would answer me and would give me the sympathy for which I longed. For a moment he was silent, and then he abruptly turned on me and spoke.

'You are enjoying your illness, and because you relish its tragedy you are really in no hurry to get well.'

Good God, what was he saying! He was accusing me of enjoying what I longed above all to get rid of — but he had not yet finished.

'Tell me, why did you go for that walk, and what were you thinking about when you looked at those stars? No, don't bother to answer, for I know. You were filled with self-pity, big with the sense of personal drama. You felt pathetic, misused and frustrated, and you wallowed in it. Well, you can have that stupid satisfaction if you want it, but don't expect to get well. You can't have both, but must have either one or the other, self-importance or health.

Preposterous! Unsympathetic. I would leave Adelboden first thing in the morning. If that was what he thought, at least I could remove myself from his presence. Then, something began to make itself heard above the inner clamour; quietly, at first, as though I were listening to a voice speaking from a long way off, and then as though it were nearer to me. 'Perhaps he is right. May not M. be able to see things more clearly than you do yourself? Would it not be better to listen to him?' I choked down the angry answer that had all but passed my lips and lay back on my pillow struggling to think.

'Yes, you are right. I admit that I felt very sorry for myself when I looked at those stars, but I can't understand it, for there's nobody in the world who wants tragedy or illness.'

He remained silent for at least a minute and then began to speak, weighing each word carefully as he uttered it. 'Men derive great enjoyment from the tragic. Look at the headlines in the paper if you want to see what people really enjoy reading about. And look also at the great plays of genius. What are amongst our greatest plays — why, the great tragedies, *Hamlet*, *King Lear*, *The Trojan Women*, and all the rest of them. Men have acquired a taste for the bittersweet.'

'But how strange that this should be,' I answered briefly.

'Suffering confers on us a kind of spurious distinction,' he continued, 'and if we cannot be conspicuous for anything else, we can at least be conspicuous as tragic figures, as disappointed men or as lifelong invalids. To feel that we are misjudged, or that we have been injured, is to infer that we have privileges that have been infringed, and then we become like kings defending their divine right.'

I got up, lit a cigarette and walked about the room. M. always took pleasure in the fantastic, but these ideas rang true. 'Let's talk about it to-morrow,' I said, 'to-night I'm rather tired.'

Next morning M. and I went for a walk and having climbed up above the level of the pine woods we rested on a rock overlooking the valley. Tiny chalets, like the toy ones my parents used to bring home from their holidays in Switzerland, clung to the slope of the hill below us and from nearby came the tinkle of cowbells.

'I've been thinking about what you were saying last night,' I began; 'all that about our secret liking for tragedy, frustration and unhappiness. I suppose it's a form of masochism.'

156

'Don't use technical terms. We tie a label on to something and then think that we've explained it. Freud tried to explain everything in human conduct in terms of sex, but it simply can't be done, and his term masochism won't help us.'

'Then how do you explain what you said about me — that I don't really want to get well? I feel that I want to get better more than I want anything else in the world.'

'Only part of you wants that, but another part either finds it's convenient to be ill, or else rather fancies itself in the role of an interesting invalid. It likes all those sentimental ideas about the consumptive genius struggling with his illness, the light that failed and that sort of nonsense.'

'Then tell me what to do.'

'First get to know yourself. It's the beginning of all wisdom.'

'There I think you make a mistake. My trouble is that I'm too introspective and think too much about what I'm doing and feeling already.'

M. took out of his pocket a small book and after turning over the pages began to read. 'Man is difficult to discover and unto himself most difficult of all.'

'Who wrote that?' I asked.

'Nietzsche.'

'Oh, that madman.'

'I see that you've got the usual misconception about him. Nietzsche wrote his Zarathustra in the state of exaltation that preceded his mental collapse. Like an over-loaded bulb, he flashed into brilliance and then, broken by a surcharge of nervous energy, expired in darkness, but in that moment of intense illumination he caught glimpses of truth that are not seen by ordinary light. We do not know ourselves; we only know our dreams, what we imagine ourselves to be.'

'Is the truth too unpalatable?' I asked, picking up a stone and hurling it down the slope of the hill.

'Much of it is,' answered M., 'and for this reason we wear blinkers. Listen to this.' He began to read again. ' "Alone with oneself! This thought terrifies the modern soul; it is his anxiety, his one ghostly fear. To become endurable to oneself an inner transformation is necessary. Too long have we lost ourselves in our friends and entertainments to be able to find ourselves so soon at another's bidding." '

I flung another stone down into the valley and it dashed against a rock and shivered into fragments, liberating sparks as it did so. 'What a lot of breaking has to be done to get at anything,' I grumbled. 'You say that I don't know myself — well, at any rate I've discovered one thing.'

'What?'

'That there's a hell of a lot of talking and quarrelling going on inside me. It's as though Jekyll and Hyde were having a scrap.'

'Not just Jekyll and Hyde, but a whole crowd of people. But that's not a very modern or original discovery, K. While I was in Vienna I read some of Tolstoi's diaries and in them he is continually harping on this inner state of conflict and confusion. You see, everything in Tolstoi was on a very big scale and therefore more conspicuous than in lesser men. Dostoievsky made this idea that man is not one but many the theme of his great novel *The Brothers Karamazov*. It's autobiographical, and the brothers represent different sides of his own character; Dimitri was the passionate impulsive animal side of him, Ivanov, the rather cynical intellectual in him, and Aloysha, the youngest and in many ways the least developed of the characters, was the spiritual side of him. Dostoievsky was rather a tragic figure, for he never found what he was looking for.'

'What was he looking for?'

'Something to live by. But we've talked enough. Let's go and have a drink somewhere.'

We got up and made our way to a café where drinks were being served, outside in the sunshine, on small tables covered with bright checked cloths.

Whether it was because of Switzerland and its fine air and sunshine, or of my many talks with M. or of both together, I do not know, but slowly and with setbacks some change occurred within me and the inner discomfort began to grow less. Life beckoned to me again and I gladly answered her summons. Muscles that had been tense for months relaxed, a face which had been stamped with anxiety lost some of its furrows, and the tone of despondency left my voice. At the end of two weeks M. and I returned to England, he to his practice and I to give my lecture before the Royal College of Surgeons. There followed for me six busy weeks during which I met many of my old friends, dined out, went to the theatre and derived other satisfactions from being in London again. On two memorable evenings I dined at 10 Downing Street and the Personage conversed with the Premier, but not on the subjects which he would have selected had the choice been left in his hands. Mr. Asquith spoke about music and the theatre and did not choose to discuss affairs of state with a potential future prime minister. The Personage was therefore unable to mention casually in subsequent conversations that Mr. Asquith had stated this to him personally, or that he knew for a fact that the Prime Minister was extremely worried about the Irish question. At the end of six weeks there seemed no longer to be any excuse for remaining on holiday and I spoke to M. of my return to Buenos Aires.

'You want to go back?' he asked.

'I must,' I answered. 'Surely after all the work I've done, all that tedious business of taking a degree, I ought to reap the advantage of it. Now that I'm qualified I can practise in Buenos Aires, and gather a rich harvest of surgical fees. I'm no longer dependent on that fellow O'Sullivan.'

'Well, you may have to go,' said M. 'We rarely travel in a straight line, but generally have to reach our goal by going a long way round. Some day you may learn that there are other ways of living.'

'What other ways?' I asked.

M. paused and then, just as he was on the point of speaking, he seemed to change his mind. 'No, I won't talk about that now,' he said. 'Perhaps you have to go back to Buenos Aires and to do many things first. You believe so implicitly in these things that you accept as being important that you do not even stop to examine their value. Go back to Buenos Aires, and good luck to you. Good-bye.' He shook my hand and then departed abruptly, as was his custom. I knew that I owed him more than I owed to anybody else in the world, but to have thanked him would have made us both feel uncomfortable. It was my last meeting with him and I sailed ten days later for the River Plate.

During the voyage I thought a great deal about what he had told me and particularly about his reference to another way of living. Did he mean by this that I should abandon my idea of making money quickly and of going into politics and should settle down in England to an ordinary medical career? No, he had implied some more radical change than this. I had the impression that he looked upon me as being a man who was walking along a road which led nowhere, and prior to that last conversation he had more than once hinted that when the day came that I discovered the futility of my journey he would have something to tell me. The different way of living of which M. had spoken was obviously something more than a mere alteration of plans, and knowing M. as I did, it probably entailed a complete reversal of values. In any case, I would have to get to know myself better. How ridiculous that sounded. It was almost as though I said to myself; 'Allow me to introduce you to Mr. Kenneth Walker, the Buenos Aires surgeon,' and as though another part of myself replied; 'Glad to meet you, Mr. Walker; we can now sit down together and have a nice heart-to-heart talk.' But when one came to think about it was it really as ridiculous as this? I recalled that part of *Peer Gynt* where the old man returns home from his numerous adventures and, peeling an onion, enumerates the many parts that he has played in life, the gold-digger self, the prophet, the emperor, and then searching in vain for the kernel he exclaims: 'There isn't one! To the innermost bit, it's nothing but layers, smaller and smaller. Nature's a joker!' It was not so difficult to believe that even if one was acquainted with one's external wrappings one might have very little knowledge of the inmost 'self'. Or was Peer Gynt right and was there no inmost self at all but only a bundle of outer wrappings. No, I would not neglect M.'s advice simply because at first sight it had seemed to me to be fantastic. I would do what he had told me to do.

CHAPTER XIV

PRACTICE IN BUENOS AIRES

FROM the moment I landed in Buenos Aires I thought very little more about what M. had said, for the business of settling down to practice took all my attention. A house had to be rented, furniture bought at auctions, instruments purchased and a housekeeper and servants engaged. All these things were eventually achieved and I was at last able to settle down to harvesting the reward for all my previous hard work. How different it was to be living in one's own house instead of in the cramped quarters of the British Hospital, and to be a free man instead of a slave of that fellow O'Sullivan. Besides, I was even now beginning to make money and the little room on the ground floor which I used as a waiting room was filled every day with a cosmopolitan crowd which included Anglo-Argentines, newly arrived Englishmen, Frenchmen, Germans, Scandinavians, Turks, in short, representatives of all the European countries and even of China and India. As I sat at my desk deciding all these people's fate, I had the feeling of power that I imagined a judge must enjoy when dispensing judgment in the law courts. Here at last was success even although there still existed certain annoyances. O'Sullivan had seen to it that there was no vacancy for me at the hospital, and this meant that I was unable to make use of its beds. Another difficulty was that the price of land, instead of continuing to rise, was now beginning to fall. But what did these things matter provided that my practice went on growing? Besides, an utterly unexpected financial windfall more than compensated for any losses I might have incurred. Shortly after landing, my friend Dr. O'Malley had made me an extremely flattering offer. He was the best English-speaking physician in Buenos Aires with a large and profitable practice, but in spite of this and of the fact that I was only a beginner and he a man of established reputation he had actually invited me to become his partner and to take a half of all our combined fees. If we were to work loyally together, there could be no possible doubt that within a very short time we would have the best of all the Buenos Aires practices. 'Think about it, and give me your answer when you've come to a decision,' he had said. But what was there to think about, for O'Malley's terms were so outrageously generous that only an impulsive warm-hearted Irishman could have offered them. A few days later I called at his house to give him my answer. 'We'll settle our business in my study over a glass of wine,' he said. 'Now, sit down, and remember that you really know very little about me and that you have the right to ask me any question you like. For all you know to the contrary I may be a villain.' I hesitated, for I had heard rumours and some people had even gone so far as to advise me to have nothing to do with John O'Malley. He was the type of man who made enemies as easily as he made friends, and as nobody had lodged any very definite charge against him I had put down their antagonism to professional jealousy. But now I was going into partnership with him, and there was one particular point that it was essential that I should clear up.

'There is only one rumour about you to which I have ever given any thought. I don't know whether you are aware of this, but there are people who say that you take drugs.'

O'Malley smiled and his smile was so open and so disarming that I regretted that I had spoken. 'Oh, you've come across that old gossip, have you?' he said. 'I confess that I thought that that ancient libel was now dead. Well, I might as well explain to you how it started. I expect you know that before O'Sullivan chucked me out of that damned hospital of his I married a nurse. There was no harm in that but we soon quarrelled and parted, and it was she who started this picturesque rumour. What can I say? I can only assure you, on my word of honour, that it's a damned lie.'

'That's enough for me,' I said, and without any document or formality other than a grasping of hands and a toast to the future success of our practice O'Malley and I went into partnership.

Practice in Buenos Aires is utterly different from practice in England and advertising in the press was not only permitted, but was accepted as being right and proper. Every morning in the *Standard* there would appear a whole column of medical notices, including my own. One could also learn in the social column of the paper that Dr. Fulano de Tal, lately returned from a tour of all the great European clinics, had now opened up-to-date and luxurious consulting-rooms at 440 Calle Cordova. Turning to other events one was informed that, on leaving the nursing home Señora de Paso, wished to express her great appreciation of all the kindness she had received there and that she wished especially to thank Dr. Blanco for the wonderful operation that he had performed on her, an operation that had undoubtedly saved her life. It was necessary to keep a careful eye on these notices, for if one failed to do so one might discover later that a rival practitioner had gone into larger print and that a visit to the newspaper offices was necessary to make suitable adjustments. There was no medical council in Buenos Aires to keep an eye on the ethics of practice, and collecting new patients was partly a question of wits.

One day my old friend Muller appeared unexpectedly in my consulting-room with the request that I should meet him later for a talk. 'Dine with me at my club to-night, and afterwards we can discuss the questions I wish to put to you.' Muller was in touch with all that was happening in the railway world and I saw from his manner that something big was brewing. I accepted his invitation to dinner and waited for the moment when he would tell me the reason for his obvious excitement. It was not until we were in the smoking-room after dinner that he showed his hand.

'What can one put in people's coffee to make them sleep?' he suddenly asked me. 'It must be something that doesn't taste and preferably something that is not too dangerous.'

'Good heavens,' I gasped, 'you're not starting to imitate the Borgias, are you? Why do you put me a question like that? I'm only a doctor, not an expert poisoner.'

'Well, you see, it's like this,' he said, drawing his chair closer to mine. 'You know Fernandez, the man who now has a controlling interest over the Paraguayan Railway, but who started as a cook; well, I've been talking to him and it appears that the usual revolution is starting in Paraguay. It was he who put to me this question. You see, he's in with the rebels, and soon they'll be closing in on Asuncion. Now, a dinner to all the officers of the garrison finishing with something in their coffee, to send them off to sleep, would save a great deal of bloodshed, wouldn't it? Instead of getting killed, they would all wake up comfortably next morning to find that a new government was in power.'

'I see your point,' I answered, 'and I agree that it isn't worth getting killed for the sake of politics. Morphia might do, but it would be difficult to judge the correct dose; those who, like me, have a passion for coffee might never wake up again, and others who took too little of it would never go to sleep. Besides, although the trick would probably save blood, and it's the chief duty of a surgeon to save blood, I don't think that, strictly speaking, this sort of business comes under the heading doctoring.'

'Well, leave that for the time being,' said Muller after a moment's pause. 'I asked you because I wanted to oblige Fernandez. But there's something else I want to talk to you about. A big American syndicate, the Far-quhar group, has just arrived in the country with the intention of buying up all the big refrigerator plants and some of the railways too. I have found out that they are going to get control of the Central Paraguayan Railway. Now, I'm very well known in the railway world here, and if I were to start buying shares for a rise, everybody would smell a rat. What I'm going to suggest is that you should do the buying, not in a small way, but buying in great blocks of shares up to sixty or seventy thousand pounds worth.'

'But what about the money?' I queried. 'I'm not a financier, and even the little I've made has gone in the land slump.'

'Don't you bother about that. I'll work the banks and then we'll sell out afterwards at a handsome profit and go fifty-fifty. It's as safe as houses.'

Certainly the proposition sounded a good one and if it succeeded, as Muller was sure it would, I could shake off the dust of Buenos Aires within a comparatively short time. I sat in silence, my judgment groping for an answer. This was the way all the successful people around me were making money, and with Muller to help me, I might easily do the same. Then from deep down in my being there suddenly rose to the surface a caution that came from my Scottish heritage. 'No, I don't like it, Muller,' I answered. 'What it really comes to is that you want to use my name and although it is not a very distinguished one, I don't care to sell it. Thank you very much for the offer, but if I buy, I'll only buy what I can manage to carry.'

Muller saw that my mind was made up, and although he was obviously disappointed with my answer, he bore me no grudge. We parted good friends and next day I bought on margin four thousand pounds worth of Paraguayan railway shares. It was more money than I possessed, but I would sell them as soon as they rose.

With O'Malley to back me my practice grew so rapidly that I was soon too busy with professional work to be able to give attention to the more rapid methods of making and losing money. One of the great advantages

of having a partner was that from time to time I could get away to some
estancia for a short holiday. There I would spend my time shooting or
lending a hand with the cattle and, as before, I found it a great relief to
escape for a while from the narrow streets of Buenos Aires and from the
equally narrow outlook of those that thronged them. After the sun had
gone down we would sit round a roaring fire on the pampas, eating
carne con cuero, each man lopping off from the roast his favourite cut. How
much better this meat roasted in its skin tasted than the expensive pro-
ducts of the Sportsman's Grill and what a pleasant contrast were the yarns,
told round the fire afterwards as we drank our *maté*, to the smoking-room
stories I had heard at the English Club. But these nights on the pampas
were a trifle unsettling, for although Selous was now playing a minor part
in the drama of my life he still made his voice heard. 'How ridiculous it
is to be in South America and yet to be content to have seen nothing of
that great continent except the Argentine and Paraguay.' When Theodore
Roosevelt, the ex-cowboy president of the United States, arrived in
Buenos Aires, on the eve of his journey in search of the source of the
River Negro, the explorer within me ran amuck and for two days my
whole professional career again hung in the balance. Would my offer to
accompany Roosevelt in the capacity of a Spanish-speaking doctor be
accepted or not? In the end the sturdy Teddy Bear — never have I seen a
man so like one — decided that no doctor to the expedition was necessary.
Our fate is settled by trifles; Roosevelt's decision allowed me to settle
down again in my consulting room, but it brought for him disaster.
When he eventually reached civilization again he was stricken with an
illness from which his health never fully recovered.

Success is a powerful hypnotic, and with increasing prosperity I ceased
to ask myself uncomfortable and seemingly futile questions and became
contented with my lot. I had many friends by now and in a certain
quinta on the outskirts of Buenos Aires there was someone who was
rapidly becoming more than a friend. It was in this carefully tended garden of the Trevor family that I was generally to be found, whenever my
practice allowed me a few hours respite from work, talking to Margaret
or telling her stories. We would sit for hours on the part of the garden
wall that was shaded by a big eucalyptus tree, peopling the world to which
we had retired with the creatures of our fancy. *The Wind in the Willows*
was her favourite book and she was thrilled when I told her that I knew

the author of it and had once visited with him the quiet backwater of the Thames in which the baby otter was found nestling at the feet of Pan. 'Oh, do write to him and ask him to write another book about the big animals that live in forests and jungles,' she had petitioned me. I had done what was asked of me and Kenneth Graham had answered that whilst he knew about the friendly little woods of England and their inhabitants, he was utterly unfamiliar with jungles and great forests. Why, therefore, did not I myself, who had visited such places, write this story for my friend? His suggestion lay for years germinating within me and it eventually found expression in my first book, *The Log of the Ark*, written in collaboration with my friend Geoffrey Boumphrey. Knight-Paton remembered his vow that he would not marry until he was forty, but the knights of old wore tokens of their ladies in their helms, and there was no reason why he should not do the same. Some day when Margaret had grown up — she was now barely sixteen — I would marry her, but for the present I must keep the secret to myself however difficult it might be. Sometimes, when off my guard, I would approach too near it and then, suddenly taking fright, I would beat a hasty retreat into the imaginary world in which she and I met and played. It would be easier for me if I could let her know that there was a secret even although she were not yet permitted to share it. In my consulting room was a golden and turquoise box which I had bought from a Tibetan woman on the borders of Sikkim. I removed from it the paper Tibetan prayer it contained and wrote at the end of it, in Hebrew characters, a reference to the twentieth verse of the twenty-ninth chapter of Genesis. 'And Jacob served seven years for Rachel; and they seemed unto him but a few days for the love he had for her.' Then I gave the amulet with its prayer and its new cipher to Margaret and told her that some day, but not now, I would help her to read it. Romantic and sentimental, yes, but adolescent love is generally of this nature, and mature as I was in years and in worldly experience, with regard to love and the life of the emotions I was still adolescent.

A comforting glow had now been cast over my life in Buenos Aires, but this new light was as dependent for its continuance on favourable conditions as the transient hues of a rainbow are dependent on the light of the sun. Two events soon occurred which disturbed my peace of mind, the first connected with my partnership with O'Malley. Nobody could have been a more loyal colleague than O'Malley had shown himself to be, but his behaviour was often so erratic as to disturb me. Could it be attributed simply to his impulsive and emotional nature, or was there some other explanation of it which I had not yet been able to discover? O'Malley was so often absent now from his consulting room that more and more of his work devolved on me. Perhaps this was merely the result of fatigue and ill-health, for it was obvious that he was far from well. He suffered terribly from insomnia and because of this he had to retire frequently to the Cordova Hills for a rest. But there was that queer experience in his yacht also to be accounted for, that time when I had taken over the tiller to allow him to retire to the cabin for sleep. A *pampero* had suddenly whipped the waters of the river into demoniac fury and, not knowing what to do, I had called to him for help. Why had he failed to answer my summons and left me alone to struggle with the storm? More by good luck than by judgment I had managed to save the boat from shipwreck and when at last I was able to leave the tiller and to go below I had found him fast asleep. Was it only exhaustion, or was it something else? A doubt entered my mind, so shabby that I feared to name it.

Things grew worse and O'Malley was so often ill that I could no longer count on his help when I had a case in need of a physician's care. 'I'll be back on Tuesday, or Wednesday at latest,' he would say. 'Would you mind looking after my patients?'

'Of course not, but what's the matter?'

'Oh, it's that damned neuralgia again, and I can't get any sleep. A few days' rest will soon put me right. Thank you for carrying on.'

But the rest never seemed to have the desired effect, and when I called at his house to make inquiries, I could never get any satisfactory news of him. O'Malley was the type of man who collects round himself a band of admiring women, and chief amongst these was Miss Bellamy, his devoted housekeeper and secretary. She guarded him so carefully that when he was resting nobody was ever allowed to disturb him.

'How is the doctor to-day?' I would ask when she opened the door. 'A little better,' she would answer, 'but I don't want you to see him at present. I've just managed to get him off to sleep.'

That was all I could ever extract from the woman who ministered to O'Malley's needs as devotedly as any mother looks after a weakly child. She was indeed such a zealous protector that nobody, and not even his greatest friends, could get near him. The day came when I refused to be shut out any longer. 'I'm sorry,' I said, 'but I must insist on seeing him,' and pushing my way past the outraged Miss Bellamy I made for the doctor's room. He was lying on the bed, and the heavy curtains shut out all the light so that it was impossible to see whether he was awake or asleep. I drew them and a shaft of sunshine fell on a face as pale as that of a dead man. This was clearly no ordinary sleep, and when I lifted the eyelids and looked at the pupils, I noted that they were tiny. Then I pulled down the bedclothes and saw a number of tell-tale marks, the pricks made by a hypodermic needle. At the same time I became aware that Miss Bellamy was standing on the other side of the bed.

'Please go away,' she said, struggling with her tears, 'and please, please say nothing about it.'

'I'm fond of him too,' I said, 'and his secret is safe with me. But you and I have got to help him to break this off.'

'He has struggled so hard and so bravely with it,' she said. 'Sometimes he manages to reduce it and then because he has some worrying case and he can't sleep, up it goes again. But what can we do?'

'You'll have to take him off to the hills for an indefinite period, and I'll do my best to look after his practice. He must take at least two months off. Let me know when he has had his sleep out and is able to talk to me and I'll come round and make all the necessary arrangements.' And in this way my partnership with O'Malley ended as quietly and as unobtrusively as it had begun, but not my friendship. Drugs have the power to injure the body, to cloud the judgment and to make of an honest man a liar, but no amount of morphia could destroy the charm of John O'Malley. I could no longer remain in partnership with a man whose professional judgment was not to be trusted, but I could be his friend.

I was fated to suffer other losses than that of a delightful partner and of a half share in a lucrative practice. A few weeks after O'Malley had gone to the hills I ran across Muller as he was crossing the Plaza Constitucion and as soon as he caught sight of me his face assumed a worried expression. 'I wanted to see you,' he said, catching at the lapel of my coat. 'It never rains but it pours.'

'Making too much money?' I asked, in an effort to be jocular.

'No. I'm afraid it's serious. It's this Farquhar business. Haven't you heard the news? They've gone bust.'

'So Paraguayans aren't rising?'

'No, they've fallen fifteen points. Better cut your losses and get out.'

'That means good-bye to all my savings, at least a thousand pounds. Thank heaven I bought no more.'

I had lost all my money, but by cabling to my stockbrokers in England to sell immediately I could at least avoid running into debt, and I did so. But the Farquhar Syndicate was not the only group of irresponsible gamblers that was getting into trouble. In Europe, Germany had been speculating in ships and armaments, France was beginning to look with concern across her poorly-protected frontiers and, worse still, a small group of conspirators was hatching a plot in a room in Sarajevo. When the irresponsibility and foolishness of the individual are multiplied so that they begin to act on the scale of those great aggregates of individuals known as nations, the madness of war is not very far distant. Premonitory rumbles were now reaching South America from Europe, rumbles which suddenly ended in an explosion.

It was the fourth of August, 1914, and on that historic evening I happened to be in my sister's box at the opera listening to the music of *Il Pagliacci*. The curtain had come down on the clown's domestic tragedy, and we had opened the door of the box to pass into the foyer. Then, seemingly from nowhere came the rumour that England, after two days of hesitation, had aligned herself with France and had declared war on Germany. War, yes, war and England! Deep within me there was a stirring and a hurrying and I caught a glimpse of a knightly figure in full armour, clambering on to his war horse. 'A cause, a noble cause, a crusade!' he was shouting. 'At last I have a mission worth living for and, if necessary, worth dying for.' Knight-Paton was no sluggard when war was afoot, and at the first sound of tramping armies he was firmly seated on his charger. A buzz of excited conversation came from the little group of Britishers which had collected in the foyer. 'Thank heaven we've come in,' exclaimed a middle-aged Englishman who lived six months of every year in Buenos Aires in order to escape paying income tax. 'I was beginning to be ashamed of my nationality. Well, we shall all have to do our bit for the old country.'

'I will, of course, offer my services immediately,' I heard myself saying, outwardly calm, but inwardly standing up on stirrups and pointing a sword to the skies.

'Surely you can't leave your practice,' said my brother-in-law.

'This alters everything. Practice or no practice, I'm going. It would be quite impossible for me to stay out here with all that happening at home, even if I wanted to, which I don't.' My words contained more meaning than I realized at the time. Knight-Paton had found a cause, a service to be rendered to mankind, spurs to be earned. This indeed altered everything, for nothing could hold back a zealous knight prepared for war. The other figures retired rapidly into the wings of my private theatre leaving to Knight-Paton the centre of the stage. Selous had no use for wars since they offered no means of confining danger within reasonable limits, but his protests passed unheard. The Personage saw that everything was against his grand scheme for becoming rich and taking up a political career, but he realized also that his best chance of its being saved lay in the possibility that the war would be over before I had time to take part in it. In the meantime he must lie low.

On the following day I dispatched a cable to Sir Anthony Bowlby, offering my services in any capacity in which they might be needed. All that remained to be done, until I received his answer, was to make arrangements for what was likely to be a very prolonged absence from work. Patients still thronged my waiting room and amongst them Prussian officers who were obviously preparing to find their way back to their country by one of the circuitous routes still left open to them by the Allied fleets. I also operated on an Austrian lady the morning after our declaration of war against her country and inoculated volunteers for the British forces against typhoid. By now hundreds of my countrymen had already left for England and I waited with growing impatience for the reply to my cable. At last it came. NOT REQUIRED AT THE MOMENT WILL CABLE WHEN WANTED BOWLBY Knight-Paton not required! The thing was preposterous. I would wire immediately to somebody else. Another telegram was dispatched. The Personage took comfort in the postponement of my departure.

A month later two letters arrived by the same post, the first from my stockbrokers informing me that, with the full approval of my brother in London, they had gone against my instructions to sell Paraguayan Centrals as they were expecting them to rise; the second was to the effect that the Duchess of Westminster had established a hospital in northern France and that I was invited to join its surgical staff. The bad news in the one letter was cancelled by the good news in the other; a great deal of money had been lost, but Knight-Paton's honour had been retrieved. It was true that Paraguayans were now worth practically nothing and that I was at least a thousand pounds in debt, but what did that matter to a crusader on horseback? A knight's fortune or misfortune lay in the battlefield, and not in the haunts of the merchants, and if the bankers wanted their gold, well, let them follow Knight-Paton to the wars.

A week later I removed my name from the column of advertisements in the *Standard*, left my house and my belongings in the care of a friend, paid a number of farewell calls and sailed for Europe. Little did I guess that for four long years Knight-Paton would control my movements, carrying me, a helpless prisoner on his war-horse, into Armageddon and exposing me to unnecessary danger for no purpose other than that of displaying his own courage. Selous had jeopardized my career, but Knight-Paton was made of sterner stuff; he was prepared if necessary to kill me, provided my end was glorious and there were enough spectators present to make the sacrifice worth while.

CHAPTER XV

KNIGHT-PATON GOES CRUSADING

How immature I was compared with those young men who offered their services to their country in somewhat similar circumstances a quarter of a century later. In *The Last Enemy* Richard Hilary explains that he got so tired 'of the sop about our "island-fortress" and "the knights of the air"' that he determined to write his book 'in the hope that the next generation might realize that whilst stupid, we were not that stupid, that we could realize only too well that all this had been seen in the last war, but that in spite of that and not because of it, we still thought this one worth fighting'. It was not so with me; I accepted without question all the fashionable catchwords of the day and I was simple enough to believe that I was about to take part in 'a war to end war'.

When we sailed from Buenos Aires the two German raiders, the *Emden* and the *Kronprinz*, were still prowling in the Southern Atlantic and to evade them we maintained a zigzag course by day and at night steamed without lights. These tactics were for us the first faint intimations that we were at war. When we reached England we found surprisingly little outward change, for the fashionable slogan at that moment happened to be 'business as usual'. I stayed in London only long enough to obtain a Red Cross permit to proceed to France. It was at Boulogne that the war seemed actually to begin. The car that had been sent from Le Touquet to meet me was stopped outside the town in order that our papers might be examined by the French military authorities. The light of a lantern flashed on fixed bayonets and on grave Gallic faces bending over the driver's permit to proceed. Knight-Paton was thrilled by this first dramatic tableau of war etched against the background of night, but as we drove on and drew near to Le Touquet the war seemed again to recede. The road now passed through pine woods and, slowing down, the car eventually stopped in front of a pleasant villa in which I was told that the hospital staff was housed. Across the way lay the great casino, now converted into a hospital, but its windows were so bright with light and outwardly it appeared so gay that I had difficulty in believing that it was crowded with wounded men.

What a friendly place was Le Touquet, and how far it seemed from anything as brutal as war. But for the periodic arrival of trainloads of wounded and the dramatic influx of men into the brilliantly-lit foyer of the casino, limping through the entrance hall or carried past it crumpled up on stretchers, I could have imagined myself to be on holiday. Not that there was any absence of work, for when a convoy arrived I was sometimes in the operating theatre for eight hours at a stretch, groping in wounds for ragged lumps of metal, washing out the earth of the trenches, removing, amputating, sewing and splinting. Yet, somehow, it was not like work, so friendly, so pleasant and so willing did everybody seem to one who had been in exile and had missed his country far more than he had thought.

Through the wards moved a very active and efficient Duchess, tall, beautiful, teasing and humorous. Small wonder that all men were subdued by her charm and that the hospital could always obtain of the military authorities whatever favours it required. And one of the favours Knight-Paton soon needed was a military permit to visit the front. We had plenty of cars and amongst others the Duchess's fine Mercedes, and when work happened to be slack we would make excursions to the forward area where the great sausage balloons were strung along the line and the deep-throated guns were growling. For visitors, the war provided a very pleasant and interesting outing. At Cassel an excellent lunch could be obtained, with choice wines and liqueur brandy and coffee served afterwards in the garden behind the inn. There, filled with good food and smoking cheap cigars, we could sit at our ease and watch the Great War in progress. Yes, life was worth living, for we were doing our bit, and doing it in comfort, but somehow — why are you hesitating, Knight-Paton? And what are you saying? 'C'est magnifique, mais ce n'est pas la guerre!' Nonsense, you're doing useful work in your right place, amongst friends, and in one of the best-run hospitals in France. What more can you want? Remember that you are a doctor and not a combatant officer, a doctor who happens to be needed most here at the base.

It was at Le Touquet that for the first time in my life I became exercised on the subject of dress, for I had come to France under the auspices of the Red Cross, and its regulations compelled me to wear a brassard and a large emblem in my cap. Marked with these insignia I could not possibly be mistaken for an officer, and Knight-Paton was highly indignant that such should be the case. 'I will not wear these abominations and be branded a civilian wherever I go', he said, and he slipped the unsightly emblem into his pocket. But officialdom was too obtuse to understand his aesthetic sensitiveness, and after my third arrest in the streets of Boulogne a document arrived at the hospital which curtly stated that Mr. Kenneth Walker was to be deported from France for being improperly dressed. What made his conduct more serious in the eyes of the authorities was that the insignia of the Red Cross were actually found in the offender's pocket. Wires were pulled, colonels were entertained to dinner, and in a short time Temporary-Captain K. M. Walker's name made a hurried appearance in the *Gazette*. The hated brassard and hat-badge could now be flung on to the rubbish heap and Knight-Paton had the thrill of purchasing spurs, a Sam Browne belt, six stars and a swagger cane. I became an officer and a gentleman and regained my peace of mind.

At the approach of autumn the machinery of war slowed down and the output of its chief product, maimed and nerve-shattered men, began to fall. For the time being there was little for me to do, and with the approval of General Sir Anthony Bowlby, now consulting surgeon to the forces, I returned for a fleeting visit to Buenos Aires in order to settle up my affairs. Again I found myself on a darkened ship, but this time not as volunteer but as a hero returning from the wars. Buenos Aires received me as such. I attended a reception at the Phoenix Hotel, delivered a lecture on war impressions, wrote articles in the *Standard*, gave inside information on the probable duration of hostilities, and was back again in France before the General Staff had had time to complete its plans for the offensive which, this time, was to win the war. Back in France, but not at Le Touquet, for Knight-Paton had carried his disappointment at being compelled to work at the base to Bowlby, and as the result of this great man's influence I had been posted to a château actually only five miles distant from the line. I was to be in sole charge of an operating centre to be organized in the village of Habarcq, in the neighbourhood of Arras. To that château were soon brought men who were so badly wounded that they would have died had they been forced to make the longer journey to the casualty clearing stations, and there, with the help of the personnel of a field ambulance and of two army sisters, I did my best to piece together the maimed and the dying.

For a year I worked in the château of Habarcq, depressed when cases went wrong, elated when they recovered, conscience-stricken when I was guilty of an error of judgment, and missing badly the comfort that comes from sharing the responsibility of a vital decision with some surgical colleague. It was difficult and exacting work and I became more and more disheartened by this lonely struggle against heavy odds. It was my job and I told myself that I must carry on with it however disappointing were my results. But there could be no doubt that Knight-Paton was again becoming restless. He knew intimately the line around Arras, and had established a close liaison with the ordnance repair workshop, which was quartered in the château yard, a liaison which led to his making frequent visits forward to lend a hand in examining, not damaged men, but damaged guns. It was the war itself and not the wreckage wrought by war that thrilled him, and the more he thought of it the more convinced he became that at all costs he must get even nearer to it and study it more closely.

Knight-Paton was dissatisfied and was beginning to dream about giving up surgery and becoming a regimental M.O., but there could be no doubt that permanent residence in one sector of the front had many advantages. Not only did I know the neighbourhood as few people knew it, but I was in touch with all the local news, with many staff officers and with the movements of troops. This brought me a number of privileges. For example, a squadron of the R.F.C. was quartered in the neighbourhood, and through my friendship with its C.O. I managed eventually to extract from him the promise of a joy-ride over the line. Joy-rides were forbidden, but if anything untoward happened, it could always be said that I was taking part in a test of some new aeroplane. It was an exciting moment when one morning I climbed into the open cockpit of an F.E. Fighter and when, in preparation for taking off, the pilot began to taxi across the aerodrome into the wind. I had never been in the air before, and I was not only going for a flight, but for a flight over the great battle of the Somme. Leaving behind us the familiar landmarks of Arras, we headed south and, craning my head over the edge of the cockpit, I could see that we were approaching the region of the Somme. Directly below me were the Gommecourt trenches which we had attacked at such a deadly cost a few days before. A few minutes later we reached country so ravaged by war and pockmarked with shell-holes that it seemed that no life could survive there. I felt that I was looking through a telescope at the desolate scenery of the moon rather than at the familiar earth. Yet in that desert of mud below me, thousands of human beings, too small to be seen, were engaged, at that very moment, in a life-and-death struggle. As though to assure me that such was the case, from time to time a tiny puff of smoke would appear on its surface and then leisurely drift away, leaving behind it yet another wound on the face of the earth. How could I have imagined that this war was a noble conflict between the forces of good and evil, when now that I viewed it in perspective I could see so plainly that it was only a struggle between rival bands of ants? An evil wind had swept through the formicaries of the world leaving behind it chaos and destruction. I recalled that day in Africa when I had transferred ants from one ant-hill to another and how the warriors had rushed out from the invaded citadel to strangle the strangers, although to me they seemed to be of the same breed. Some force, as impersonal and as irresistible as that which had produced the response of those African ants, was now at work on the world below me and, as a result of its action, thousands of men were struggling and dying in the mud of the Somme battlefield.

The plane climbed upwards into keener air and purer sunshine, and as it drew away further from the tortured earth I became conscious of an increasing sense of freedom and detachment. My mind seemed to be gliding through space, a small island of consciousness, as detached from all else as was the plane in which my body was riding. Here in this serene air ordinary thoughts had become so heavy that they dropped towards the earth, whilst emotions, buoyant and free, speeded upwards to the sun. What a clumsy tool was the intellect on which I had set such store, and how incapable it was of expressing what, in this exalted state, I now felt. I was happy without knowing why, I was wise with a wisdom for which I could find no words, and again I had that feeling that, if I could only struggle a little further upwards, I would be able to touch the fringe of a great mystery. Never before had I known such a sense of freedom; for the time being I had shaken off the shackles which bound me to the earth and, what was of far greater importance, to myself. Then, as the plane circled over Peronne, it started to bank so steeply that I was dragged back again into the small cockpit in which I was sitting and forced to maintain my position by clinging to the machine-gun projecting over my head. My pilot had spied a tiny hostile plane coming in our direction and, distrustful of my fumbling gunnery, had decided that it was wiser to turn and to wing it for home. In another fifteen minutes we landed on the airfield on the outskirts of Arras and the earth swallowed me up again. Everything had become as it had been before and I even forgot that it was possible to live in a freer air and to be a disembodied spirit moving over the face of the earth.

On his return to Habarcq, Knight-Paton gave a thrilling eye-witness account of the battle of the Somme and, oblivious of what he had so recently felt, he again became enthusiastic about the great adventure in which he and some hundred thousands of his countrymen were engaged, the war to end war. And on the scale and the level of the ant-heap his enthusiasm was not misplaced, for war brings to the surface not only the baser, but the finer qualities of men. Nobody could be in better company than in the company I enjoyed. I had seen so much that was noble and lovable in those amongst whom I was living and working that my chief fear was that an order might come which would remove me from them and send me back to a casualty clearing station or, worse still, to the base. But I was fortunate. Colonel Johnson, D.D.M.S., of the Nth Corps, was devoid of brain and, like many stupid people, he was as brave and as stubborn as a buffalo. He happened to approve of a surgeon who appeared to be at least as keen on the war as he was on his surgery, and when I expressed to him my fear of being sent back to the rear, he listened to me with sympathy. 'I quite agree with you, my boy', he said, 'those fellows at the base are shirkers, and if you tell me what you want, I'll put up any proposal you like to make to army headquarters.' I suggested to him that it would be a good plan to create for me an entirely new medical post, namely, that of consulting surgeon to the front area. There were consultants further back, so why not pay more attention to the work of the regimental officers and give them their own consultant, a consultant to the trenches. The D.D.M.S. liked the idea of having yet another officer attached to his staff, and thanks to his powerful support, I eventually became what I wanted to be, a surgical specialist to the whole of the Nth Corps front area. My post allowed me to go where I liked, to do what I liked and to be free of all interference, provided that I kept on the right side of the D.D.M.S. Nothing could have suited me better.

Towards the end of the winter whispers went abroad of a great spring offensive that would bring this costly war to a satisfactory end. Staff officers, seated in high-powered limousines, drove up in great numbers to Arras, and the D.D.M.S., who had little liking for office work, spent most of the day at his desk at Corps Headquarters drawing up reports and looking at maps. Something big was brewing and, long after he had known all about it, the surgical specialist to the Nth Corps was told in strict confidence by the D.D.M.S. that preparations were being made for a great offensive on the Arras front. 'I'm going up there to look at some of the big caves', he said one day, 'and I would like you to come along with me.' I was his blue-eyed boy, and this old gentleman with the white hair and blue eyes, who had killed more young regimental doctors than any other senior member of the medical service by insisting that they should go over the top with the second wave of attack, thought very highly of me, or perhaps not of me but of Knight-Paton. I hurried along beside him to the eastern outskirts of Arras beneath which lay the great caverns from which the Spanish builders of the city had once quarried chalk and that afternoon we wandered together in the bowels of the earth and visualized the caves as dressing stations thronged with wounded. There in that capacious alcove, situated only a few hundred yards distant from the front line, the corps surgical specialist would set up his operating table and deal with those cases which were urgently in need of attention. Never before in any war had a surgeon been able to carry on his work so near to a battle. In a few hours everything had been settled, and that night Knight-Paton dreamt of his glorious position in the van of the great offensive and of the decoration he would wear when it had been won. No one had ever before performed a major operation a few yards from where a man had fallen, and seldom had a medical officer been given a better opportunity of distinguishing himself. For many weeks I had been scheming to take part in the battle of Arras and now everything had been settled in conformity with my plans.

With the coming of spring a growing activity was to be seen on the Arras front. Long lines of troops trudged along the dusty roads leading to that area, new gun emplacements were dug, ammunition dumps reached a prodigious size, and a web of light Decaville railways was laid down by engineers talking with a strong Canadian accent. As an advanced operating centre was no longer needed at Habarcq, the château reverted to its former state and became a field ambulance headquarters.

Freed for the time being from all surgical duties, I lived with a field ambulance of the third division quartered in Arras. That city was rather like the red and white armlet worn by the D.D.M.S., in that it was a place of sharply defined contrasts, the flaming red of war and the serene white of peace. Although it was under continuous shell and machine-gun fire, a few stout-hearted civilians still carried on their trade there. I could buy tubes of Chinese white for my paintbox — I had taken to sketching as a hobby — at the chemist's shop on the right-hand side of the main street, and after my shopping I could lie back, in great comfort, in a hot bath at the Officers' Club, and could watch through the open window a dog-fight, high above the city, between German and English planes. But the enemy had noted the activity behind this part of the line and was not slow in making himself unpleasant. Life above ground became more and more precarious, and we took therefore to our cellars and dugouts. Having much time on our hands, these subterranean dwellings became the centres of a great deal of social activity. Friends were continually dropping in at the École Normale, at which I now lived, to suggest some outing. 'Come over', they would say, 'to where the fifty-second division is quartered and we'll take tea off old Morrison, the M.O. of the Rifle Brigade.' 'Right', I would answer, and would collect my tin hat and gas-mask. Then in all probability there would follow a short conference as to how we should go. 'The best way', one of us would suggest, 'is down Iceland Street and then by the main sewer along to Manchester. There's a nasty bit in the Rue St. Michel where we come above ground, but after that it's all right as far as the crater. Morrison's cellar is near the sugar refinery.' So arm-in-arm we would saunter down the attractive sewer-system of Arras, the different branches of which had been labelled by the sappers, Oxford Street, Piccadilly, Pall Mall and Manchester. I can remember well one such expedition to Blangy, a south-western suburb of Arras and a place I had known before Arras had begun to receive so much attention. I had visited it when a Scottish battalion under the command of Winston Churchill had been holding that part of the line. There was a tree there under which this gallant commander could often be seen sitting and reading Shakespeare, oblivious of the 'whizz-bangs' which the Germans were sending over. Stopping for a moment to read a notice that informed us that, in future, the sewers were for use of the staff only and that nonentities like ourselves must walk above ground, we eventually reached Manchester, and from thence made our way to Blangy. There on that particular afternoon we found Morrison overwhelmed with work, and with five bad stretcher cases on the floor, still awaiting his attention. 'That naval gun is becoming nasty', I said, as I started to lend him a hand. 'Not a bit of it', he answered, 'it was that poor blasted fool of a Tommy in the corner.' Morrison nodded in the direction of a stretcher completely covered by a blanket. 'He found a dud shell and thought it would be useful as a weight to keep his blankets round his feet, so he slept with it as a bedfellow for a week — did you ever hear anything like it? And then, hitching his blankets this morning, the damned thing fell to the ground and went off. Sorry I can't give you fellows tea, or even a drink.' We assured him that it didn't matter and that we would go on to the aid post in the Rue des Portiers. 'You'll find Patrick Brown there,' said Morrison.

So Patrick Brown, the Caius wit, the man who *had* to be funny, was here in Arras. Once already in France I had run across him still struggling, with the help of alcohol, to maintain his name as a wit. I wondered what he would do when alcohol began to fail him. Would he fall back on drugs? He could never afford now to stop being funny. But perhaps, in our different ways, we were all like Patrick Brown, pedlars of some personal stock-in-trade, publicity agents for some line in individual cleverness or virtue, dressers of our personality's shop-windows. What indeed was I doing myself in this shell-scourged city except keeping up a reputation for fire-eating amongst my friends and play-acting to the gallery? Such uncomfortable thoughts as these passed through my mind as I helped Morrison to bandage and splint a shattered arm, and when I had finished I said: 'I don't think I want to meet Brown, for I'm rather tired of his funny stories. Let's go back.' The others readily agreed.

During the return journey I talked very little, and my companions, putting down my lack of spirits to that common ailment, war-weariness, suggested dropping in at the field ambulance in the Hôpital St. Jean for a drink. But I wanted to be alone and, making an excuse about having to go through my equipment in the cave, I returned to my billet. My thoughts were still on Patrick Brown, the man who had to be funny, the slave of his own wit. It seemed ridiculous to put it like that, and yet it was a true description of him. He was like a man who had lightheartedly taken a drug and, having acquired the habit, was compelled to go on taking it in increasing quantities until in the end it killed him. And it was not only the drug addicts and the professional wits who found it impossible to give up their vocations. Look at the fellows who gained a reputation for doing stunts in aeroplanes, and who had to go on doing them until in the end they 'stunted' themselves out of life. Still, one mustn't push that idea too far or it would land one into accepting psychological determinism, the doctrine that we were so many clockwork toys that went on doing their particular tricks over and over again until the machinery finally ran down; the idea that, like the physical world outside us, our actions were determined by iron laws, that we were unable to move off the line of rails along which we were fated to run, even by a fraction of an inch. A mechanical world, inhabited by robots! What a dreadful view of life that was. I must put such unhealthy ideas out of my head. Besides, it simply wasn't true that I had come to Arras merely for self-display and not for the good of others. Because I knew the regimental M.O.s personally, and to some extent shared their life, they were prepared to listen to me and to accept new ideas about the early treatment of wounds which they would have turned down immediately had these ideas reached them from the back area. Look at the way they had taken to the Thomas' splint after I had shown them that it could be put on over the clothes and almost as quickly as that inefficient old splint the Long Liston. I was doing good work here and I wasn't just indulging in exhibitionism. It was ridiculous to think that I was like Patrick, a slave of my own personality Such ideas were thoroughly unhealthy.

A few days later the artillery bombardment worked up to a crescendo and all unnecessary expeditions above ground ceased. The last time I had walked along Imperial Street a whizz-bang had landed in the trench five yards ahead of me, but fortunately just beyond a bend, and even Knight-Paton realized that sightseeing was an insufficient excuse for getting killed. On April 8th, on the eve of the great attack, we were lined up in the cave in front of the D.D.M.S. to listen to a stirring message from our divisional commander. It ended with the words: 'May the traditions of the Third Division be upheld, and may the name of the Division become famous in the annals of our country and be a terror to the enemy.' King Harry had perhaps done better on St. Crispin's Eve, but Deverel, the divisional commander, was not much of a poet, and he must have sweated blood to produce even this. Still, what did his speech really matter, for message or no message, we were on the eve of one of the biggest battles in history and it was thrilling to think that one was in it.

That night our ambulance sat down thirteen to mess and those amongst us who were stretcher-bearer officers were under orders to move forward into battle position within a few hours. Those new inventions, of which we had heard rumours, the tanks, were rolling forward above our heads and around us in Arras some thirty thousand men were waiting, as we were, for zero hour. For miles to the north and the south the same sort of thing was happening that was happening here in this cave. As with us, young officers would be dropping in everywhere to say good-bye before taking up battle positions, final orders were arriving, last letters were being written home. I shook hands with many of my old friends and wished them good luck and, for the first time since I had landed in France, I felt thankful that I was a doctor and not a combatant officer. This contentment with my lot was intensified by a short 'breather' above in Iceland Street, where the machine-gun bullets were now making a noise like swarms of angry bees and the roar of the artillery was so shattering that I was glad to return to the quiet of the caves.

Two hours later the wounded began to arrive and, working in my alcove with my two excellent orderlies, Latham and Forbes, I was soon too busy to dream about the 'greatest battle in history'. There was a steady flow of stretchers along the passages and soon the usual crop of wild rumours reached us. Not only had Tilloy, the Harp and Vimy Ridge been taken, but our troops were now well beyond the 'Brown Line'. It was even said that the cavalry were moving up and that the enemy was now on the run. I paid a hurried visit to the world above, breathed in great chestfuls of fresh air, enjoyed a few minutes of sunshine and then returned to my burrow. The divisional wounded had now been cleared and, as the second attack had not yet been launched, there would probably be a respite from work.

About tea-time there occurred in the cave an unforeseen incident. An eight-inch, armour-piercing shell landed in the Rue des Temples, above our head, and a few minutes later some hundredweights of chalk fell with a crash on to the floor, almost burying beneath it two strange companions brought together by the hazards of war, Wilson, a lieutenant of the 'Blues', and a young wounded German. Hardly had we rescued them when more than a ton of ceiling crashed to the very spot on which their stretchers had previously been lying. The shell which had caused this downfall had at the same time cut the main coming into Arras and water now began to trickle from the cracks spreading in the ceiling. Everyone looked up at the water suspiciously and, as the trickle swelled to a downpour, and as more chalk came to the ground, suspicion changed to anxiety. I went to the mess to see what was happening there, and, as I entered it, a large piece of chalk fell on the table and smashed all the glasses. I returned to where I had come from to find that someone had given an order and that sappers were hurrying about everywhere carrying pit-props, which they were wedging between the roof and the floor. As well might one have attempted to have held up a falling railway bridge with clothes-poles, and it was obvious that disaster was imminent. We were forty feet below the level of the surface of the earth; would we ever see it again? A deep rumble came from the direction of the outlet into Iceland Street as a hundred tons of solid chalk tumbled to the ground. One exit was blocked, and how long would it be before the other was cut off? I recalled the final act in *Samson and Delilah*, which I had seen, three years ago, in the Buenos Aires Opera House, and wondered whether a similar spectacle was to be enacted in this cave. But it was ridiculous to think of that; disasters of that sort happened at the time the Bible was written, but not nowadays, and not to me and my friends. Then word was passed round: 'Evacuate the wounded and then abandon the cave.' Hurriedly and in good order, the cave was emptied and, after marshalling his army of two men, Knight-Paton escaped with them to the world above. It was a dramatic moment, but he intended that it should be made more dramatic still. Having ordered his two men to continue their retreat, he returned alone to the cave of roars and rumbles, seized a handful of tubes of catgut and needles off the surgical table in the operating alcove, and then made again for the outer air. The objects that he had salvaged were worth in money some three or four shillings, but as signs of heroism their value to him was beyond the price of rubies. Was it unfortunate that there was nobody present to witness the deed but himself or did this make it all the more disinterested and heroic?

We stumbled along in the outer darkness, and sleet battered against our steel helmets as we groped our way in the direction of our new billets, the girls' school further along the street. Every now and then the whole scene was lit up by gun flashes. All the roads in Arras were full of jammed traffic, of patient horses and of shouting men, illuminated by falling shells and answering gunfire. What infernal luck that the weather should have broken just as our offensive seemed to be going so well. I was tired, and snuggling into the rough army blankets laid out in the cellar of that high school for girls, I was soon sound asleep.

During the next few days Arras resembled a patient convalescing from a sharp attack of pneumonia. The crisis had been passed and the invalid was now beginning to take notice of her surroundings, to think of the future and to be interested in all the things that, during her illness, had been laid on one side. Tricolours were hung from windows and groups of civilians were to be seen digging in derelict gardens for buried valuables, or wandering disconsolately among the ruins of their homes. Dead horses and other victims of the bombardment were dragged into shell-holes and buried, and streets that had been almost deserted for years now rumbled with traffic. Yes, Arras was convalescing, but symptoms of the old trouble still persisted in the shape of that cursed naval gun which still dedicated itself to the work of annoyance. But gun or no gun, I was supremely happy. For a year now I had been living amongst the best of comrades, sharing their hardships and their pleasures and convincing myself — in spite of those doubts that had troubled me high over the Somme battlefield — that I was taking part in a glorious adventure. How rich I was in friends and what splendid times we had together, playing polo mounted on the clumsy ambulance horses and riding down partridges in the devastated land behind the trenches. My contentment was increased by the sharpness of the contrast between my present life and my former life in Buenos Aires, and I realized now how unhappy I had been in the years before the war. At night I would often dream that I was back in my old consulting room about to restart my work. This dream was always accompanied by a feeling of deep despair. Then, just as I was on the point of sitting down at my desk to take up my life again at the point at which it had been broken off, I would be awakened by a shell whinnying overhead, followed by a crash and the clatter of falling bricks. 'Thank heaven the war is still on and that I'm not back in Buenos Aires', I would murmur to myself, and then, turning over in bed, I would go contentedly to sleep.

The battalions that had borne the brunt of the recent attack were to be marched back to rest and, on the eve of their departure, a farewell tattoo was held in the main square of Arras. Many of the battalions were Scottish and their massed bands played the stirring music of the Highlands. Thirty pipers and forty drummers marched backwards and forwards with kilts and sporrans swaying to the wild lament of the hills. This was no descriptive movement in a concert hall to which we were listening, but a dirge which was being played for those who had actually fallen in battle. Here were to be heard pipes in their right setting and, standing there in the great square at Arras, I felt that for the first time I really understood the music of my country. Every nerve in my body tingled to the sad song of the pibroch. Its magic swept me along with it and converted me suddenly into a clansman, whirling a claymore round his head and leaping down the hillside, to repel the advance of the invader. I would do something magnificent; I would charge a machine-gun emplacement single-handed, hurl myself at the strongly-entrenched enemy, make a ring of light around me with my claymore, and then, shouting 'Scotland for ever!', I would gloriously fall. The music suddenly stopped, and at the word of command, the massed bands turned to the left and marched down the road in the direction of Duissan. For a few moments I stood there dazed. What an astonishing effect the music had had on me, almost as though I had been hypnotized. Five minutes ago I had wanted to hurl myself to death just because the air had been thrown into vibrations by a number of bagpipes. If the right note is struck a glass will vibrate so violently that it is liable to fall in pieces. Was a man as helpless in the presence of the right stimulus as a tumbler? It would almost seem that this was the case. Scotland's music was as powerful as its whisky and it was small wonder that the old Scottish chieftains kept their pipers near them so that, at the right moment, their followers might be flung into vibrations of such warlike fury that they would gladly rush to their deaths. Our modern chiefs at Whitehall, living in a more civilized age, were achieving a similar result by means of skilful propaganda, and what was propaganda but the application of the right emotional stimulus? It was ignominious to think that we were so responsive to the appropriate manipulation that we could be made to do almost anything that was required of us. A clever person was able to play on us in the same way that a skilled performer played on a musical instrument. Hamlet had said something about that. I had learnt the play at school and could recall his words: 'Why look you now, how unworthy a thing you make of me.

You would play upon me; you would seem to know my stops; you would pluck out the heart of my mystery; you would sound me from the lowest note to the top of my compass.' No. I would not think any more along these lines, for they were leading me back to the idea of psychological determinism, the idea that had so troubled me on the day I had heard that Patrick Brown was in Hammond's dressing-station. With so many alternative philosophies to choose from it was ridiculous to adopt what was clearly a philosophy of despair. I was a man who did what he wanted to do. Yes, but what decided what I wanted to do? Damn it, I was moving in that old direction again.

News came later that the Third Division, the division to which I was so proud to belong, was about to be withdrawn from the Third Army front and to be sent off to the Ypres salient. This meant that I would have to say good-bye to all my friends. A few days before the division moved, Snoddy, Mann and I went for our last ride together. It was one of those clear summer days about which poets have so much to say, with birds overhead, bees on the wing, the air heavy with the scent of flowers and nature decked in her best. We had made a compact not to talk of war, and we spoke instead of our friends at home, of hunting in Ireland, of what we wanted to do when all this was over and of how nice it would be to live in the country and to hunt twice a week. At the edge of a wood we dismounted, tied our horses' bridles to a low branch and then lay down on our backs in the sunshine. The soft ground was spread with a delicate carpet of velvety grass, while overhead in the spacious canopy of the sky some bird was singing, so high up that we could not make out its form. The sweet scent of earth rose from the ground and, as we lay there, some primitive energy seemed to be flowing from the great mother of us all into the bodies of her children. I remembered the Greek story of the giant who from time to time renewed his strength by lying full length on Mother Earth, and I understood now what this legend meant. Energy came to us from the earth and if we lived too long away from her, abandoning her and breathing only the confined air of cities, we became weakened in body and mind. Gratefully we drank in the beauty around us and were contented to lie there relaxed and silent. Basking in sunshine is a full-time occupation, and talking seemed to be unnecessary. Our mounts cropped the short grass behind our heads so that we could hear their contented munching and the occasional champing of bits. Snoddy's old charger, 'The Slug', was the first of the party to speak. Raising his head, he looked round and gave vent to a contented whinny.

'Good old Slug,' said Snoddy, getting up and loosening the curb-chain. 'You're having a day off like your master and you're making the most of it, aren't you? Lord, why can't this go on always?'

'Because we shall never sheath the sword until — what was it that old blighter Asquith said about his sword?' asked Mann, without moving his head from the soft mound on which it was resting.

'I can't remember,' I answered, 'but I think it was something about "until the wrong has been righted and the oppressed have been freed".'

'Well, we're more than oppressed,' said Snoddy, 'why can't we get away from this damned conflict and lead a decent life somewhere else? I'm fed to the teeth with all this murdering and frightfulness. Did you hear about my quiet luncheon party the other day? Everything went swimmingly until a shell removed the next room just as we were sampling some port I had scrounged from a cellar in the Rue Centrale. How can a fellow enjoy a few moments of blessed peace with that sort of reminder of what's going on?'

We murmured our sympathy.

'And when we'd settled down again there was another interruption,' continued Snoddy.

'Another crump?'

'No, an old French woman dashed into the room without even knocking and tore down all the Kirschner girls that I'd pinned up for decoration. She drew crosses on the wall with a piece of chalk instead and then disappeared again into the bowels of the earth.'

'Who was she?'

'Haven't a notion, but I expect it was her house.'

Snoddy lay silent for a moment and then suddenly exploded. 'I wish to hell I could get a nice cushy job at the base. If I did you wouldn't see me for the dust I'd raise getting there.'

'There isn't even standing room for people like us at Boulogne,' said Mann, 'though why our surgical friend here doesn't take a decent job and live in comfort is more than I can tell. There's nothing to stop *him*.'

'Well, why the blazes doesn't he?' asked Snoddy, throwing a small pellet of earth at me so as to ensure an answer.

'Perhaps he's looking for a decoration,' suggested Mann, 'and hasn't yet learned that they're not to be found up here.'

'Maybe you're right,' I answered. It would be difficult to give any explanation to Mann and this one seemed as good a one as any other.

'Then get back to Boulogne as quickly as you can,' replied Snoddy. 'You're like a man fishing upstream when all the salmon are being netted at the mouth of the river. You'll never land anything up here.'

We lay on the ground, each with his own thoughts, and then Snoddy got up and came over to squat beside me. We were friends and although we never discussed the links that drew us together, we knew that they were strong ones. Perhaps, if I'd been asked, I would have talked of Snoddy's freshness, of his amusing Irish candour and of the attractiveness of his youth, whilst he, on his part, might have spoken of the value of friendship with an older man who had seen so much more of the world than he had and yet who always met him on an equal footing. But how can one talk in cold intellectual terms of that which draws two people together? The alchemy of the emotions cannot be expressed in any chemical formula. Snoddy and I were fond of each other, and that was enough.

'Tell me, old idiot,' he said, lowering his voice so that Mann could not hear, 'why don't you get out of all this mess and go and do your proper job at the base?'

I could not be insincere with Snoddy but would have to find some explanation that bore some resemblance to the truth. But what was the truth? Did I know it myself?

'We are frightfully complicated creatures, Snoddy,' I began at last, 'and the more one sees of oneself the more complicated one seems to become. I find that I am not just one person, but a crowd of them, all of them wanting different things and moving in different directions.'

'And one of them won't move in the direction of Boulogne?'

'Yes, there's one fellow who wants to be terribly brave. And in the name of goodness, why?' I asked, raising myself on my elbow and speaking more loudly. 'We all know that this war is a madness and that there's no such thing as a war to end war and that the world cannot be made safe for democracy and, for that matter, for anything else. So why should I do it?'

'You seem to be getting as disillusioned as the rest of us,' interrupted

Mann who had overheard my last words about the war. 'Didn't you tell me once that it was a crusade against tyranny?'

'Heaven knows what I told you.'

'Then what is the war if it isn't what you thought it was?' persisted Mann.

'A bickering among ants, anything you like,' I answered impatiently.

'Or an amusing game for ex-cavalry officers who are too old to play polo, and fancy themselves as divisional commanders,' suggested Mann. 'But anyhow it's no good talking about it. Let's go home.'

We rose, pulled up our horses' noses from the sweet-smelling grass, mounted and rode slowly back to Arras. Mann had a new charger and, wanting to try its paces, he went off at a canter, but Snoddy and I rode home side by side.

'Why can't you take a firm grip on the neck of that fellow and make him do a right-about-turn?'

I lifted up my reins and looked at Snoddy puzzled.

'No, not the horse,' he laughed, 'but the fellow you were talking about.'

I let the reins fall again from my hands. 'It may seem a funny thing to say,' I answered, 'but I don't think that I have much control over him. Somebody at home once told me to try to get to know myself, and one of the things that I have discovered is that I'm much more like a passenger in this voyage through life than like a captain. I don't agree with that fellow Henley.'

'Then I should stop being so introspective,' said Snoddy, 'it doesn't sound healthy. Come on, the Slug's liver is out of order and I want to give him a good gallop.'

The two horses bounded over the soft turf, flinging up great chunks of earth behind them. Soon we had overtaken Mann and, breaking off abruptly into a walk, we continued the rest of the way home together.

CHAPTER XVI

IS ONE RESPONSIBLE?

THE fact that the Third Division had moved out of the area and that my patron the D.D.M.S. had been got rid of by the method the army used when saddled with an unpopular officer, namely promotion, rendered my position extremely precarious. At any moment an officious clerk sitting in some office might point out to his superior officer that Captain Walker was apparently unposted and that if a surgical specialist were needed at a C.C.S. his services would be available. If I were to retain my unscheduled post of consultant to the front area I must justify it by means of some new line of research. Advocacy of the Thomas splint in the early treatment of fractured femurs was no longer a satisfactory excuse for all the regimental M.O.s now recognized its value. Preaching that old gospel to the already converted would not serve my purpose. There were two new ideas worth considering, namely, the study of the onset of wound shock and an examination of the possibility of protecting certain vital areas of the body by means of some form of light armour. I decided to take up both of these researches as soon as I had finished my temporary job as regimental M.O. of the West Yorks. Before the Third Division had left I had volunteered to act as regimental M.O. to this battalion until a new one arrived from the base. It was good to be with a battalion again and Colonel Smythe was one of the best C.O.s that I had ever met. If those in higher positions had been as efficient as he was the war would not have dragged on so long, but unfortunately men as efficient and enterprising as the colonel were seldom promoted. The West Yorks had very few wounded, in spite of the fact that the enemy plastered our trenches so heavily with trench mortars by day that working parties had to be out every night to repair the damage. One evening a private, accompanied by a tall sergeant of the solid, unimaginative, courageous and seasoned soldier type, was carried into my aid post shivering and shouting.

'Where's he wounded?' I asked.

'He's not wounded at all,' answered the sergeant, 'only scared. He was working with my party in the sap in front of Fish Trench and they suddenly began dropping some of them "pine-apples" round about us. Before you could say "knife" he had lost his head and was running down the trench yelling about his wife and saying he was going home, and all that sort of nonsense.' The sergeant looked at the pale, undersized man on the stretcher with a good-natured grin and then shrugged his shoulders. 'We couldn't quieten him, so we roped him to a stretcher and brought him down to you, sir.'

'It's only a question of time and how much a man can stand, isn't it, sergeant?' I said. 'We all reach our breaking-point eventually.'

'Yes, but that doesn't apply to him, sir. He's only just joined us and hasn't seen anything yet.'

'Well, leave him here with me and I'll talk to him and see what I can do about it.'

The sergeant saluted, started to leave and then turned and spoke to me in a lower voice. 'The colonel sent his compliments and would you let battalion headquarters have a medical report.' He then put his hand to his mouth and whispered: 'It's a question of disciplinary measures being taken, or of his being sent back to a hospital.' Having said this he left, and I knelt down at the side of the stretcher and looked at the pale trembling form that lay on it. My patient was staring vacantly at the ceiling through dilated pupils and his lips were moving unceasingly.

'What is it?' I asked. 'What's the matter with you?'

'No, no. I can't stand it no more. Please don't make me, please don't, sir. I'd rather do anything than go back again into that hell. Really, sir, I can't stand it. I swear to God I can't.'

Was he responsible for deserting his post? Would it have been a physical impossibility for him to have stayed where his duty lay or had he deliberately disobeyed orders? Should he be given the rest for which he was clamouring, or was he to be sent back again into what he had called 'that hell' and what for him was undoubtedly a hell? These were the questions to which I had to find an answer, and like a blind figure of Justice, but a figure of Justice without any scales, I knelt on the ground beside his stretcher. Was he responsible for his actions, this little pale clerk of a man, swept by a cruel fate out of some quiet office into the trenches of Lagnicourt? He was sensitive, too, for I noted his hands and his face and the tell-tale twitching of the corners of his mouth. A man like that had not been fashioned for this brutal work of killing, and what to that fine burly sergeant was only 'some pine-apples dropping about' was for him a veritable man-made inferno. Yes, but was he responsible for deserting his post? Could he have withstood the effect of those heavy percussions on his sensitive nerve-endings, and was it physiologically feasible that by some supreme act of will he 'might have inhibited the sudden mobilization of his body for flight? Did the body govern the will or did the will, if properly exerted, govern the body? Could he, being the person he was, have acted otherwise than he had done? According to the colonel, this was a medical question to be decided by doctors, but was it not rather a problem that for centuries had defeated the best philosophers. Was I myself indeed responsible for anything I did, or in this universe was everything predetermined, even the verdict I was about to give? How strange that I of all people should have been called upon to produce an answer, I, who only a few weeks ago was speaking of my doubts to Snoddy. Black Hawk would, of course, have said that a man who is a man was capable of bearing anything, and Knight-Paton would have scorned my patient as a poltroon and a cur who had betrayed a noble cause. But it was I and not these actors within me who must find an answer to this question, the 'I' in me that could stand aside and think and act. Or was there no such person?

The clock in my dugout ticked loudly, the man turned slowly on his stretcher and from behind me came the noise of footsteps. I looked round and I saw that it was the colonel who had entered my dugout.

'I happened to be passing by and I thought that I would save you the trouble of sending me a report. What do you make of him?' he said, looking sternly at the stretcher. I waited and then at last the answer came, but as though it had been given by another person to whose voice I happened to be listening.

'In my opinion he's not responsible.'

'Well, it's a medical question,' said the colonel simply, 'and you doctors ought to know. But tell me, what makes you say this?'

I bent over the stretcher and raised the man's upper lip with a finger. 'His mouth is in a shocking condition and with all that septic absorption going on you might almost look upon him as being drugged. And a drugged person is like a somnambulist, irresponsible for his actions.'

'All right. If that's what you think we'll have him evacuated as sick.

But, of course, you know —' He took me by the arm and led me towards the stairs — 'we have to be severe with these fellows. If I were to send a man away just because he was scared I might lose half of my battalion in a few months. And I would be held responsible for it, wouldn't I?'

'I suppose you would,' I answered. 'It's a bloody business.'

'You're right,' he said, then nodded cheerfully and climbed the stairs leading to the trench. I sat for a long time by the stretcher and thought, and then, noting that the morphia I had given my patient had taken effect, I went out and made arrangements for his evacuation.

Three weeks later the new M.O. for the West Yorks arrived, bringing with him orders for me. I was to proceed forthwith to Grévillers to attend a meeting at which the subject of wound shock was to be discussed. It was obvious to me that Gray, the consultant to the Third Army, had been responsible for calling this meeting, and I was glad to go. He and I had often discussed together the factors that caused some men to collapse completely on receiving a trifling wound, whilst others remained in good physical condition even though they were suffering from a shattered limb. It was pleasant to be going back for a spell and the discussion was bound to be interesting. How lucky I was to be able to retire for a time from the front whenever my nerves began to feel the strain of living there. As I clattered away from the waggon-line on my horse I turned round in the saddle from time to time to take a last look at all the landmarks I now knew so well; there in the distance was the ruined factory chimney on which the artillery took a line, there was the sunken road, and there on the right were the trenches occupied by the battalion on our flank. At this very moment they were being plastered and I could even see one of those damned plum-puddings sailing through the air. I hoped that the wretched K.O.Y.L.I.s, who were in that part of the line, would succeed in dodging it.

Next day I reached the large army hut in which those attending the meeting were assembling and Colonel Gray, who had noted my arrival, came up immediately to shake hands with me. 'Congratulations,' he said, 'on the splendid work you're doing forward. That method of using the Thomas splint has undoubtedly saved thousands of lives, and we now want you to help us with this business of shock. It's a big thing we are tackling and Army H.Q. is behind us.'

The meeting proved a great success, a number of motions were passed, a 'shock committee' elected and a scheme for the study of physical collapse outlined. I was to be in charge of the investigations in the Third Army forward area, and was to be given a laboratory at some C.C.S. which I could use as my base. Otherwise I was free to go wherever I liked, to be my own master and to attach myself for rations to any unit I cared to join. The job seemed to be in every way as good as my previous one and I left the meeting in high spirits. I was again immune from all orders and could follow my own fancies provided I could manage to call them 'shock investigations'. For this I needed badly wounded men, caught at the very moment of wounding, so that the earliest signs of shock might be studied. I would measure the fall in their blood pressure, take samples of blood, estimate the haemoglobin, count the corpuscles and observe shock phenomena with the cold, detached eye of the scientist. Where would I be able to get hold of wounded men immediately after they were hit? Clearly it would be ridiculous to parade the warmest parts of the line, looking for trouble, and even the melodramatic hero within me saw that this was impracticable. A much better plan was to get wind of the raids, now being carried out every week on some sector or other of the Third Army front, and be the first person to greet the raiders on their return. I would start by getting in touch with brigade headquarters.

The brigadiers were unexpectedly helpful. 'Certainly we'll do what we can to assist you. Major Thorpe, make a note that Captain Walker is to be informed of all raids on our sector. We must, of course, disguise the message. How shall we put it?'

'Invite me to a tea-party and give me a map reading. I'll know what that means.'

'All right, a tea-party,' answered the brigadier, smiling. 'Anything else?'

'It would be a help if I could have some idea of the size of the raid. Say only a few cups, or quite a number are needed.'

So from time to time I received wires from some brigade headquarters inviting me to tea. After collecting my shock-kit I would set off for some part of the line to return next day tired and dirty, but with my field message-book filled with entries that to me seemed of the greatest importance. Sometimes when I reached the appointed place, it was only to find that the raid had been cancelled; the wind had veered a few points to the east and thereby spoilt the chances of a good smoke-screen, the Bangalore torpedo had failed to explode under the enemy's wire, the divisional commander had changed his mind, or the enemy had noted our preparations and was obviously on the alert. On other occasions conditions remained favourable and, like a privileged spectator sitting in the stalls, I watched one of these miniature assaults. First, the raiding party, with faces blackened and hearts cheered by rum, would assemble in the dugouts of the front line to be addressed by their officers, now wearing Tommies' uniforms but with revolvers hanging from halyards round their necks. All buttons and badges had been cut off and pockets emptied of papers, so that if anyone was captured no unnecessary information would be given to the enemy. Then, having heard the plan of campaign, the party would sally forth and wait on the firestep, the officers' eyes glued to their synchronized watches. 'Ten seconds, nine, eight, seven, six, five, four, three, two, one — zero hour.' Over the sandbags they went and at the same moment our barrage came down on the enemy's support trenches with the precision of a machine. Damn, those Verey lights from the enemy front line went up too soon, and the rockets sailing into the air from the support trenches were too prompt. They must have been expecting this, and here comes their reply. Pretty bloody. Then I would hurry back to the aid post and thank my stars that I was not out there in no-man's land but here in a dugout.

'How long have they been gone?' I would ask my companion, the regimental M.O.

'Ten minutes.'

We would wait in silence, our thoughts out in front with that 'Nigger Minstrel' party, fathered by the divisional commander and mothered by rum. How strange life was, with all that happening out there, and my mother at home getting into a stew because Ellen, the prim housemaid, had failed to turn out the drawing-room properly last Tuesday. Had human existence any meaning or was all life on the earth what the scientists believed it to be, the chance appearance of a sort of fungus on the satellite of a third-rate star! 'Listen, there is something happening outside. Yes, they're coming back.' We would hasten out of the dugout to find that the raid had been a great success and not too costly. But one of the officers was lying on the bottom of the trench with his arm smashed to pulp. 'Quick, a stretcher, and bring him to the aid-post.'

We're back again and the dugout is so full that there's scarcely room to move. First, that badly wounded boy; cut away his tunic and bandage his shattered arm to his chest so as to steady the grating fragments. He looks shocked but how can I take his blood pressure and play about with instruments with him in such pain? I'm damned if I will. Let him have morphia and get him back as quickly as possible to the C.C.S. where they can deal with him properly.

How grand those men were, and how much their thoughts were for others. They showed sympathy and understanding even for their wounded prisoners. I can recall one night when after I had seen to our own men I started to examine a muscular young German with a gaping wound in the buttock. 'Here, hold his leg,' I called to a cockney raider, who was hovering round the stretcher like an inquisitive sparrow. 'He's got a nasty flesh wound here from something or other,' I said.

'Bayonet, sir,' chirped the sparrow, 'right through the fundament.' He spoke as one with knowledge. 'How do you know?' I said, as I painted the skin with iodine. 'Here, help me lift him up while I get this bandage under him.' Together we raised that fine young German, heaved him on to his side and placed a folded blanket under his head to act as pillow. 'Take care he does not topple back while I see to this other fellow.'

The sparrow's eyes twinkled. 'I'll look after him all right. Now then, Jerry, you lie quiet. We're going to send you back to Blighty and in a couple of weeks you'll be as right as rain.'

My work was over, no more stretchers were arriving, and the wounded were nearly all evacuated. The last to leave the dugout was the fine young German, with his faithful sparrow in attendance. I called the cockney back just as he reached the door. 'Here, you needn't bother about him any more. Why are you so interested in him?'

A look of pride came into his face. 'Well, you see, sir, he's my first bag, and ain't he a beauty?' The sparrow took stock of his fine prisoner, his eyes travelling lovingly over his six feet of brawn and muscle. Small wonder that the staff had issued strict orders against fraternization, for left to themselves and freed from the influence of newspapers, military authorities and politicians these men were so goodnatured that they would soon have made friends of their enemies.

Blood transfusion was the most valuable of all the methods that we were studying for the combating of shock, and more especially of shock combined with haemorrhage. How wonderful it was to see colour creeping back into blanched lips and grey faces as blood was returned into empty veins, and what a boon it would be if the forward area could benefit from a method that was doing so much good further back. It was up to us to discover some way of bringing this about. Robertson, who had come to us from Yale, eventually supplied the key to this problem. He showed us how, by filtering off the blood corpuscles and adding to them a solution of dextrose, the corpuscles could be kept fresh on ice for from two to three weeks. My laboratory at the C.C.S. now became a factory for the preservation of blood, and in quiet periods we drew off pints of the precious fluid and stored them in a cold dugout. When an 'invitation to tea' arrived now, I no longer attended the party as an empty-handed guest but brought with me a precious gift. With my large ice-box, containing two flagons of blood, slung round my neck I looked like one of those old-fashioned players of hurdy-gurdys who once paraded the streets of London carrying with them their boxes of music. All that was really needed to complete the resemblance was a shivering monkey dressed in a scarlet coat and cap. I lacked the monkey but Duke, the large wolf-hound that had attached himself to my person, often came with me to act as a substitute. However doubtful might be the benefit of this treatment — and we no longer believe that corpuscles alone are very efficient — the effect of the magic box on the men's morale could not be doubted. 'There's a bloke up here in the trenches who revives you from the dead by pumping blood into you', was excellent news to those who were about to go over the top. So the organ-grinder became quite a well-known figure on the Third Army Front. It was only the higher ranks of the Army Medical Service that were inclined to be critical. 'Blood transfusion in the trenches', some of the old regular colonels would say, 'who ever heard of such nonsense! That sort of thing is all very well at the base, but not up here.'

Whilst transfusion was an important measure in the treatment of shock, it was not the only one. Something also had to be done to lessen the hardships of the journey back to the C.C.S. and, in order to study the effect of different methods of transport, I spent some weeks accompanying the wounded on long rides in ambulances or on Decaville railways, counting pulses, measuring blood pressures, estimating haemoglobin, and making copious notes in Army Book 153. Next, motor experts were interviewed and new shock absorbers and spring racks tested out. Various methods of supplying heat to chilled and exhausted men were improvised, and the value of hot-air chambers, charcoal stoves and electric blankets compared. Reports from time to time found their way back through the usual channels to come finally to roost in one of G.H.Q.'s capacious pigeon holes.

At intervals the shock committee met to discuss results. It was obvious that much had been achieved but also obvious that much remained to be done. The amount of blood available was insufficient for our needs and this being the case the committee decided to tap new sources. I travelled from Arras to London, a journey that in wartime took two days and entailed a vast amount of jolting. In spite of this the emulsion of corpuscles arrived in good condition. If it could travel in one direction, it could also travel in the other, and the Medical Research Council hastily summoned a committee of distinguished physiologists to consider the matter. At it I met Fletcher, Starling, Bayliss, Bainbridge and Dale, and I asked them whether they could help us. 'We'll do anything you like,' they answered, 'and if you want a sort of Cross and Blackwell in London for preserving blood, you shall have one. All that is needed is a little propaganda.' It was suggested that a pint of royal blood followed by donations from the Gaiety would prove to be such excellent propaganda that all the volunteers that were needed would present themselves. 'And, think,' I said, waxing enthusiastic, 'think of the thrill of the wounded officer who awakes from shock to discover that the blood of Gladys Cooper is coursing through his veins.' The theme was a rich one and we talked blood until late in the afternoon, Sir Walter Fletcher promising to ask the Air Ministry to fly fresh supplies straight out to France. By the time that the meeting broke up everything had been settled, and next day I started on my return journey delighted with the success of my mission.

Two afternoons later I was leaning out of the broken window of a battered first-class carriage wondering why the train had come to a stop five miles outside Arras. And what did that drumfire mean? Some of my disgruntled fellow-passengers were talking to a French railway-official on the line who was trying to make them understand that something unusual was happening on the Arras front and that the train could proceed no further. The 'something' turned out to be Ludendorf's great 1918 offensive which was destined to push the Allies back to within a few miles of Amiens and to all but lose the war for them. For the next few days rumours were plentiful; the Germans had advanced in the south to a depth of twenty miles; Gough's army had lost touch with the French; German cavalry had been seen in our rear and four German divisions had driven a wedge between us and the French. So far Arras held, but it was like the strained hinge of a door that has been forced too wide open. What would happen? Nobody really knew.

The weeks that followed were weeks of confusion, of retirement along roads crowded with broken units and lost detachments, roads hopelessly blocked by transport. Every day new orders were issued, to be counter-manded a few days later, and rumours were so plentiful and so contra-dictory that in the end we believed nothing. I was no longer 'shock' expert to the Third Army, but a medical tramp temporarily housed in a C.C.S. back in the neighbourhood of Doullens. All the refinements of medical treatment had been jettisoned, for the fate of the Allies was hang-ing in the balance. If Amiens were to fall, we should lose touch with the French and be pushed back to the Channel ports. To have bothered any longer about such superfluities as the treatment of wound shock would be as futile as to start to redecorate the cabins of a sinking ship. In the midst of all this confusion a messenger arrived at the C.C.S. to which I had attached myself, summoning me to Army Headquarters.

The D.M.S. looked grave when I entered his office. 'What I'm going to tell you,' he said, 'is highly confidential and on no account must you talk about it to anybody, even to your superior officers.' It was an excel-lent beginning and Knight-Paton felt immensely important at being thus taken into the army's confidence. The D.M.S. continued: 'The staff has decided that Doullens must be held at all cost and arrangements are being made to garrison it with a picked body of troops. At this very moment the citadel is being strengthened and being stored with supplies for them. Should the enemy advance further the whole town and its surrounding country will be flooded and the garrison will be left to hold out as long as possible. It is obvious that some sort of provision must be made for the treatment of badly wounded men. Now, Captain Walker, you have always shown a liking for adventure —' here the general smiled — 'and it is for this reason that I have decided to offer you the job of remaining with the garrison. Of course, you appreciate that it will be impossible to get away.' My knees gave slightly, but I pulled them stiff. Damn it, I didn't want to be killed or to be made a prisoner, but here was the army taking me into its confidence and counting on my gallantry. What could one do?

'Certainly, sir,' answered a voice that I had some difficulty in recognizing as my own. 'Thank you very much for the honour you have done me.'

'By the way, have you got a brassard? In such circumstances it will be wiser to wear one.'

'I'll get one from the quartermaster.'

'Well, good-bye, and good luck. You will receive fuller orders later.' It was a special occasion and the D.M.S. rose and grasped my hand. I saluted and left his presence.

Did I really appreciate the honour of being called upon to become a prisoner or perhaps to die for my country? A thousand times, no. It was flattering to realize that the army had picked me for this job but what upset Knight-Paton was the fact that the news was highly confidential and that nobody except the D.M.S. would know about his mission. What was the good of being a hero in private? It was no fun at all. That afternoon I obtained from the quartermaster a brassard, for the Red Cross armlet that had once caused me such shame and distress at Boulogne had now become the symbol of my honourable mission. I fingered it as it lay in my pocket and wondered whether I should post to England a special letter inscribed 'To be opened only on the news of my death.' That was what people did, didn't they? No, it would only upset the relative to whom I confided it and very likely to no purpose. After all, the line in front of us might not give, so that Doullens might not have to be defended desperately.

That afternoon I sat by myself on a small hillock on the outskirts of Doullens watching a line of men wriggling up a zigzag path that ended in a tunnel. Great stores of ammunition were being transported into that hole and deposited in caverns beneath the citadel. A lurid picture of the future formed in my mind. Between me and that rock there stretched a great sheet of water and immense guns were pouring an endless stream of shells across it into the doomed citadel, perhaps from this very spot on which I was sitting.

Desperate men fought on in the citadel, but fire was creeping down the passages and Knight-Paton, one of the few survivors, knew that the end had come. How utterly different and peaceful it all looked now, with this gentle breeze ruffling the poplars and turning their green into tremulous silver. I looked above my head at a pattern of birds in the sky, rooks making their way home at the close of the day to the rookery in that dark clump of elms over there. Must I give all this up for the sake of my country? No, that was a lie. If I were to die it would not be for my country, but for the sake of satisfying a senseless craving inside me for the heroic. At all costs, and however contrary it might be to my true nature, I was being forced to play the part of the hero. What was I doing at this very moment but posturing before myself, a man playing before a mirror, an actor overcome by his own mock-heroics. Yes, mock-heroics, for no germ of nobility lay in what I was proposing to do. I was as irresponsible for my actions as had that poor trembling clerk in the West Yorks aid-post been irresponsible for his. Was it only for the purpose of revealing that there was nothing real in me, nothing but posturing and pretence, in short to show me that I was a sham, that M. had told me to watch myself? I rose abruptly from my seat and returning to the C.C.S. I offered my services in the theatre in the hope that a few hours of hard work would direct my thoughts elsewhere. M. had been right. It was a painful thing to catch sight of oneself.

A week later news reached us that the military situation was improving and that the Australians had not only held their ground, but had even managed to advance a little. In a fortnight we learnt that Foch had been made generalissimo of the Allied Armies, and that the retreat was at an end. I had been let off and the armlet in my pocket would never have to be worn. Another piece of good news was that the Third Division had moved back again into the Third Army area so that I could now rejoin Snoddy and others of my old friends in the field ambulance. Then quite unexpectedly a telegram arrived ordering me to proceed to London forthwith. On arrival I was to report for instructions at the Ministry of Munitions. I said good-bye to my friends, and, annoyed by these absurd orders, I made my way to Boulogne.

What on earth had I to do with the Ministry of Munitions? I puzzled over this mysterious wire during the journey home and it was only when I had nearly reached London that I began to connect it with a memorandum I had sent in to G.H.Q., some six months previously, on the subject of chest wounds. While acting as a regimental M.O. I had been impressed by the number of men killed in the trenches by small fragments of grenade or mortar entering the front of the chest and ripping open the roots of the great blood vessels. These fragments had very little penetrating power and I had suggested that if a thin sheet of steel were to be slipped into a pocket in the back of the box respirator, when worn in the 'alert' position, many of these deaths could be avoided. It was quite possible that this strange order had something to do with that old memorandum of mine.

Next day I presented myself at the gloomy hotel in Northumberland Avenue in which the Ministry of Munitions was lodged and I was taken up immediately to the room of the Controller of Trench Warfare Supplies. To my surprise this official turned out to be my old friend Arthur Asquith. He had lost a leg in the Battle of Arras and was now attached to the Ministry.

'I'm glad you've come to join us,' he said. 'You see, I happened to come across your memo when I was going through the records in this office and I thought your suggestion sufficiently important to be shown to my chief Winston Churchill. He's keen on the idea of armour protection and he immediately gave instructions that you were to be brought home. Next year tanks are to be developed on a very big scale, and instead of having to march up to battle positions, men will be carried there in armoured cars. That being so a small addition to the weight of their equipment won't matter much. That's the reason you've been attached to us.'

'In what capacity?' I asked.

'As expert in armour to the forces. The French have one and so I believe have the Italians.'

'And what am I supposed to do?'

'Well, I imagine you'll carry out experiments on rifle ranges, test the protective value of different steels, or any other material you may think worth trying, and from time to time confer with your opposite numbers in France and Italy.' I looked at him doubtfully, but he continued speaking. 'Of course, it's machine-gun fire that is the chief obstacle to any advance, and Churchill is keen on finding some remedy for it.'

'It's quite impossible,' I said, after a pause. 'Nothing will protect a man against rifle or machine-gun fire except a weight of armour which is far too heavy for him to carry. You can protect stationary men in a trench but not mobile infantry advancing. All that I was proposing to do was to prevent small splinters from entering certain highly vulnerable parts of the body.'

'Well, you can start on that and tackle the bigger problem later.'

'Look here, Asquith,' I said, 'it took two years for the staff to accept the tin hat even though the French had adopted it long ago; you know the military mind well enough to realize that the war will be over before they have even begun to consider the protection of vital areas against splinters. Besides I am not the right person to carry out experiments on the resisting power of different types of steel and I shall be much more useful back with my old ambulance in France.'

Asquith saw that I had made up my mind and he promised that he would have me released at once. Two days later I returned to France. I reached the ambulance on the eve of Foch's great offensive, an offensive which, unlike so many of its predecessors, met with great success. Thousands of prisoners streamed back along the roads, villages in which we had been billeted before the great retreat were retaken and we advanced so rapidly that many people began to talk about the end of the war. But optimists had so often been proved to be wrong in the past that when the war actually did look like ending many of us remained incredulous. Progress now became so rapid that, for the first time in our experience, supplies from the rear had difficulty in reaching us. The sumptuous rations to which we had become accustomed in the old days of static warfare were no longer forthcoming and we sat in our ruined billets, grumbling at the lack of food and at the poor supply of blankets. Then, suddenly, and to the great majority of us unexpectedly, the end came. The Third Division had had orders to take up battle positions for the next offensive and its ambulances were moving up to establish battle dressing-stations and aid-posts when we met the 'Gloucesters' marching in the opposite direction. They were singing songs and shouted to us as we passed them that an armistice had been declared, that the offensive was cancelled and that the whole war was over. An hour later their news was officially confirmed.

I sat alone in a village schoolroom, feeling, as my old friend Hardwick had felt years ago, after he had qualified, that my mission in life was over. For four years the wheels of my being had been running along tracks that had now suddenly come to an end. For four years there had been no necessity to think about my future and now that I was forced to do so I had no idea what I was going to do. But fortunately the war for me was not yet quite over. News came that the Third Division would form part of the new Army of Occupation and two days later we started on a long march through Liége, Namur and the villages of Belgium, up to the German frontier. Then, as had happened to me before, the unexpected arrived in the form of a telegram, which informed me that I had been posted for duty at the Royal Herbert Hospital, Woolwich, and must return to England forthwith. There was no appeal against such an order and I was forced to bid a final farewell to my old field-ambulance and to watch it marching away without me towards the Rhine. I felt lonely and dejected as I turned in the opposite direction.

The war was over and I was now a doctor at Woolwich, a doctor who walked round the hospital in a 'Sam Browne' belt and a uniform, and who was generally in a bad humour. The old sense of comradeship had gone and breakfast with the medical staff at the Royal Herbert Hospital was as cheerless as a meal in a railway station. One morning, while at this meal, a fellow-officer, who was a regular, lowered his *Morning Post* and stared at me. 'Congratulations', he said briefly, and then hid his face again behind his paper. Congratulations? What did he mean? To Knight-Paton suddenly came the answer. At long last he had won his D.S.O., the white enamelled cross with its blue and crimson ribbon, the emblem of courage of which he had so often dreamed. I rose from my chair, went over to a table, seized a morning paper, fumbled for the right page, read through a long list of names and then put the paper down again. My name was not there. But that idiot had said 'Congratulations', and he must have had some reason for doing so. Taking up the paper again and opening it at another page, my name burnt into my eyes — I had been awarded the O.B.E.! It was a decoration which in those days was looked upon with great disfavour chiefly because of the wholesale manner of its awarding.

Knight-Paton was furious, for he knew that he had been recommended for the D.S.O. and that the Third Army commander had taken the trouble to ensure that the recommendation reached the War Office by shepherding it through G.H.Q. Yes, those wearers of red tabs and scarlet hatbands at the War Office had been clever. Having obtained for themselves their full complement of M.C.s and D.S.O.s they were now engaged in enhancing their value by contriving that in future such decorations should only be awarded for bravery on the field of battle. Well, he would have nothing to do with their paltry O.B.E.s. He would have a D.S.O. or an M.C. or — nothing at all. Knight-Paton was a crusader, a follower of noble causes, but it must be confessed that while serving these causes he served also himself. Self-effacement and the doing of good works in secret did not appeal to him. He was deeply insulted.

That morning a temporary captain attached to the staff of the Royal Herbert Hospital was absent without leave from duty and if he had been looked for he would have been found in the writing room of his club writing a letter to the Right Hon. Winston Churchill, now Minister for War. In it he stated that he had been awarded an O.B.E., that he had no use for it and that he would be ashamed even to be found dead in a ditch with it. Did the Right Honourable gentleman realize that this decoration was now a music-hall joke and that George Robey was appearing on the halls in O.B.E. trousers. He thanked the Minister of War for his good intentions, but asked only that his war services should be rewarded with one privilege, namely the privilege that his name should be removed forthwith from the lists of the Most Excellent Order of the British Empire. After posting this letter the angry knight left the front of the stage to nurse his grievances in the background. I returned to my duties at the Royal Herbert Hospital, Woolwich.

Two weeks later I was summoned to the C.O.'s office. He looked at a sheaf of papers lying on his desk, took up one and gazed at me through the thick lenses that made his eyes look like bottled specimens in the medical museum. 'You are to be at the headquarters of the Blank Command at twelve o'clock sharp. See that you are properly dressed.' Outwardly I clicked my heels and saluted like a good mechanized soldier, imparting a slight tremor to the hand as it reached the peak of the cap. Inwardly a cynical knight laughed at these professional warriors who fought the war with forms and rubber stamps, who had never heard a shot fired in anger and who were always 'properly dressed'. Now he was going to visit their great chief, General Blank of the Blank Command, the High Panjandrum of Office-boys. Outside the General's private room staff officers were coming and going, and amongst them I discovered my old friend Colonel Prinne, A.D.M.S., of the 15th Division. I greeted him as a white man greets another in a land of negroes.

'I've an appointment with the great one,' I said, inclining my head towards the closed door. 'But I don't know the reason for the honour.'

'The O.B.E.,' said the A.D.M.S., looking suddenly grave.

'Oh, of course, I refused it.' (What superiority a man who has refused a proffered honour can feel!)

'Yes, but it's what you said about it that has caused the trouble. I've been in to see him and have done what I can to help you, but I'm afraid you will find him very angry.'

I did. The door had opened and at the heels of a staff officer I entered the room. In front of me, at an absurdly small table, sat an absurdly crimson general. 'A Study in Scarlet' would have been a suitable title had some painter made him a subject for a portrait. No, not scarlet, for his face was between puce and crimson with an occasional brush-mark of blue where tiny webs of veins crept forward on to his nose. His hair and his moustache were white and he was looking at me severely through eyes of a soldierly colour, a cold, steel blue.

'Are you temporary captain K. M. Walker?'

(Surely, General, that emphasis on 'temporary' was unnecessary? It is obvious that I'm not a real soldier.)

'I have here a letter from the Army Council about you,' he continued, and then began to search amongst his papers. (The Army Council! Knight-Paton was getting into high places.) 'This is a very grave matter, very grave indeed. I will read the letter to you.' His face opened and then closed again upon an eyeglass, the rim of which pressed out a thin crescent of pallor on the puce of the cheek. Couched in the best official language, the letter informed Temporary Captain Walker that after much consideration (so that was how they spent their time), the Army Council had decided not to court-martial him but to inflict on him the severest reprimand. It stated also that the Army Council was pained and shocked — (did these old gentlemen really feel so acutely?) — that one of His Majesty's temporary officers could have used such language about an honour that His Majesty had seen fit to confer on him.

The scarlet face let the eyeglass fall and the white crescent on the cheek slowly changed back to puce. 'I don't know when I've had a more painful duty to perform, and I am deeply shocked that a temporary' — again the word was emphasized — 'officer could have so disgraced himself. My staff-colonel here is honoured to wear the O.B.E.' — a thin officer with only two mean rows of ribbons here made himself a little stiffer — 'and I myself, had I received it' — we all looked at the general's chest and noted that he was starting a fifth row — 'would have been proud to have worn it.'

He had finished, and a leaden silence descended on the room. When a great actor has delivered the speech that marks the climax of the play, when the lawn sleeves of the bishop, held over the heads of the congregation, have given the blessing, it is best to leave, for what follows will only be bathos. Standing in that room I felt that my presence there was superfluous, and that the general would also deem it to be superfluous. Bringing my heels together and saluting, I made a brief apology, for I had undoubtedly been in the wrong, and then, in the words of the drill book, retired in an orderly manner. The door closed on the 'study in scarlet' and looking at the ceiling of the office outside I saw, on its whitewash, complementary splashes of green, a sure sign of ocular fatigue. Well, we were all of us probably feeling a little bit tired and it was best to admit it. Not only was my name expunged from the Most Excellent Order of the British Empire, but it was also removed from the *Army List*. I was no longer a temporary officer or a temporary gentleman but only a civilian.

CHAPTER XVII

THE END AND THE BEGINNING

THERE are times when one has the feeling that an interval has been reached in the private drama of life and that the curtain has come down while the stage is being set for another act; the main theme of the play is to be continued, but the scenery and some of the actors will be different. This feeling grew strong in me as I travelled down to Cornwall to enjoy a brief holiday and to think over my plans. I would have to come to some decision as to my future alone, for I had not seen M. since I had said good-bye to him, on the eve of his sailing for Gallipoli. 'There will be a devil of a mess,' he had said to me just before we parted, 'when the old dugouts in charge of this outfit try their hand at landing us on the beaches.' And he had been right; the expedition had been a costly failure and, when Gallipoli was abandoned, M. had been sent to Mesopotamia. I was going down to Cornwall to reach a decision as to what I should do but, when one came to think about it, did one really ever decide anything? Was one not rather in the position of a man who watches a number of weights falling into the two pans of a balance, and who is unable to influence in any way the position in which that balance will finally come to rest? One side of it drops lower, then the other, the beam swings to and fro and then, quite suddenly, one end of the balance dips down and it is at rest. That was probably a good picture of what was likely to happen in Cornwall.

How lovely is England to one who has been in exile, even when the exile has been of his own contriving. I drank in her beauty as I lay prone on the cliff, following with my eyes the wide sweeps made by the gulls as they glided over the sea, and listening to their protests at my presence. Soon I would have to return to London to take up the thread of my life again, but for a whole week I could revel in what I had missed so badly without knowing it, the beauty of my native land. Of one thing only was I certain, namely, that in future nothing would induce me to abandon my profession; I was a doctor and I would remain a doctor. It was true that I had become one more or less by accident, but it seemed that everything was determined in this way and the accident that had made me a doctor was a very fortunate one. All that I had to settle therefore was what sort of a doctor I should be. The Medical Research Council had been pleased with my work on shock and Sir Walter Fletcher had held out to me the prospect of a grant for research, when funds were available for this. It looked therefore as though I would do better to sacrifice all that work I had done in B.A. and remain now in England. Then suddenly the balance began to dip in the opposite direction as the thought of a certain *quinta* on the outskirts of Buenos Aires pushed its way into the more conscious part of my mind. Margaret would have grown up by now and this being so there would be no longer any reason why I should not tell her — but what was there to tell her? Was I now, or had I ever been, really in love with her? Had I not rather fallen in love with the picture of myself as the patient lover, the faithful friend who was waiting for that distant day when he would be able to declare his true feelings? The Tibetan charm, the lama's prayer, the Hebrew characters I had added to it, all the mystery and the romance I had interwoven with that idea, was it not with these rather than with Margaret that I had been in love? Mock heroics instead of unostentatious courage, public acclaim as a substitute for innate worth, sentimentality in place of love — was there nothing that was genuine in me, nothing that was truly my own? Was I only a crowd of posturing actors or was there some small part of me I could trust? Yes, there had been moments in my life when I had found deep within me something of a different character, something that was more real. There was that moment at the gateway to the Taj when the spiritual world had suddenly become more real to me and had seemed nearer to me than the physical world in which I was moving. I recalled also that unaccustomed detachment I had known while flying over the Somme battlefield, that fleeting liberation from self and from all the petty compulsions and desires of self, that freedom which had allowed me to see what had previously been hidden from me. At such times the rushlight of life had burnt with an unaccustomed brightness and I had been filled with a new understanding. And I remembered other occasions in my life when I had caught glimpses of the spiritual behind the material and when 'the world with its loud trafficking' had retired into the distance and I had been able to see a little further into that 'void Deep' which encloses us. Those scattered moments, when I had been able to penetrate to some hidden sanctuary in myself which provided a wider vision of life and a deeper understanding of it, at least were real. Browning had described in 'Paracelsus' what I had felt at those times:

> There is an inmost centre in us all,
> Where Truth abides in fulness; and to know
> Rather consists in opening out a way
> Whence the imprisoned splendour may escape,
> Than in effecting entry for light,
> Supposed to be without.

And yet knowing this I had continued to be ruled by trivialities, by the urge to satisfy my own small wishes, by the desire to show that I was right, by the itch to gain the approval of others, and by the lure of the 'ignis fatuus' of worldly success. *Video meliora proboque, deteriora sequor.* How many people had murmured one edition or other of that old Latin tag and had then, with a sigh, continued to follow the second-rate. Perhaps they were right and it was best to accept oneself as one was and not to cherish the illusion that one could ever be anything else. No, that was only an excuse. If one wanted anything badly enough and were prepared to pay the necessary price, one could obtain almost anything, even the bringing about of some inner change.

The machinery of government moves slowly and when, on my return to London, I called again on Sir Walter Fletcher, he was still unable to tell me when funds would be available for the research I was hoping to do. It would depend on the Chancellor of the Exchequer, on the permanent officials of the Treasury and, since medical research came under that body, on the Privy Council, in short, on everybody except Sir Walter and my-self. Well, this was not altogether unusual. My departure to Buenos Aires had depended upon the behaviour of a stranger in a Turkish bath, and my return to London might well hang on the moods of the Chancellor of the Exchequer and on his attitude to medical research. But until he and the others had made up their minds I would have to go into medical practice.

Harley Street with its tall houses, its Adam fanlights and its Georgian solidity and restraint, had always attracted me, and I thought that it might be helpful to look up some of my old friends now practising in that street. As I walked down its immense length and looked at the shining doorplates, so many names winked at me that I seemed to be a fly crawling between the leaves of the medical directory. Mr. Claud Wills, Sir Winthrop Winslow, Mr. Diocletian Dinkle — what wonderful names these surgeons and physicians had. What did Mr. Diocletian Dinkle look like in the flesh? Perhaps the man with the grey hair and aristocratic face peering through the ground-floor window of number 47 was he. No, that was probably his butler. Diocletian sounded massive and portentous, but Dinkle relieved it, the two names suggesting a combination of well-balanced qualities. Yes, Mr. Diocletian Dinkle could be counted upon to give a sound opinion, well worth a three-guinea fee. Why had not my own parents displayed more imagination and foresight when they carried me to the font?

Harley Street practices cannot be bought but must be made, and there are three legitimate methods of making them — the hospital, social and literary. The first is the most orthodox. It entails the obtaining of as many honorary appointments to hospitals as possible in the expectation that students and practitioners will eventually recognize one's worth and will send one private patients. It is the long safe highway to success, demanding of the traveller stamina and perseverance, rather than initiative and courage. For the social method special endowments are required in the shape of personal charm, attractive manners and a good memory for names and faces. The men who travel by the social road must be seen in the right places and dressed in the correct clothes; they must be good fellows, approved of by medical practitioners' wives and popular with hostesses. It was only too clear to me that I was not properly equipped for this journey. I dressed abominably, displayed mental deficiency at bridge, forgot people's names immediately after being introduced to them and quickly tired of dining out. The third, or literary, method was more promising, for the standard of writing amongst doctors was not high and I had a facility for producing readable articles for the medical journals. I decided that a judicious blend of methods one and three was the best combination for me. I would start by applying for some sort of honorary appointment at St. Bartholomew's Hospital.

In emigrating to South America in search of forbidden joys I had offended my old hospital, but she now forgave me my naughtiness. It is true that the calf killed at the return of the prodigal was not a very fat one, but what did that matter so long as I was accepted as a member of the honorary staff. This new appointment at St. Bartholomew's justified my adding yet another plate to the brass-decorated doors of Harley Street. Whether I liked that street or not — and it happened to attract me — I was now compelled to practise in it. Kings have lost their healing touch, and the shrines of the saints are deserted, but sick men still require a man who is more than an ordinary doctor to cure them. Confidence in Harley Street is for them the modern substitute for the old faith in holy relics, in miraculous virgins and in the healing properties of the waters of Jordan and the Ganges.

My new life in London was an arduous one, but it had many compensations. It allowed me to enjoy many pleasures which, by emigrating, I had previously forfeited. I was able to satisfy an old ambition and to keep a hunter, at first in the Oakley country and then later, when I became more affluent, in that of the Whaddon Chase. There could have been no finer way of renewing my acquaintance with the beauties of rural England. The sight of her undulating fields stretching away into the distance, and of hounds running on a roaring scent, there just beyond that hedge, whimpering and giving tongue, their black, white and tan flashing in the sunlight, checking for a moment and then on again, the sight of all this pageantry of rustic England made me rise in my stirrups and shout for the very joy of living. What could any man want more than to be well-mounted and to feel beneath him that quick gathering in of strength at the take-off, that lift into the air, that first view of the field beyond, followed by the sudden jolt of landing and then, after a momentary pause for recovery, that surge forward at the gallop. Every thought and care was banished except the urge to be there, there where hounds were racing across the open. No, all thoughts were not always banished, for from time to time I would catch new variations of old questions. Why had I taken that post and rails when it could so easily have been avoided by a slight detour to the left? Because I enjoyed the thrill of jumping — no, because people were looking, and there was still someone within me who insisted on showing the world what a hard-bitten rider was sitting in the saddle.

Hunting was only one of the many pleasures I had missed during my exile in South America. There was also social London waiting to be explored, not just the rather shabby London I had known in those far-off student days, but the London of society and of literature and art. Lady

Cherry now assumed the part that the Señora Torres de Castex had played for me in Buenos Aires, and, for one brief season, I perspired on crowded stairways, danced where there was not even room to stand, made conversation to bored partners and was the guest of hostesses whose names I did not even know. But for me this proved to be an alien world, a world for which my equipment was utterly deficient, and I soon tired of appearing to be other than I was. After midnight my mask of inane amiability would slip from my face, my evening bow would become unmanageable and my shirt-front, bursting through the restraining confines of my waistcoat, would bulge forward in angry protest. No longer able to grin and gibber, I would seize my hat and coat from the cloakroom and I would escape outside into the friendly night, there to find solitude and quiet.

Mayfair had proved a failure and I decided to exchange Curzon Street and Grosvenor Square for Bloomsbury and Chelsea. Perhaps I would not prove to be such a misfit in the world of art and letters. Mrs. Curtis-Allen, the wife of the writer, replaced Lady Cherry and became my cicerone. She told me that I had an interesting face, but that I failed to make the most of it. Apparently it was a face that required the help of an eyeglass, with a broad black monocle ribbon, a face that must also be offset by a stock. These additions to my countenance having been made, I entered the salons of Bloomsbury and Chelsea, looking like a nineteenth-century actor. But my mentor had not deceived me, for in this new world to look interesting was obviously the right note to strike. The devil which haunted these regions was the devil of boredom, and men and women fought him with the fervour shown by the saints in their struggles with the lusts of the flesh. To keep him at bay the correct strategy was change and distraction. Men sprouted beards and shaved them off again, women played tricks with their hair and their eyebrows, changed their sleeping partners, their politics and their views on art, and finally, in desperation, took to alcohol or to psycho-analysis. But in the end the devil of *ennui* generally got them.

It was the absence of any direction in the lives of all these clever people which discomforted me most. What did they want out of life and how did they propose to get it? These intellectuals talked very brilliantly about new movements in art and literature, about novel methods of government, improved social conditions and world progress, but when

I had left their presence and examined at my leisure all they had said, I could find nothing there but words. But what did I want myself, and would I be content with it if I obtained it? Did I want only worldly success? By success in Harley Street was meant bigger and faster cars, higher fees, more patients, less leisure, moving through life at greater and greater speed, like the cars that I rode in, and finally, if I was lucky and got to know the right people and was tactful, a knighthood. Was this what I really wanted? Here was a much more vital question and I did not feel sure that I knew the answer to it. There were so many different sides of one that wanted different things. Some time I must talk to M. about all this.

When I rang him up a few days later I was told that he had lately been demobilized, but that he had gone off to the continent. No exact date could be given for his return, but as a great many letters had arrived for him and as he had not asked for them to be forwarded, it was to be presumed that he did not intend to be away for very long. I added one more letter to the correspondence awaiting him, in which I asked him to get in touch with me as soon as he returned.

A month later I had an invitation to dine with him in Hampstead. Two years had passed since we last met and so much had happened to us both during that time that it was late in the evening before we had exchanged our news and that the subject which was the chief reason for my meeting him was broached. I introduced it by describing my adventures in Bloomsbury. 'I know some of the people you're talking about,' he said, 'and their chief trouble is that all their cleverness gets in their way. A conversation with them is like talking in a factory, where there are so many wheels turning, cranks clattering and belts flapping, that nobody can hear what is said. Why don't they try to turn off the machinery sometimes, I mean all that noisy commerce of their heads, that continual clamour of little thoughts.'

'And if they were to do so, what would they hear?'

'They might learn some of those truths which lie beyond the reach of the intellect. You see K., when we are in the presence of the great mysteries our reason must often be content to follow the guidance of our hearts. This, these intellectuals will never allow, and their minds are so cluttered up with preconceived ideas, with wrong ideas and with, what is still more misleading, with half-wrong ideas that nothing new is able to enter there. When Christ talked in the Temple he astounded the scholars with his learning but we are not told that he made any converts amongst the assembled rabbis and doctors of law. It was only the simple, unprejudiced people, like the fisher folk, who were prepared to listen to his words. "Except ye become as little children, ye shall not enter the kingdom of God." '

I quoted Nietzsche. 'Altered is Zarathrustra: a child has Zarathrustra become; an awakened one is Zarathrustra. What will he do in this land of sleepers?'

M. laughed. 'So he's no longer a man who died in an asylum and who wrote about the strong right arm and the mailed fist?'

'I've altered since those days, M.'

'My dear boy, you've altered less than you think. It's only in novels that people suddenly change. In life we remain the same, reacting as we have always done and repeating and repeating our mistakes. We are imprisoned in the closed circles of our personalities.'

'Rather a gloomy picture, that, isn't it? Surely our position isn't quite as bad as you make out?'

M. suddenly got up, turned his back on me and stood for a moment in front of the fireplace with his hands resting on the edge of the mantelpiece. Suddenly he spun round and faced me. 'You're a damned sight too comfortable about everything, including yourself, K. Now that you're beginning to be successful in Harley Street, and that life has for the moment become easy for you, you're trying to persuade yourself that you've changed, that everything is now all right and that it's a mistake to take anything too seriously. You won't face the fact that in all essentials you're the same person that you were in South America and that all that has happened is that, for the time being, your surroundings have become more favourable. No, I can assure you that change doesn't come like that. It can only be the result of continuous inner struggle and I doubt whether you have ever seen or ever will see the need for that.'

'You don't give me credit for much in the way of guts,' I protested.

'That's one of my complaints that you should have wasted so much effort over the wrong things and should have shown so much tenacity to no purpose. It took a European war to evict you out of that hole in Buenos Aires and heaven knows what will be needed to make you see that your present way of living is just as dangerous, even although it may be more pleasant, as your life out there was. You don't realize how little time we've got, perhaps only a few years.'

'Come, come, we're not as old as that.'

'I wasn't referring to our age, but to the state of the world we live in.'

'What's wrong with it?' I answered. 'Personally I find it quite bearable.'

'Everything is wrong with it. In the same way that you, so long as you remain as you are, repeat and repeat your old mistakes, so do those great composite beings, the nations, continue to revolve in fixed orbits. We are all heading for what may be the greatest disaster that has ever overwhelmed mankind. How long we've got before this happens I don't know, ten years, perhaps more, perhaps less. One simply cannot tell.'

'G od heavens, you are a pessimist. What on earth do you mean?'

'Wars, revolutions and possibly — although nobody can be certain about this — the end of all Western civilization.'

M. was one of those violent people who did nothing by halves; when he was gay, the buoyancy of his gaiety carried one up into the sky; when he was gloomy, one fell headlong with him into the depths. I was convinced that he was exaggerating and that the grim picture he had drawn of the future needed considerable toning down. 'Don't be so tragic about everything,' I said. 'Personally, I don't share your views. Why, we've only just finished a war, and although there are many fools in the world, the majority of men have learnt a hard lesson. The mere fact that the League of Nations has actually come into being and that it is not merely a pious aspiration in the minds of a few idealists, is a sign of this.'

'It won't work. So long as men go on living as they have hitherto lived, so long as there is no inner change, everything will go on as before. Humanity cannot be saved by formulas and protocols. Shifting the scenery doesn't change the nature of the actors and this is as true of nations as it is of individual men. I tell you, K., I am frightened.'

'Of what?'

M. paused, and then answered slowly: 'Of what was once known as original sin, of the fierce brutish energy of the great masses of mankind. Men no longer have any religion in common, or a generally accepted code of behaviour to guide them. They are sheep without a shepherd.'

'Well, if you're right and if nothing can be done about it,' I said, a little bitterly, 'it doesn't seem worth discussing. If the deluge is coming we are evidently for it.' I rose to go.

M. took no notice of my remark but walked over to the cupboard in which he kept his crockery. 'We'll have some coffee,' he said, 'and there's no need for you to go yet. The tube doesn't stop running for another half-hour, so you've plenty of time.'

I knew from M.'s manner that he had something more to say and I knew equally well that no effort of mine would induce him to continue talking before he intended to do so. After we had drunk our coffee he filled his pipe, made sure it was drawing, laid it down on the table beside him, and then turned to me.

'You and I are old friends,' he said, 'and I've often been on the point of speaking to you about something, but in the end I've always decided that the time was not yet come for it. You remember my saying something to you, just before you left for Buenos Aires, about a different way of living?'

I nodded.

'Well, I meant something more than just where one lives and what sort of medical practice one takes up. I was implying something much more fundamental than that.'

'I realized that at the time,' I said, 'in fact, I thought quite a lot about it during the voyage out, and I eventually came to the conclusion that you were talking about a change in values; I mean by this a change in what one thinks important and what one dismisses as unimportant.'

'All right, we'll start from that. Well, you'll agree with me that one of the most important things is to have some chart to steer by, otherwise one just goes round in circles and that's one of the reasons why human behaviour is so ineffective. How can one expect to keep any direction when one is pushed hither and thither by the flux of changing desires and shifting moods which make up one's being?'

'Then what do you recommend?'

'It isn't a case of recommending, it's a case of first seeing one's position. That was why I suggested to you that you should get to know yourself better, for the man who knows himself begins to see how complex he is and how many different sides there are to his nature.'

'Well, if that's all you wanted, you can have the satisfaction of hearing that I've already seen a sufficient number to make me feel damned uncomfortable.'

'It wasn't all I wanted, but I'm glad to hear that you are uncomfortable,

217

because the chief reason that I've not been able to talk to you about this before is that you've always been far too comfortable about yourself.'

'Hardly charitable, that, if a man must remain as he is, in which case it would surely be best for him to accept himself with as good a grace as possible and cease to worry.'

'I have never said that. I have only said that the only change that is worth anything is an inner change, and from what you've told me, I am sure that there have been moments in your life when you've fully realized this.'

'Well, perhaps there have been,' I answered, 'but these moments have come by accident, and there is nothing I can do about it.'

'There is. If you know that there are things in you of different quality, you can do everything possible to feed the higher in you and to starve the lower. You give very little sustenance, K. to that small part of you that can see more, understand more, and, in course of time, perhaps become more. Have you ever read the Bhagavid Gita?'

'A long time ago, but I can't say that I got very much out of it.'

'Then read it again, for it is one of the three or four great books of the world. I've been working at psychology for more than ten years now and I can only tell you that, in my opinion, the Bhagavad Gita contains more true psychology than whole libraries of modern treatises. But to get anything from it you must first understand a little about its symbolism and must then test the truth of its teaching by applying it, so far as it is possible to do so, to your own life. You realize, of course, that the battle-field of Kurukshetra is the battlefield of one's own life, and that Arjuna, Krishna, Dhritarashtra, Sanjaya and all the rest of them, represent different sides of one's being. For example, Dhritarashtra means literally "the man who has seized the kingdom" and it stands for the empirical ego in us which is entirely controlled by personal desires and is in almost complete possession of us. Krishna represents the higher or more godlike qualities in us. Arjuna is that part of a man which sees the warring elements within him but, although he sees them, doesn't want to commit himself too much by taking sides.' M. picked up his pipe from the table, puffed at it, found that it had gone out and put it down again. I waited for him to continue, but he only looked at me as though judging the effect of his words.

'But you haven't told me yet what I'm to do,' I said at the end of a long silence.

'I have. I've told you first to read the Bhagavad Gita and then if you like, you can come and talk to me again. We shall then have certain more practical questions to discuss. But now you must go, or you will miss the last train.'

Twenty years have elapsed since that conversation in Hampstead and the disasters of which M. spoke have swept through the world, leaving in their wake a trail of death, destruction and chaos. Again we are faced with the necessity of rebuilding our ruined world and again we are relying on protocols and formulas to save us from future destruction.

This time peace is to be maintained, not even by a balance of power backed by nominal subservience to a moral law, but by the will of the Great Powers. The world's theatre is under new actor-managers who are willing to take the leading parts in the drama of the United Nations provided that they are not bound by the rules to which the lesser actors must subscribe. Old tragedies are to be replayed by the former cast, but on a larger stage and against a new backcloth.

In the smaller playhouse of my personal life a great deal has also happened but these new events are too near to me to be seen in their true perspective. This, as I have said before, is no ordinary autobiography but an effort to demonstrate some of the laws under which we live. To render them clearer I have shown them in action in my own life, supplying not only the demonstrator, who lives in the present, but the object on which he demonstrates, which lies in the past. These now tend to draw together and, because for clear exposition a demonstrator must not stand too near to his rabbit, the moment has come at which it is better that both should retire.